THE METAPHYSICS OF APES

The Metaphysics of Apes traces the interpretation of the ambiguously human-like great apes and ape-like ancestors of present-day humans. It shows how, from the days of Linnaeus to recent research, the sacred and taboo-ridden, animal–human boundary was time and again redrawn to cope with these challenges. At stake was the unique human dignity, a basic idea and value in the West which was, and to some extent still is, centrally on the minds of ethnologists, archaeologists, and primatologists. This book is thus the first to offer an anthropological-cum-epistemological analysis of the burgeoning anthropological disciplines in terms of their own cultural taboos and philosophical preconceptions. It maps their unwilling retreat from the notion of human unicity and from the relentless policing of the animal–human boundary.

Raymond Corbey is Lecturer in the Department of Philosophy at Tilburg University and holds the Chair of Epistemology of Archaeology at Leiden University, both in The Netherlands. He has published extensively on the history of philosophical, scientific, and colloquial views of humans, animals, culture and cultural others, as well as on the history and epistemology of anthropology. He participates in the Dutch research program *Thoughtful Hunters,* on Neanderthal cognition and communication, and is the co-editor, with Wil Roebroeks, of *Studying Human Origins: Disciplinary History and Epistemology* (2001).

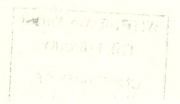

The Metaphysics of Apes

Negotiating the Animal–Human Boundary

RAYMOND CORBEY

Tilburg University and Leiden University

CAMBRIDGE UNIVERSITY PRESS
Cambridge, New York, Melbourne, Madrid, Cape Town, Singapore, São Paulo

Cambridge University Press
40 West 20th Street, New York, NY 10011-4211, USA

www.cambridge.org
Information on this title: www.cambridge.org/9780521836838

First published 2005

Printed in the United States of America

A catalogue record for this publication is available from the British Library.

Library of Congress Cataloguing in Publication Data

Corbey, Raymond, 1954–
    The metaphysics of apes : negotiating the animal–human boundary / Raymond Corbey.
      p. cm.
    Includes bibliographical references and index.
    ISBN 0-521-83683-2 (hardback) – ISBN 0-521-54533-1 (pbk.)
    1. Primates – Evolution.   2. Apes – Evolution.   3. Fossil hominids.
  4. Human evolution.   5. Human-animal relationships.   I. Title.
    QL737.P9C67   2005
    599.93'8 – dc22
                                                       2004020243

ISBN–13   978-0-521-83683-8 hardback
ISBN–10   0-521-83683-2 hardback

ISBN–13   978-0-521-54533-4 paperback
ISBN–10   0-521-54533-1 paperback

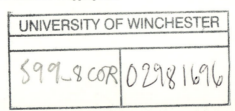

Origin of man now proved. – Metaphysics may flourish. – He who understands the Baboon would do more towards metaphysics than Locke.

Charles Darwin, in Notebook M (Darwin 1987: 539)

Contents

Contents

Preface

My ongoing fascination with the ape–human boundary was sparked by my doctoral research in the 1980s on the animal/human distinction and the interpretation of evolution in German philosophy in the 1920s, in particular in the work of Max Scheler and Helmuth Plessner. Most of the research resulting in the present monograph was done in an immensely stimulating context: the multidisciplinary research program "Changing Views of Ice Age Foragers" (1993–1998) at Leiden University, sponsored by the Netherlands Foundation of Scientific Research (NWO). Two conferences and their participants added to the inspiration provided by that setting: *Ape, Man, Apeman: Changing Views since 1600*, in Leiden in 1993 (Corbey and Theunissen 1995), and *Studying Human Origins: Disciplinary History and Epistemology*, issuing from the above-mentioned research project, also in Leiden in 1998 (Corbey and Roebroeks 2001a).

Over the course of the past ten or so years, I have been tolerated as a philosopher among archaeologists and anthropologists at Leiden University, and as an anthropologist among philosophers at Tilburg University – an always rewarding and often demanding road, not only for myself. My interest in both continental European and Anglo-American philosophy, both human sciences and life sciences, and both intellectual history and present-day epistemological issues has added to the complexities of being an interdisciplinary mediator.

Preface

I would like to thank numerous colleagues, friends, and students who provided continuous feedback over the years, in particular archaeologist Wil Roebroeks (Leiden), ethnologist Wiktor Stoczkowski (Paris), and archaeologist Tim Murray (Melbourne), who were always prepared to give me a hard time when needed. The project also profited much from early interaction with philosopher and science historian Gerlof Verwey of Nijmegen University, science historian Bert Theunissen of Utrecht University, and Claude Blanckaert and his research group on the history of the human sciences in Paris. The late Frank Spencer's bibliography (Spencer 1986) and encyclopaedia (Spencer ed. 1995) of the history of physical anthropology proved invaluable resources.

While finalizing the manuscript, an inspiring setting was provided by the Centre for the Evolutionary Analysis of Cultural Behaviour at University College London, directed by Stephen Shennan, and the courses, at UCL, given by primatologist Volker Sommer and palaeoanthropologist Mark Collard. Language editors Mark Vitullo and Marianne Sanders of Tilburg University regularly went beyond idiom and style, and Gabrielle Delbarre and three anonymous referees made valuable remarks on the final manuscript. Felix Corbey helped with the index. Smithsonian Institution Press has kindly permitted the use of passages from my chapter 'Negotiating the ape–human boundary', in B. Beck *et al.* (eds.), *Great Apes and Humans: The Ethics of Coexistence*, Washington, DC, 2001.

A note on terminology : to avoid unnecessary confusion, "hominids" is used throughout the book in the traditional sense of modern humans and their closely related bipedal ancestry (other *Homo* species, *Australopithecus, Paranthropus*, etc.), with the exclusion of the Great Apes.

Introduction

This study explores a number of crucial episodes in the fascinating struggle concerning the status of human and non-human primates in various sciences since the mid-seventeenth century, against the background of European thought, religion, and cultural imagination. The history of scientific approaches to primates, including early hominids, is characterized by an enormous increase in empirical knowledge of their systematics, evolution, ecology, behaviour, and cognition. But, as the case studies in the following chapters show, it has also been a permanent struggle with the most significant, most heavily tabooed dividing line within nature; an enduring activity of drawing, policing, displacing, denying, and bridging the metaphysical, religious, and moral boundaries between humans and their closest relatives in nature. The thesis of this book, to be developed and substantiated step-by-step, is the following: that the history of the anthropological disciplines to a considerable degree has been an alternation of humanizing and bestializing moves with respect to both apes and humans, a persistent quest for unambiguousness and human purity, and an ongoing rebuff of whatever has threatened to contaminate that purity. This thesis is proposed for its heuristic value, for further corroboration and refinement or, alternatively, for partial or complete refutation, with sound argument.

Chapter 1 analyses attitudes towards animals in general and apes and monkeys in particular in the history of European culture and thought. It also explains what is meant by "metaphysics" in the book's title. Chapters 2 to 6 explore how metaphysical views of the place of humans in nature have guided – and, to some extent, continue to guide – the accumulation and interpretation of empirical data on various newly discovered humanlike beings in various anthropological disciplines. Although the chapters deal with episodes from various fields and periods, with their own idiosyncratic logic and concepts, and can be read as more or less separate essays, their overall organization is roughly chronological and cumulative. They are connected by the underlying theme, the so sensitive ape–human boundary, and the book's unitary approach, that of intellectual history combined with ethnological and epistemological viewpoints. As the various chapters range over a broad, interdisciplinary canvas of specific vocabularies from various periods, and apply still other viewpoints in analysing those vocabularies, some effort and patience will be required from readers not equally familiar with all of these fields. Technical concepts will be kept to a minimum, explained as clearly as possible, and illustrated with examples.

Chapter 2 traces the how and why of the rebuff of apes and apishness in the seventeenth- and eighteenth-century natural history of primates, steered by the Christian grand narrative of immutable essences and nature as God's harmonious, hierarchical creation. It also gives attention to the debate on linguistic capacities as a sign of the humanness of apes at the end of this period. Chapter 3 analyses the idea, persistent since the mid-nineteenth century, that as high as humans have ascended, the brutish nature of their apish ancestors is still, quite literally, within them. Subsequently, in Chapter 4, it is shown how twentieth-century palaeoanthropology has been preoccupied not only with the discovery of ever more "natural" facts concerning human evolution, but also with the interpretation of those facts in terms of human unicity and the concomitant dichotomizing of the archaeological record into still beastly and already "fully human" hominid ancestors.

Chapter 5 deals with another episode from the continuous policing of the animal–human boundary in the history of the anthropological disciplines: the idea of the specialty, in nature, of "symbolic man" in American and French ethnology. In both language areas, this idea has contributed a great deal to the disciplinary identity of ethnology. In the second half of that chapter, ethnology is compared to behavioural biology, which, in a reverse process, analyses the behaviour of humans in the same terms as that of animals – a levelling of the animal–human boundary that has provoked sharp protests from ethnologists. Chapter 6 rounds off the series of episodes with a look at the dramatic changes in perspective with regard to the great apes as a result of the research on their sociality and their behavioural and cognitive capacities that has been conducted since about 1960. Attention is also given to recent debates on their moral status, which stress their humanness in a moral and philosophical sense.

The episodes from the history of natural history, evolutionary biology, cultural anthropology, palaeoanthropology, and primatology covered in Chapters 2 to 6 show interconnections as well as tensions between scientific categorizations, on the one hand, and philosophical, moral, and vernacular categories and appreciations, on the other. A category is a group, class, or concept that is deemed to be elemental, basic, or primitive, and not susceptible to further division. It is suggested below, in Section 1.2, that the ethnological theory of ambiguity can aid in understanding important aspects of categorizations in the history of anthropological research. Chapter 3 adds some theoretical reflections on parody and symbolic inversion, and shows how insights from narratology help in understanding various – profoundly narrative – constructions of the "natural" order and human nature. Chapter 7 continues these theoretical explorations by returning to the case studies on a more abstract level. This final chapter provides an analysis of the how and why of the aforementioned interconnections and tensions in terms of the "epistemology" of anthropology: the study not of anthropological data as such but of our – various and often conflicting – methods of treating this data in terms of cherished basic assumptions.

As sketched, the animal–human and, more specifically, ape–human boundary will be traced from the mid-seventeenth to the late-twentieth century through various disciplines: natural history, biology, palaeoanthropology, ethnology, primatology, and also, occasionally, psychology and philosophy. Most of these disciplines can conveniently be subsumed under the heading "anthropology," in the sense of twentieth-century American anthropology's traditional "four fields": cultural anthropology (or ethnology), biological or physical anthropology (including palaeoanthropology and primatology), archaeology, and linguistics. In this sense, the present book provides an alternative history, epistemology, and – to the extent it uses such anthropological viewpoints as sketched below in Section 1.3 – anthropology of anthropology, in a specific key.

ONE

Ambiguous Apes

It is part of our human condition to long for hard lines and clear boundaries.

Mary Douglas (1966: 162)

In the Spring of 1999, thousands of baboons were roaming the South African landscape eating crops. A number of business people, in an attempt to turn this agricultural disaster to their advantage, launched a large-scale project to process baboons in specially constructed slaughterhouses and sell their meat for consumption. This initiative created a storm of protest. It does not require having read primatologist Shirley Strum's sensitive analysis of the family life of Peggy and other clever and caring baboon mothers, as described in her book *Almost Human* (1987), to be able to imagine the feelings of the protesters. One Dutch newspaper quoted an animal rights activist who commented that apes were so close to humans that eating them virtually amounted to cannibalism.

Apes and monkeys are among the most prominent inhabitants of the misty borderlands between beast and human in Western cultural imagination. They are the animals perceived to be closest to humans because of their general appearance and, since the seventeenth century, because of their anatomical similarity to humans. In the late eighteenth century, as well as in recent decades, their presumed linguistic capacity has provoked debate. In the nineteenth century, evolutionary affinity positioned them even closer to humans, and still more recently, biochemical similarity and proficiency in tool making and deception have closed the gap even further.

The history of human dealings with non-human primates ranges from worshipping them as ancestors or spirits to hunting them for meat, amusement, or trophies; from casting them as literary or cinematographic characters to putting them on show in zoos, in circuses, and on television; from trying to teach them language to infecting them with lethal viruses for medical purposes. Apes and monkeys have not only been vilified as intrinsically evil creatures but also interpreted as basically noble, not yet perfected but perfectible "natural man." They have played a great variety of ritual, cultural, and symbolic roles in Western culture, serving as characters in the narrative articulation of human identities and human origins, and as vehicles of moral and cultural criticism. How humans have treated them has depended to no small degree on how they have interpreted them in myth, ritual, religion, folklore, literary fiction, the plastic arts, philosophy, and various sciences.

More than other animals, monkeys and apes have left their mark on the fundamental concepts and discussions of human nature and human origins. Apes have been, and still are, "good to think [with]," a phrase coined by Claude Lévi-Strauss meaning that humans in small-scale societies identify with totemic animals as an articulation of their social identity as different from that of their neighbours (Lévi-Strauss 1963: 162). Apes and monkeys in the West, however, have mostly been negative totems, underlining that we, humans, are *not* apes; we are different. Nowhere in the study of the animal world, it would seem, is the emotional involvement of the human species so great as with its own ancestry and next of kin.

Ironically, our fascination with apes is only rivalled by our rebuff of apes. When confronted with non-human primates or with reconstructions of what their early hominid ancestors may have looked like, humans tend to feel somewhat baffled by the paradoxical experience of recognizing something human in them, while at the same time tending to deny any identification with these beastly creatures. "The Orang-Outang," the prominent eighteenth-century natural historian Buffon wrote, using a term which in those days still referred indiscriminately to both the African great apes and the Southeast-Asian orang-utans, "which does not speak, nor think, nevertheless has a body, members, senses, a brain, and a tongue entirely similar to those of man, for it can initiate or imitate all human behaviours, and . . . yet it never really performs any action of man" (de Buffon 1749 etc., XIV: 61). Studying apes, as a primatologist put it more recently, creates "an empathic unrest" because they "evoke the subjective appreciation of animals as experiencing, judging, and striving beings," begging interpretations of their behaviour in terms of subjective valuations and calculated intentions (van Hooff 2000: 126).

Section 1.1 of the present, introductory chapter offers a historical survey of European views of apes since Antiquity, including a clarification of the term "metaphysics" in the title. The gradual discovery of apes and – apelike – early hominids is reviewed in Section 1.2. These ambiguous creatures were interpreted against the background of Christian and rationalist views with regard to the animal–human boundary, and in the context of the partial demise of those views since the nineteenth century, when the conviction that humans are part of, rather than separate from, nature began to take a firmer hold. Another, equally substantial part of the story is composed of the various mechanisms articulating cultural identity in terms of animal otherness, as will be seen in Section 1.3, which also briefly touches upon differences with various non-Western societies. The present chapter's title, "Ambiguous apes," refers primarily to non-human primates, ambiguously similar to ourselves, but can also be taken to regard humans themselves without getting too far off the mark. During the Middle Ages, humans were regarded as intermediate between the rest of creation and the Creator by Saint Thomas Aquinas and other scholastic thinkers; during the nineteenth century, they stood uneasily erect between the crouching ape and the soaring angel in bewildered Victorian minds.

1.1 Traditional Views of Apes

Western perceptions and appreciations of non-human primates were to a certain extent similar to those focussed on animals in general, but at the same time apes and monkeys were seen and treated as special because of their uncanny similarity to humans. Views of monkeys have predominantly been condescending and unflattering. In the Platonic dialogue *Hippias Maior*, possibly authored by Plato himself, Heraclitus is quoted as saying that the most beautiful of apes is hideous in comparison to man and that the wisest of men is an ape beside God (Plato 1982, 289a). Like the Roman poet Ennius three centuries later, in his well-known dictum "Simia quam similis turpissima bestia nobis" – "How similar the monkey, this ugliest of beasts, is to ourselves" – quoted by Linnaeus in his *Systema naturae* (Linnaeus 1766: 84), the dialogue's author was probably referring to either the Barbary ape, *Macaca sylvana,* or to the baboon. Both could be found in the relative vicinity, and were, therefore, the best known non-human primates in the Mediterranean area. Their similarity to the human primate was detailed by both Aristotle and Galen.

In Christian contexts, these primates were seen as hideous, foolish, and obscene. Common Christian images were those of the monkey as *figura diaboli* – "image of the devil" – and sinner, an image of man in a state of degeneracy. Patristic writers applied the negative monkey icon to pagans, heretics, and other enemies of Christ. The medieval association of monkeys with sin and the devil, with hideousness, frivolity, and, especially, impulsivity and wantonness, persisted in modern times. "Monkey" is still a powerful category of verbal abuse. "As an unworthy pretender to human status, a grotesque caricature of man, the ape became the prototype of the trickster, the sycophant [defamer], the hypocrite, the coward, as well as of extreme ugliness," H. W. Janson writes in his classic on apes and ape lore in the Middle Ages and the Renaissance (Janson 1952: 14–15). Not only Adam as the original sinner, but also the sinful, bestial aspect of human nature since the Fall have been associated with the monkey; so have Eve, "female" qualities of guile and sensuality, and the fallen angel Lucifer and his cohorts (*ibid.*: 109).

At the end of the Middle Ages, the image of the monkey was secularized from sin to folly. The simian sinner became the simian fool, and the monkey's role as prototype of all-too-human qualities persisted into modern times. The hideous monkeys of Antiquity and the Middle Ages also provided sources of ideas and terminology concerning the great apes and early hominids discovered by Europeans in recent centuries. Other testators of interpretive tropes were the devil; the monstrous or Plinian races, situated at the margins of the known world by Pliny the Elder and other authors; the sylvan Satyr, fond of Dionysian revelry; and the medieval *homo sylvestris* (Husband 1980), the mostly savage and impulsive, but sometimes idyllic Wild Man of the woods. The names and positive or negative attributes of these various characters have resurfaced regularly in the history of primate taxonomy, palaeoanthropology, and the popular imagination with respect to apes and primeval "apemen."

The originally American–English slang expression "to go ape" conserves elements of the traditional stereotype of apes and monkeys. According to the *New Oxford Dictionary of English* (Pearsall and Hanks 1998), it means to go crazy, to become excited, violent, or sexually aggressive; to display strong enthusiasm or appreciation. "To monkey" means to ape or mimic someone's manners; to mock, make a jest of; to play mischievous or foolish tricks; to fool or mess about or around; to waste time, or spend time aimlessly; to tamper with. To monkey around is to goof off or manipulate, seemingly aimlessly; to make a monkey of someone is to humiliate that person.

While eighteenth-century pictures of great apes show peaceful, rather human-looking creatures living happy, natural lives in God's harmonious creation, in the second half of the nineteenth century and most of the twentieth century they were typically depicted as ferocious, bloodthirsty monsters, involved in a hard evolutionary struggle for survival and, in the case of our apish ancestors, the ascent towards humanness. In the context of imperialist and colonial expansion, apes, among other "wild" animals, in particular the gorilla, came to be seen as powerful personifications of wildernesses to be fought heroically and conquered by civilized Westerners. Small-scale non-state peoples were seen as "savages" and associated with the negatively perceived monkey and, as "contemporary ancestors," with the bestial beginnings of humankind.

A colonial propaganda film made in the 1950s in the Belgian Congo on behalf of the Belgian government was still typical of this traditional negative attitude towards apes. It circulated widely in Belgian cinemas, programmed on Sunday afternoons for families with children. The footage shows in great and, by present-day standards, shocking detail how scientists of the Royal Belgian Institute of Natural Sciences shoot and kill an adult female gorilla carrying young. Subsequently, the body is skinned and washed in a nearby stream, with the distressed youngster sitting next to it. The adult's skeleton, skin and other body parts were collected for scientific study and conservation, while the live young gorilla was sent to the Antwerp zoo.

Just a decade later, such a cruel scene had become unthinkable as suitable for Western families with children. The publicity around field studies of great apes in the 1960s brought about significant changes in the way Westerners felt about them (cf. Reynolds 1967; Morris and Morris 1968). A forceful new icon was the picture of a young Jane Goodall and a likewise young chimpanzee reaching their fingers to one another, as portrayed in a 1967 issue of *National Geographic.* Early hominids too started to appear in illustrations and museum dioramas as peaceful human-like beings in idyllic natural settings, although pictures of monstrous brutes wielding clubs persisted to some degree, as did less positive views of apes, especially baboons.

Caliban, the wild native of the tropical island upon which Europeans shipwrecked in William Shakespeare's *The Tempest* (1611), is a quintessential bestial European Other, an avatar and condensation of earlier figures such as the Plinian Races and the Wild Man. This ambiguous being, a monster, as the text states some forty times, "a thing most brutish" (Shakespeare 2001 I, ii, 356), a "thing of darkness" (V, i, 275), "as disproportioned in his manners [as] in his shape" (V, i, 290–91) lusts after the young and attractive Miranda, and is enslaved by her father, the prince and scholar–magician Prospero, a paragon of civilized humanness. The Beauty-and-the-Beast theme, already present in the ancient theme of sylvan satyrs abducting shepherdesses, resurfaces on many occasions in the European imagination: in Emmanuel Frémiets statue of a gorilla snatching an African female, displayed at the 1859 Salon de Paris (see Figure 4 on page 78; cf. Ducros & Ducros 2000); in the interaction of Anne Darrow and an apish monster in Merian Cooper's 1933 film *King Kong* (Jensen 2002: 108 ff.); in the monstrous aliens confronted by an attractive female in Ridley Scott's film *Alien* (1979) and its sequels; or, with the beast cast much more positively, in Peter Høeg's brilliant morality tale *The Woman and the Ape* (Høeg 1996). Through the ages, the Caliban character has been staged as a brute primitive, a noble savage, the missing link, an unemancipated slave, a colonial native, and a postcolonial citizen. The chimpanzee appears as a noble Caliban in Jane Goodall's and Dale Peterson's book *Visions of Caliban: On Chimpanzees and People* (Goodall & Peterson 1993) – a far cry from the ferocious orang-utan in Edgar Allan Poe's *The Murders in the Rue Morgue* (1841).

Our focus, however, will not be on the literary, artistic, and popular imagination of apish others, but on the nature, role, and origin of basic, deep-level conceptual assumptions of an ontological, metaphysical nature with respect to the status of humans and animals in the anthropological disciplines. It is an examination of how such assumptions are related to folk, moral, religious, and explicitly philosophical views and categorizations, held in wider and other contexts. Anthropological approaches to how people perceive, categorize, and deal with their world – such as ethnobiology, the analysis of native categorizations of living nature – will prove to be handy tools of analysis in this respect. They will be applied, however, not to non-Western peoples but to anthropologists themselves.

The resulting history, anthropology, and epistemology of anthropology is not only (disciplinary) history for history's sake, to be reconstructed as adequately as possible. It is also aimed at the clarification of conceptual and epistemological issues as they are presently at stake in the study of human and non-human primates. One possible, and promising, angle of approach to present-day anthropological discourse is the study of its historical genesis: how and why present-day views and discussions arose and persisted, changed, or disappeared – temporarily or definitely – in the history of anthropology. Such an enterprise is, inevitably, to some extent "presentist": dictated by present-day concerns, possibly at the expense of an adequate reconstruction of the past for its own sake, as it really was. It is intended that this presentism be put to good use in clarifying some key issues in the anthropological disciplines.

The idea, highlighted in Chapter 5, of a unique "symbolic man," and symbolic capacity as an animal–human boundary marker, is one of the clearest examples of a topos from disciplinary history that is crucial to present-day anthropological research, germane as it is to the identity of cultural anthropology as a discipline. The *homo symbolicus* idea is also pivotal in recent discussions in palaeoanthropology on when, how, and why "behaviourally and cognitively modern humans," of the extant type, appeared (Chapter 4), and in such controversial issues as the cognitive capacities of chimpanzees, among other animals (Chapter 6).

This book concerns the metaphysics of apes, and in one sense they, not humans, should be its main protagonists, although I am not sure that is the case in the end. Non-human primates have continually been forced into ancillary roles as privileged figures of otherness or alterity assisting articulations of human identity. Ironically, this study itself probably, and perhaps inevitably, does not completely escape from that "speciesist" pattern, nor, on the other hand, from a certain amount of "primatocentrism" at the expense of other animals. Its author was mainly formed in two intellectual traditions that tend to afford a special status to humans, to wit continental European philosophy and cultural anthropology, and in this text wrestles to come to terms with their basic tenets and, in both cases, contested disciplinary identities.

It is good to be explicit about what is meant by "metaphysics of apes." Metaphysics, according to the *New Oxford Dictionary of English*, is the branch of philosophy "that deals with the first principles of things or reality, including questions about being, substance, time and space, causation, change, and identity (which are presupposed in the special sciences but do not belong to any one of them); [it is] theoretical philosophy as the ultimate science of being and knowing" (Pearsall and Hanks 1998). This is the *first* sense of this book's title: apes have always been assigned a certain metaphysical or ontological – these two terms are used synonymously in the following – status in the grand scheme of things.

Furthermore, metaphysical or ontological assumptions on the status of apes have, as was touched upon earlier, figured as conceptual or theoretical foundations in scientific research. In this *second* sense, "metaphysics" refers to basic convictions that guide the accumulation, categorization, and interpretation of data – and at the same time may encode cultural values and perceptions, and express and validate social agendas. This corresponds to another general usage of "metaphysics" according to the same source, usually as "metaphysics *of . . .* ," to wit "questions of metaphysics as they relate to a specified subject or phenomenon; the underlying concepts or first principles on which a particular branch of knowledge is based" (*ibid.*).

A *third* sense in which we can speak of the metaphysics or ontology of apes is that of ethno-metaphysics or ethno-ontology, by way of "ethnobiology" as the (anthropological) study not of living nature as such but of how cultures use and conceptualize living nature. In the present casuistry, it is analysed how Western citizens have dealt with apes and apish beings in terms of their world-views. *Fourthly,* stretching the concept to its limits, there is a "metaphysics of apes" in the sense of a *genitivus subjectivus*: the way in which chimpanzees, bonobos, gorillas, orang-utans – among two-hundred-odd extant species of non-human primates – themselves see the world.

The first three intimately connected senses of the phrase "metaphysics of apes" are the ones primarily referred to in the following. The issue of how apes themselves see the world is primarily, with the exception of Chapter 6, addressed indirectly, through the scrutiny of various interpretations that have been given of their subjectivity. An explicitation, finally, and in the *fifth* place, of the metaphysical and epistemological stance which informs the following historical explorations themselves can be found in Chapter 7 – there is no escape from metaphysical assumptions, not even, or perhaps especially not, when they are analysed.

The complex traffic in popular images of apes in recent decades is matched by marked differences in the preconceptions and assumptions of different researchers. Those assumptions "determine what constitutes data, which questions are relevant to ask of data, and how data should be organized, measured, or, most generally, interpreted" (Clark & Willermet 1997: 5; cf. Corbey & Roebroeks 2001a, and, specifically with respect to archaeology, Murray 1992). There is a chronic lack of consensus between as well as within the various disciplines and subdisciplines which contribute to the study of primates, early hominids, and human cultures. The resulting inconsistency even in the definition of basic concepts and terms at times precludes any common basis for discussion. "I think the major problem with anthropology today is the fragmentation that has taken such a deadly grip," the British anthropologist Robin Fox stated in 1993 with regard to anthropology and its four fields (in Walter 1993: 450). Against this background of theoretical and disciplinary fragmentation, the preconceptions of a number of past and current approaches to human and non-human primates in anthropological disciplines will be clarified. Special attention will be given to the pivotal role of the idea of human unicity, and to the opposite conviction that human nature is part and parcel of the living world, and should, therefore, be studied in the same fashion.

1.2 The Discovery of Apes and Early Hominids

The history of discoveries by European human primates of other extant and extinct primates – in particular the great apes and early hominids – is a richly chequered one. In Europe, such monkey species as macaques and baboons were relatively well-known since Antiquity, as such or from descriptions and pictures. The great apes – orang-utan, chimpanzee, and gorilla – were, however, discovered only gradually between 1650 and 1850, in the context of trade and colonial expansion in Africa and Southeast Asia. During the same period, a number of apelike characters gradually disappeared from the then-prevailing amalgam of representations, when it became clear that they were fictive beings.

The first apes were brought to Europe, alive or dead, from West and Central Africa. Nicolaes Tulp of Amsterdam described a chimpanzee in 1641, and Edward Tyson dissected one in London in 1698. Apes and monkeys were put on display in market places and early animal gardens, or kept in the menageries of wealthy noblemen and citizens, adding to their owners' prestige. In the late eighteenth century, the first orang-utans from Southeast Asia reached Europe. The Dutch physician–anatomist Pieter Camper had the opportunity to study some in the menagerie of Stadholder Frederic Henry in The Hague in the 1770s.

It was many years before medical anatomists and natural historians managed to discriminate clearly between chimpanzees and orang-utans. *Orang-Outang* and *homo sylvestris* were terms generally and indiscriminately used during the seventeenth and eighteenth centuries for "the" human-like ape from the tropics, specimens of which arrived on merchant traders returning from Africa or via Africa from Southeast Asia. The former term, Orang-Outang, was borrowed from Malay, spoken in the Southeast-Asian Archipelago where Europeans traded, and referred to orang-utans (*Pongo pygmaeus*). In Europe, it came to refer to any large human-like ape from the tropics: orang-utans from Southeast Asia as well as chimpanzees (*Pan troglodytes*), bonobos (*Pan paniscus*), and gorillas (*Gorilla gorilla*) from Africa.

The other term used for apes, *homo sylvestris*, was exchangeable with "Orang-Outang" and literally meant the same, "human from the woods," in Latin. Originally, in the Middle Ages, it referred to hairy beings, half beast, half human, believed to live deep in the European forests and to be wild, licentious, and dangerous. When the term came to be adopted for tropical apes, it brought some of these connotations with it, which, remarkably, were to some extent not unlike the connotations the apes had among the humans in their tropical origins. Both the Orang-Outang and the Wild Man from the woods were believed to regularly capture women and rape them. Both terms for the newly discovered creatures suggested their possible or partial humanness, as did the English term "man-ape." *Menschenaffe* in German and *mensaap* in Dutch still carry that suggestion. The humanness of "the" Orang-Outang immediately became an issue for anatomists and natural historians. In eighteenth-century speculative thought and literature, it was hailed as the uncorrupted "natural man" by Jean-Jacques Rousseau and Lord Monboddo. Together with human "wolf children," who grew up in isolation, it figured in philosophical speculation on speech and human nature, the history of humankind, and the ideal society.

Another confusing circumstance, in addition to a shared tropical origin, was the fact that most "Orang-Outangs" which arrived in Europe were young animals. With the sparse knowledge then available, it proved difficult to sort out differences between individuals due to age, gender, species, and subspecies. The apelike beings from traditional lore that sooner or later turned out to be fictive constituted another complication. It was only in the late eighteenth century that detailed anatomical comparison proved chimpanzees and orang-utans to be different animals, the one from Africa, the other from Southeast Asia. Gorillas were recognized as a separate species in the 1840s (Savage 1847). The bonobo or pygmee chimpanzee (*Pan paniscus*), finally, was first described as a species differing from the common chimpanzee (*Pan troglodytes*) in 1933.

The existence, at the roots of humankind, of "apemen," quite literally halfway between apes and humans, had been a subject of some speculation since the late eighteenth century, and was a direct implication of the mid-nineteenth-century theory of evolution by means of natural selection. A whole series of early hominids was indeed discovered from about 1830 onwards (Reader 1988), although some of the early finds were not immediately recognized as such. Like the extant apes earlier on, this second group of apish others, not from the present but from the past, not only created scientific havoc but also fed into the arts, and Western thought – from Friedrich Engels' speculations on the evolution of labour through Sigmund Freud's views of the origins of war, to feminist anthropologists in the 1970s hailing Woman the Gatherer instead of Man the Hunter as the bringer of Civilization.

The first Neanderthal remains were discovered in Belgium, Gibraltar, and Germany in 1829, 1848, and 1856, respectively. Skeletal material of *Homo erectus* from Java and China followed in 1891 and the 1920s, respectively. Since the 1950s, the same species or a closely related one has been found in several parts of Africa as well. A spectacular nearly complete skeleton of a teenage male was found at Nariokotome, Northern Kenya, in 1984. *Homo erectus* was initially called *Pithecanthropus*, literally "apeman," by Eugène Dubois (1894), the species' discoverer. The German evolutionist Ernst Haeckel had suggested this name in 1866 for "the" – at that moment still hypothetical – missing link between ape and man. Dubois' fossils, a femur and a skullcap thought to belong together and suggesting bipedality but a small brain, qualified for that position (Haeckel 1866, I: clx; *cf.* Theunissen 1989).

With the first fossil of *Australopithecus africanus*, found in South Africa in 1924, not just a new species but another genus entered the

FIGURE 1. Fossil brains of australopithecines, a group of bipedal early hominids, from Sterkfontein, South Africa. These so-called endocasts are made of now petrified sediments which filled the cranium after death. The brain volume is below 500 cc, while later *Homo* species range between 600 and 2000 cc. The form of the brain as revealed by endocasts has played a role in discussions on the presence or absence of brain structures associated with language, in particular regarding the earliest *Homo*. John Reader/Science Photo Library.

stage. The fossil, apelike yet hominid, and, as in the case of the Orang-Outangs, difficult to interpret because it was juvenile, generated much controversy. More robust specimens of australopithecines were found in Africa starting in the 1940s, among them an impressive skull first called *Zinjanthropus boisei* and then *Australopithecus boisei*, and popularly known as Nutcracker Man, in 1959. *Australopithecus afarensis*, a much earlier species from Ethiopia, named in 1978 and popularly known as "Lucy," is but one of a series of australopithecines (see Figure 1) that have since joined the ranks of the hominid family, including new genera such as *Ardipithecus*, *Orrorin*, *Kenyanthropus*, and *Sahelanthropus*, found in recent years. In the *Homo* genus, the Neanderthals were joined by, among others, the earlier species *Homo heidelbergensis*, discovered in Germany in 1907; the earliest-known, African *Homo*-species, *Homo habilis*, in 1959; and, very recently in 2003, by the baffling, pygmy-sized and small-brained *Homo floresiensis*.

As important as the discoveries of physical remains were those with regard to the nature, chronology, and ecology of technological and cultural behaviours of early hominids. The Acheulean handaxe tradition was highlighted as early as the 1840s in the writings of Jacques Boucher de Perthes (1847 etc.), who collected handaxes in quarries along the Somme river in Northern France. Other nineteenth-century discoveries in Europe were Upper Palaeolithic ritual art, portable as well as on cave walls, and Upper Palaeolithic burials. In the course of the twentieth century, archaeology came of age. A wealth of archaeological data on palaeolithic societies was accumulated, not the least of which as a result of systematic excavations, for example, the Oldowan stone technology, traces of the early use of fire, a variety of patterns in the use of space, and subsistence activities such as scavenging and hunting. It also became clear that the early hominids lived much earlier than previously thought. Spectacular specific finds in recent decades were 3.5 million-year-old footprints of australopithecines in fresh volcanic ashes at Laetolil, Tanzania, and 450,000-year-old spears, very probably meant for hunting, in Schöningen, Germany.

The scarcity and ambiguity of early, palaeolithic, archaeological data, in particular, have provoked much discussion, for example, with respect to the identification of the earliest hunting behaviours, use of fire, burials, and base camps, and with respect to the use of present-day foragers and non-human primates as models for the past.

While there has been considerable progress since the nineteenth century in our knowledge of the behaviour patterns of early hominids, the same cannot be said with respect to our knowledge of apes. That chimpanzees have some technology and nonsymbolic cultural traditions, and that great apes in general are quite sophisticated cognitively, became clear only in recent decades. Some chimpanzee groups tailor twigs down to size and use them to fish termites from their holes, while others use hammers and anvils to crack nuts. It was also discovered that they have complex social lives, including political coalitions, are capable of deceiving others, occasionally hunt cooperatively, and occasionally kill conspecifics. In captivity, they recognize themselves in mirrors, and can learn to communicate proficiently using arbitrary symbols. Traditionally, most of these behaviours were cherished as markers of human unicity, a concept which now came to be challenged by these very discoveries.

Sherwood Washburn once characterized the history of scientific dealings with non-human primates and early hominids as a progress from a data-poor and nonsense-rich to a more sophisticated, data-rich era (Washburn 1982: 38). In a sense, that is a correct observation, but it needs qualification, for this progress has not been unequivocal. In the interpretation of the new data, old ideas often persisted, as shall be seen time and again when studying the interactions and tensions between data and ideas in the following chapters. Even at the core of currently fashionable scientific theories, there are certain elements of traditional European metaphysics.

How Western humans coped with the baffling, newly discovered human-like apes and apish human ancestors can partly be understood in terms of traditional views of non-human primates, as sketched in Section 1.1, but must, of course, also be seen in the context of traditional European views of animals and nature in general. In Western societies, the ecological dominance of humans over other species was associated with grand ideas and narratives explaining why this was a "natural" and desirable state of affairs – justifying the human's high and central position and the animal's low and marginal place in nature.

There has always been a good degree of tension between views that stress discontinuity and those that stress continuity between humans and animals. Until recently, the former generally prevailed, notwithstanding the efforts of sceptics and materialists, the Aristotelian idea of one nature which humans are part of, the writings of Michel de Montaigne, the British empiricist tradition in philosophy, the materialism of a number of Enlightenment thinkers, the tendency to stress continuity between humans and the rest of nature in folk conceptions, an ever-growing amount of empirically discovered similarities between humans and other living beings, and concomitant forms of philosophical physicalism, materialism and naturalism.

While monkeys have often been cast in the role of image of man, *imago hominis*, Judaeo–Christian religion holds humans to be *imago Dei*, the only beings created in the image of God, as is written at the beginning of *Genesis*. It is immediately added there that as such, humans reign over the rest of nature, and can put the animals to their use – the *homo dominator* theme, although more benign interpretations stress human stewardship over and responsibility for the rest of life. Greek philosophy, with its doctrines of the immutable, archetypal essences of all living beings, constitutes the other main root of the conviction of human unicity so characteristic of European cosmology. It soon merged with Judaeo–Christian views. While all living beings have souls, only humans have a *nous* or rational soul, called *anima rationalis* by medieval authors, which constitutes their essence (*essentia*) and the "essential" difference from the ape's or any other animal's essence.

The medieval conception of a *scala naturae* or ladder of nature forming the Great Chain of Being persisted in post-medieval Europe. It lasted well into the nineteenth and to some extent even the twentieth century. In this harmonious hierarchy of unchanging species, from worms to angels, created by a transcendent Almighty, the steps between adjacent species were very small, as authoritative Christian metaphysicians like Saint Augustine and Albert the Great had argued. They synthesized Greek views of the natural world – Platonic and Aristotelian – with Christian theology. On the one hand, this continuity between adjacent species implied close affinity and similarity between humans and apes. On the other hand, paradoxically, discontinuity was claimed – humans were the only beings created in the image of God, but still within the same cosmic or natural order. Even the nineteenth-century evolutionist metaphor of a "missing link" between ape ancestor and human descendant has its roots in the Christian notion of nature as a Great Chain, stressing a connection as well as distance at the same time.

The idea of the unique rationality and dignity of humans and the strict metaphysical and moral boundary between them and animals which it implied was reinforced with new arguments by such rationalist philosophers as René Descartes and Immanuel Kant – notwithstanding the milder views of empiricist and materialist thinkers. By positing the absolute transcendence of God with respect to created nature, Judaeo–Christian thought had already begun to remove subjectivity from nature, perceived as sacred and as full of personal beings in the animistic, mythical world-views preceding Christianity and to some extent persisting alongside and within it. Modern Cartesian philosophy, in its turn, further widened the abyss between humans, conceived as autonomous rational subjects, and the rest of nature, including (other) animals, by interpreting the latter as purely material and mechanical, and as such, available for humans.

In the second half of the nineteenth century, evolutionary theory reinforced and renewed the painful rapprochement between humans and other animals which was in many ways suggested by developments in comparative anatomy and natural history. The theory of evolution merged with the eighteenth-century idea of an ascent to civilization and reason. Human's apish ancestors were thus held at arm's length, as were non-Western peoples living in small-scale societies. The latter came to be viewed as still half-beastly relics from the past, so-called "contemporary ancestors," "primitive" in the negative and not just in the neutral sense of being the first. In this context, it was not so much the different eternal essence of humans that constituted the cleft between them and their apish ancestors, but the long, heroic ascent to civilization and the rationality achieved exclusively by Western citizens as the paragon of humanness.

1.3 Citizens and Animals

Another source of unfavourable views of animals in general – parallel and in addition to the effects of Judaeo–Christian cosmology, Aristotelian ontology, and modern rationalism – was of a somewhat different order. European citizens looked upon themselves as "civilized" and behaved as such. Decent people had to behave, dress, eat, defecate, make love, and so on, in a proper manner, and had to control their "animal" impulses. In European culture, as in a number of other cultures, animals and their "beastly," "uncivilized" down-to-earth behaviour provided models of how not to behave. They served as forceful symbols of uncivilized conduct, as in such expressions as "you behaved like an animal" or "they treated those people like animals" and in forms of verbal abuse. Citizens subjugated animals and usually classified them according to their utility instead of their inherent characteristics. Even Linnaeus still classified dogs according to their human uses.

While many individual species of animals – such as the lion, the pig, the lark, the horse, the rat, and the eagle – played variegated specific, and context-dependent, positive or negative symbolic and heraldic roles, the beast as such was usually a paragon of brutishness, a "natural symbol" (Douglas 1970) of impulsiveness. European citizens associated their own bodies and bodily functions with beastliness. They associated peasants, the working classes, non-Western peoples, and various infamous professions and undesirable humans, with animals and animality, with "untamed," "still uncivilized," and "low" nature (Frykman and Löfgren 1987; Corbey 1993b; Blok 2001). Many European citizens expressed their own identity in terms of the exemplary otherness of the uncivilized animal: we are not (like) it.

Other cultural mechanisms, deeply ingrained in culture, added to the infamy of animals and the negative effects of the articulation of the citizen's identity. Westerners tended to conceal from themselves part of their dealings with animals. Those living in cities and towns had less frequent contacts with animals. Such common cultural activities as slaughtering and hunting, still shocking to children, have increasingly been hidden from public view and are quickly looked upon with indifference when people grow up. More recently, the large numbers of livestock in identical cages have made individual animals anonymous, while food terminology such as "sausage" or "hamburger" tends to dissociate what humans eat from the live animals as they know or hardly know them.

Such distancing and distorting mechanisms, including representing animals as dull, brutish, or even evil beings, or as lacking in real subjectivity and feelings, facilitated exploiting them in a variety of manners (Serpell 1986). As all cultures do, Western cultures have world-views which specify which organisms can legitimately be exploited. A sharply drawn animal–human boundary enables humans to go on killing and eating millions of certain animals every year, apart from the many other things they do to or with other animals. At the same time, they usually refrain from killing and eating other humans, as well as pets, which are considered and explicitly represented as fellow beings. A more specific form of misrepresentation has been the projection by humans of impulses they have experienced in themselves and felt uneasy about – for example lust, vanity, aggression – upon monkeys and apes.

The uncanny apes stood and still stand betwixt and between human and animal, being not completely the one, nor the other, and in a sense both at once. The same holds for prehistoric "apemen." Such ambiguous beings challenged the possibility of drawing a neat boundary line between "man" and "beast" as two fundamental categories of the moral order and alimentary regime. The apes' puzzling similarity to humans, their mirror quality – which includes a whole repertoire of emotions, gestures, and other behaviours humans immediately recognize – made them a potential threat, or alternatively, a challenge, to human identity, and even, sometimes, an ideal for it. This resulted in complex reactions of humans to their closest relatives. In the case of a threat, humans often vigorously reaffirmed the ape's brutish animality and low status, thus neutralizing its disquieting familiarity and maintaining the fence between themselves and animals.

According to Mary Douglas, ambiguity is essentially a threat of disorder, and often provokes an intensification of the cultural struggle for order. Douglas, a British neo-Durkheimian (cf. Section 5.1) ethnologist, has studied the ways in which peoples culturally conceptualize themselves and their environments. She argues that, in particular, it is those entities and situations which are ambiguous with respect to established classificatory grids applied to reality which are suitable to expressing and symbolizing things.

Entities such as dirt, menses, and faeces, or animals living both on the land and in the water, are ambiguous. They fall in the boundary area between two fields or classes of phenomena or violate the boundary between classes. Their transgression of, or ambiguity with respect to, respected boundaries and the difficulty in pigeonholing and comprehending them makes such things uncanny and frightening. It is this quality of physically marginal entities that makes them symbolically central – powerful carriers of meaning and emotion. Ethnographers have been able to document this time and again in various different cultures. From all that is available in the environment, the ambiguous is among the best suited means of expressing human meanings and feelings. It is precisely such things which are chosen to be manipulated in rituals, to be subjected to taboos, or to be used to curse and to insult people. "Wherever the organic erupts into the social, there is impurity; birth, death, sex, eating and defecation incur impurity and are so hedged with rituals," according to Douglas (1975: 214). What is ambiguous in terms of how humans culturally categorize their world, according to this approach, quickly becomes taboo, insulting, dangerous, and dirty. The unclear is unclean.

"[A] violent reaction of condemnation [is] provoked," writes Douglas (1966: 56), "by anything which seems to defy the apparently implicit categories of the universe. . . . In this way the permanence and value of the classifications embracing all sections of society are emphasized." Her analysis sheds light not only on how the Lele of the Congo Basin deal with such ambiguous animals as the scaly ant-eating pangolin or on the food taboos mentioned in the Old Testament, but also on the obsession with keeping apes and monkeys at a distance in the history of Western culture and science. This would seem to be another case of pollution avoidance, "the reaction which condemns any object or idea likely to confuse or contradict cherished classifications" (*ibid.*: 48). Such manoeuvres clarify and maintain social definitions, and guard against threatening disturbances of the moral, social, and natural order; indeed, such is the case when humans are classified with apes. Social order presupposes unambiguous rules as to what can be used, eaten, or killed, and what cannot. For Douglas, "dirt is a kind of compendium category of all events which blur, smudge, contradict, or otherwise confuse classifications. The underlying feeling is that a system of values which is habitually expressed in a given arrangement of things has been violated" (Douglas 1975: 51). Pollution behaviour, in short, is "the reaction which condemns any object likely to confuse or contradict cherished classifications" (Douglas 1966: 48).

Another British ethnologist, Victor Turner, has suggested that the concept of the liminal can be applied heuristically quite widely. Literally, "liminal" means on the *limen*, Latin for verge or border. Turner has pointed to the prominent role of monstrous entities and behaviours in the so-called liminal phase of rites of passage, when the person's status is no longer the old one, but not yet the new one, and, indeed, categorially ambiguous (Turner 1969). This suggests that apes and early hominids being depicted as monstrous, in physical appearance as well as behaviour, may be related to their liminal or categorially ambiguous position in the European cosmological framework. "Monstrous" behaviours such as cannibalism, incest, rape, and nakedness are frequent attributes of early hominids in nineteenth- and early twentieth-century representations. These behaviours correspond to what a third well-known British ethnologist, Edmund Leach, has identified as three universal foci of taboo: food, sex, and clothing (Leach, 1982: 118).

The theory of pollution and taboo as developed along slightly different lines by Douglas, Turner, and Leach, with its neo-Durkheimian underpinnings, is not uncontroversial. It is not presented here as the complete or definitive explanation of a range of remarkable phenomena around how the ape–human boundary has been drawn in the history of anthropological disciplines, but it is suggested that it has considerable heuristic value. It aids in understanding much of the casuistry laid out in the following chapters, and also, to give but one example here, the severe emotions provoked in the Netherlands and beyond around 1908 by an initiative by Herman Bernelot Moens. Backed by some scientists of repute, he lobbied for large-scale experiments involving hybridization of African humans with chimpanzees, in order to better understand the origins of the human species (de Rooy 1995). Moens' project created a major scandal and never got off the ground.

The analysis of the Indian caste system by another prominent neo-Durkheimian, the Frenchman Louis Dumont, can be of help in the present context as well. The manners in which nature was categorized and dealt with in Western societies exhibit interesting similarities with the Indian caste system as he analysed it. In Dumont's view, the caste system reflects an overarching hierarchical "sociocosmos" of traditional ideas and values (*idées/valeurs*). The status of individuals and their place in that hierarchy is determined by their dignity or purity, a central religious and moral value, and the "principle according to which elements... are ranked in relation to the whole" (Dumont, 1970: 66; cf. *ibid.*: 21). The distinction between pure and impure is germane to the system. There are strict rules with regard to all sorts of exchanges and activities, such as diet, marriage, work, and burial. These rules maintain strictly separate but at the same time interdependent castes, hierarchically ordered in terms of purity and pollution. Pollution takes place when those rules are broken, and purification rituals may become necessary.

Dumont's analysis of the caste system in his book *Homo Hierarchicus* (Dumont, 1970) and other research based on his theoretical tenets has been criticized as being too exclusively focussed on the pure/impure distinction; for too idealistically and holistically overstressing the caste society as a cosmological system; and for underplaying variability, individualism, conflicts, oppression, as well as historical change (e.g., Khare 1996). Nonetheless, and despite the fact that he contrasted the hierarchical holism of the caste system with the egalitarian individualism of modern Western societies, Dumont's approach is helpful when it comes to discussing the position of animals – and, for that matter, the position of non-Caucasian "races" – in nature as a moral order in Western worldviews. The role of animals in the West is to some extent analogous to that of the subservient, infamous Untouchables, outcasts who traditionally handled impure things – corpses, dung, meat – and did impure work. At the same time, however, animals are crucial to the system they complement and have their "natural" place in it. The position of humans in the West, on the other hand, resembles that of the "pure" Brahmin in India. In both cases, Dumont's three central analytical categories, hierarchy, separation, and interdependence, can be applied fruitfully, showing holistic aspects of modern Western culture despite its, and Dumont's, stress on individualism. Both animals in the West and Outcasts in India have a considerable potential for causing pollution.

As will be explored with respect to the burgeoning anthropological disciplines, apes, monkeys, and apish ancestors threatened the social and cosmological order of Europeans with their considerable ambiguity and potential of pollution. At the same time, however, while apes were considered to be low and defiled socially and humanly speaking, they were symbolically central – potent and dangerous signifiers. They formed a powerful semiotic realm in terms of which people in the West articulated their self-identity as not-animal, as having subdued the animal deep inside themselves through civilized constraint. Animals are good to think and to symbolize with, some more than others, but apish beings turned out to be especially suited to expressing, signifying, and dealing with things human, including aspects of human behaviour humans themselves considered immoral and unacceptable.

The element of threat was dealt with and the semiotic potential used in, for example, monkeys or apes on show – in the streets, in amusement venues, in circuses, or on television – provoking both sympathy and ridicule, identification and rebuttal. The manners taught to such monkeys "imitate European forms of culture or politeness and amusingly transgress, as well as reaffirm, the boundaries between high and low, human and animal, domestic and savage, polite and vulgar," Stallybrass and White write in their brilliant analysis of the cultural imaginary of transgression of the European middle classes. The performing monkey, mimicking humans, is a grotesque exemplary Other of citizen identity which must be "transformed into Same ... but at the same time, the Other's mimicry of the polite is treated as absurd, the cause of derisive laughter, thus consolidating the sense that the civilized is always-already given, the essential and unchanging possession which distinguishes the European citizen from the West Indian and the Zulu as well as from the marmoset and the manteger" (Stallybrass and White 1986: 41; cf. Rooijakkers 1995).

In summary, human identity in European societies was articulated in terms of animal alterity. Traditional cosmological schemes were at play here, and had moral implications. People defined and redefined themselves through exclusion of what was perceived to be low and dirty. Concealment, stereotyping, and various other devices served for "distancing" beings which were put to human use, made to suffer, or killed. Undesirable other humans were perceived as "apish" or "bestial." The various aspects of attitudes to animals – cognitive, emotional, motivational, moral, aesthetic, and cultural – were part of a typical modern "habitus" of the European middle classes in the sense defined by the French sociologist, Pierre Bourdieu: a corporally embedded regime of appreciation and feeling, which includes opinions as well as uneasiness, shame or disgust regarding what is considered improper or unbecoming to the "civilized" citizen (Bourdieu 1984; cf. Frykman and Löfgren 1987).

The distorting mechanisms, together with European discursive traditions, converged – and to a considerable extent continue to do so – to a strictly drawn and heavily tabooed, theoretical and moral animal–human boundary, which is not only preached but also practiced. Animals are put to work or eaten. All kinds of human practices, from hunting and killing to circuses and zoos, were, and still are, legitimized by the view that animals are lower beings. Such practices, as well as the worldwide ecological dominance of the human species as such, were and are connected with, and justified by, the idea, or ideology, of the unicity and unique human dignity of "man" as the sole creature created in the image of God, or the sole being viewed to have risen to reason and rationality. "Dignity," from the Latin word *dignitas* (merit, worth), carries such meanings as "the quality of being worthy or honourable; worthiness, worth, nobleness, excellence ... honourable or high estate, position, or estimation ... nobility or befitting elevation of aspect, manner, or style; becoming or fit stateliness" (*New Oxford Dictionary of English*, Pearsall and Hanks 1998).

The idiosyncratic, extremely hierarchical character of Western views of apes, and animals as such, is brought out more clearly still when these are compared with views and practices among non-Western peoples. This is a highly interesting subject in its own right, which within the framework of the present book we can look into only briefly. Non-modern, pre-state foraging and tribal peoples have conceptions of animals which generally are of a more egalitarian spirit than those held in the West, and seem to be related to the degree of egalitarianism in their society. In such cultures, what is called "nature" in the West is usually conceived of, and dealt with, as part of the overarching social world. Here, as in Europe before the spread of Christianity, humans maintain reciprocal relationships with the spirits and ancestors that also dwell in the forest or the landscape. Gifts, services, civilities, complaints, and other messages are exchanged with them (cf. Ingold 1994a; Bird-David 1999).

The Sakkudei, for instance, who live in the tropical rainforest of the Mentawei Islands off Sumatra, offer pigs and chicken as sacrifices to the spirits of the forest. In return, these spirits show the hunting Sakkudei their benevolence and give them their blessing by letting them catch some of their animals. The flesh of monkeys, thus acquired, is eaten ritually, and the skulls of these animals, who to the spirits were what the sacrificed pigs were to the Sakkudei, are kept permanently in the houses of the village as a sign and guarantee of their solid relations with the beings of the other world (Schefold 2002: 430).

The roles of non-human primates in traditional Chinese and Japanese culture illustrate differences as well as similarities with the roles they have played in the West. In China, the gibbon (*Hylobates lar*) has been celebrated for centuries in prose, poetry, and art as the aristocrat of the animal and primate world. As Robert van Gulick documents in great detail in his wonderful, beautifully edited essay *The Gibbon in China: An Essay in Chinese Animal Lore* (van Gulick 1967), it was "the traditional, purely Chinese symbol of the unworldly ideals of the poet and the philosopher, and of the mysterious link between man and nature . . . it initiates man into abstruse sciences and magic skills, and it is his calls that deepen the exalted moods of poets and painters on misty mornings and moonlit nights" (*ibid.*: iv). As such, the gibbon, aristocrat among the animals and favourite animal of aristocrats, sharply contrasted with the vulgar macaque in travelling monkey shows. The macaque exemplified the trickery, inconstancy, and restless curiosity of humans, and, as such, was closer to the monkey lore of the European tradition.

During the early period of Japanese history, the Japanese macaque's – *Macaca fuscata* – similarity to humans made it a revered trickster figure, a sacred mediator between humans and the deities in nature, or the animal deity closest to humans. Neither Buddhism, nor Confucianism, Taoism, or Shintoism assumes the sharp boundary between humans and other primates present in Western traditions. In later times, the macaque became profanized into a trickster–scapegoat, mocked for its vain efforts to behave in a human fashion in monkey shows in the streets. Interestingly, the monkey trainers were Burakumin outcasts, practicing occupations involving "dirty" work and substances and regarded as "naturally" impure and morally inferior to other Japanese. For the contemporary Japanese, the ambiguous macaque has assumed yet another role, that of a highly reflexive clown, turning itself into an object of laughter while challenging the basic assumptions of Japanese culture and society (Ohnuki-Tierney 1987; cf. Ohnuki-Tierney 1995).

Some traditional vernacular, philosophical, and religious categories and terminology with respect to nature, animals and, specifically, monkeys persist in certain research traditions in professional Japanese primatology, in addition to work in more Western modes, which predominates. Japanese primatologists tend to adopt a more intuitive, empathetic approach to monkeys than do their Western counterparts, and base their work on traditional Japanese views of nature. This gives rise to quite different, more or less anthropomorphic conceptualizations of the mental and social life of the Japanese macaque, African chimpanzees, and non-human primates in general, as analysed in detail by Pamela Asquith in her doctoral thesis *Some Aspects of Anthropomorphism in the Terminology and Philosophy underlying Western and Japanese Studies of the Social Behaviour of Non-Human Primates* – a less accessible and well-known work than it deserves to be (Asquith 1981; cf. Asquith 1986, and Asquith 1995). It is not just a certain inclination due to cultural and religious influences, but concerns a carefully considered interpretive methodology. The *kyokan* – "feel one" or "sympathetic" – method, for example, establishes "a mutual communication between the human observer and the monkey. . . . Specific thoughts and feelings are attributed to the monkeys and emotions and ploys of the animals are given human labels so that terms such as 'secret plot,' 'timid,' 'duty' and so on appear frequently in reports" (Asquith 1981: 361).

At a time when objectifying observation predominated in the West, Japanese primatology pioneered naming individuals and provisioning food – continuing a practice of Shintoist nature worship – in order to be able to study animals more closely. Individuals were identified, and their relationships and rank position carefully mapped. All living things were deemed to be connected, including humans and monkeys, and monkeys to each other. The attention to individual animals, as one Western primatologist visiting Japan and reflecting on its primatological tradition wrote, "amounts to a momentous theoretical contribution to the study of social animals. The ideas that individuals matter, that their identities are linked to their place in the whole, that they need to be followed over time, and that human empathy helps us to understand them, are so obviously correct that armies of scientists now apply this perspective, often without knowing where it came from" (de Waal, 2001: 193–194). It is telling, finally, that many Japanese primatologists attend yearly memorial services held in several sacred locations for the souls of monkeys that have died in the course of their research.

Back now to nineteenth-century Europe. How appalling the idea of a transmutation of ape into human must have been to the Victorian imagination is difficult to imagine nowadays. It was as shocking and threatening as the replacement, in evolutionary theory, of divine meaning and reason by blind contingency in natural and human history. For this reason, Darwin himself hesitated for decades before broaching the matter of human origins explicitly. "What is the question now placed before society with the glib assurance which to me is most astonishing," the British conservative statesman Benjamin Disraeli asked in a speech in Oxford on November 25, 1864. That question, he answered according to *The Times* of November 26, was "Is man an ape or an angel? I, my lord, I am on the side of the angels. I repudiate with indignation and abhorrence those new-fangled theories." Disraeli's answer tellingly evokes the dilemma posed by the rise of a new cosmology which no longer explained humans *meta*physically with the help of discursive thought, but traced their origin to the physics of lowly animals and the rest of nature with the help of empirical sciences. This cosmological sea-change resulted in grave problems for Western human identity, for which the exclusion of animals, not their inclusion, had been constitutive. It forced humans into reluctant retreats from, and renegotiations of, the notion of their own specialty.

Evolutionary theory suggested new ontologies which replaced meaning by chance, mind by matter, the supernatural by the natural, and essence by variation and change. These ontologies threatened to dethrone humans by treating them as just another animal species under the sway of coincidence. An answer to this menace was immediately sought in narratives of progress, under the influence of Enlightenment thought: humankind's beginnings may have been humble, but it had acquired a higher standing in the course of its "ascent" towards proper humanness. It was this move, the temporalization of the hierarchical scale of nature, which provoked the following aphorism from Friedrich Nietzsche, one of the sharpest critics ever of traditional Christian metaphysics as well as Enlightenment rationalism. It is entitled "The new seminal feeling: our definitive transitoriness:" "Previously people tried to attain a feeling of majesty by pointing to their divine origin: this road is now forbidden, for at the gateway stands the monkey, next to other hideous beasts, and emphatically gnashes its teeth, as if to say: no further in this direction! Therefore, they now try the opposite direction: *whither* mankind moves now has to prove its majesty and relationship to the divine. Alas, nothing comes of that either" (Nietzsche 1999, III [1887]: 53–54).

How the idea of the divine origin of humans affected eighteenth-century scholarship on primates, human and non-human, is explored in the next chapter; the idea of an ascent from the ever-encroaching ape is delineated in Chapter 3. From angel to ape, and up from the ape again through secular progress as a remedy to the danger of bestialization; these are crucial episodes in the history of notions of human status. Such remedies notwithstanding, the new, materialist, or at least empiricist and agnosticist, world-views have been spreading since. One of their widely read recent spokesmen, evolutionary biologist and science writer Stephen Jay Gould, for example, has time and again asserted "the unpredictability and contingency of any particular event in evolution," emphasizing that "the origin of *Homo sapiens* must be viewed as such an unrepeatable particular, not an expected consequence . . . humans can occupy no preferred status as a pinnacle or culmination. Life has always been dominated by its bacterial mode" (Gould 1997: 4; cf. Dennett 1995).

TWO

Crafting the Primate Order

Then the Lord God said, "It is not good that man should be alone; I will make him a helper fit for him." So out of the ground the Lord God formed every beast of the field and every bird of the air, and brought them to man to see what he would call them; and whatever man called every living creature, that was its name.

Genesis, II: 18–19

During the seventeenth and eighteenth century, several chimpanzees from Angola and, subsequently, orang-utans from Southeast Asia reached Europe, some dead and some alive. This chapter reconstructs how, by their humanlike physique and behaviour, these strange creatures baffled physician–anatomists, natural historians, and philosophers, from Tulp and Tyson (Section 2.1) through Linnaeus (Section 2.2) and his critics (Section 2.3) to Rousseau and Monboddo (Section 2.4).

The backdrop against which Europeans tried to come to terms with apes, in addition to persisting Christian beliefs, was the Enlightenment, a movement and climate of opinion which encouraged the critical and even sceptical exploration of traditional beliefs, including religious dogma, with the help of rational argument and empirical observation instead of the authority of texts or the Church. This quite heterogeneous movement was associated with the scientific revolution and the concomitant rise of a more mechanistic world-view. Reason was seen as the most characteristic and significant (also in the moral sense) feature of humans, helping them to understand a basically rational world and achieve historical progress towards civilization and perfection. Although the authority of the Church was criticized, Christian world-views persisted, often to some extent transformed by the new faith in rationality.

The first specialized studies on great apes were written by two seventeenth-century humanist physicians who, in the tradition of Galen and Vesalius, were trying to sort out the comparative anatomy of humans and other living beings. Their publications set the stage for later research. In the eighteenth century, non-human primates created controversies among natural historians who classified all natural beings they could lay their hands on in search of the "natural system" of Creation. The Christian idea of a harmonious *scala naturae*, created by God with humans on top, provided the conceptual backbone of their scientific interpretations.

However, when Carolus Linnaeus classified humans as *Primates*, in the same genus with apelike beings, this was immediately perceived as a threat to the unique dignity and special place of humans in creation. Guided by metaphysical agendas, Buffon, Blumenbach, and Camper again separated humans from apes. Camper's craniofacial morphology interpreted the degree of prognathism – forward projection of the jaws and teeth – in the animal world as physical evidence of gradation in nature, placing snoutless humans on top. Reversing the metaphysical hierarchy assumed by the natural historians, the philosopher Jean-Jacques Rousseau pointed to the tropical apes as exemplary, natural humans still uncorrupted by society.

2.1 *Homo sylvestris*

Two physicians and anatomists, Nicolaes Tulp of Amsterdam and, somewhat later, Edward Tyson of London, tried to cope with the anatomical as well as metaphysical problems posed by the "Orang-Outangs" that were brought back from the Tropics. Their publications set the agenda for

FIGURE 1. Engraving of, probably, a chimpanzee or bonobo, published in 1641 by the Dutch physician and anatomist Nicolaes Tulp. He was convinced that such newly discovered living beings, brought back from the tropics on merchant ships, corresponded to the satyr of ancient Greek and Roman folk beliefs. From Tulp 1641.

several generations of research and discussion in comparative anatomy, natural history, and philosophy, and had an impact upon the literary imagination as well. They interpreted human and non-human primates in terms of viewpoints issuing from a complex interaction of empirical observations, religious and metaphysical views, ancient mythology, animal lore, stories from travelogues, and monkey allegories and iconography. The authority of tradition and written sources still carried weight, next to and combined with one's own observations.

Nicolaes Tulp was a well-to-do Protestant physician, burgomaster, and professor of anatomy and surgery in Amsterdam. In Rembrandt van Rijn's painting "Anatomy lesson of Dr. Tulp," exhibited in the Mauritshuis in The Hague, he appears in the latter capacity. In 1641, he published a short essay entitled "Homo Sylvestris; Orang-outang" in a book of *Observationes medicae* which soon became a classic and appeared in six editions until 1740 (Tulp 1641: 274–279). The essay describes the results of his observations of a juvenile female ape (see Figure 2), probably a chimpanzee or a bonobo, from the menagerie of Stadhouder Frederic Henry, Prince of Orange, in The Hague. A Dutch physician in the East Indies had reported that such creatures were called "Orang-Outang" by the local population, and Tulp was the first to apply this name to a tropical ape in Europe, in this case, a chimpanzee from Angola, where the Dutch traded along the coast.

In his essay, Tulp confirmed what others before him had already suggested: the hairy, impudent Dionysian satyrs, described by ancient authors such as Pliny the Elder and familiar from literature and art, really existed. He therefore proposed calling the animal from the Stadhouder's menagerie *Satyrus indicus*, literally, satyr from the Indies. Remarkably, the satyr, according to Greek and Roman myth, and the orang-utan, according to local beliefs in the Southeast Asian Archipelago, as well as the Wild Man of the woods in the European medieval imagination were all chasers and rapists of women (cf. Figure 4, page 78). This is, likely, not entirely coincidental, as incorrect sexual behaviour is a widespread ethnocentric perception of cultural others. Tulp tended to overestimate the Orang-Outang's resemblance to humans, as late eighteenth-century natural historians would point out, and in particular failed to notice that the Orang-Outang was incapable of a fully erect gait.

While Tulp had dissected humans, but never a chimpanzee, Edward Tyson, another proponent of the medico–humanistic tradition, reported in 1699 in detail on his careful and meticulous dissection of an ape. Primatologists disagree on the species to which this specimen belonged, not least because it was a juvenile, and thus difficult to classify. On the basis of the detailed engraving which accompanies the essay, most believe it was a bonobo, but it has also been argued that it may have been an orang-utan. The infant had arrived in London in 1698 on a ship from Africa and had soon died of an infection.

In *Orang-Outang, sive Homo Sylvestris, Or, The Anatomy of a Pygmie*, a classic of comparative anatomy and a founding text of primatology, Tyson adopted Tulp's terminology, adding the term "Pygmie," which ancient and medieval authors used for a fabled race of dwarfs situated in Africa. Step by step, the distinguished London physician and lecturer compared the details of this particular Orang-Outang's morphology with those of humans and two species of monkey. Carefully analysing and tallying differences and similarities, he found 48 features which resembled those of humans more than those of monkeys, against 34 which bore a greater resemblance to monkeys. "The catalogue of both are so large," he concluded, "that they sufficiently evince, that our Pygmie is no Man, nor yet the common ape: but a sort of animal between both, and tho' a Biped, yet of the Quadrumanus-kind: tho' some men too, have been observed to use their feet like hands, as I have seen several" (Tyson, 1699: 94).

For Tyson, this astonishing being was an intermediary form between human and monkey, yet another link in the Great Chain of Being. The dedication of his book, to Lord Falconer, a high-ranking member of the nobility and a patron of science, sums up his interpretation: "The animal of which I have given the anatomy, coming nearest to mankind; seems the nexus of the animal and the rational, as your Lordship, and those of your high rank and order of knowledge and wisdom, approaching nearest to that kind of beings which is next above us; connect the visible, and invisible world" (*ibid.*: iv). The human being, in Tyson's view, was "part a brute, part an angel, and . . . that link in the creation that joins them both together" (55). In a subsequent "philological essay" which complemented and reinforced his anatomical digressions, he argued that the "cynocephali," "sphinges," "pygmies," "satyrs," and other creatures ancient authors thought were other species of humans were, in fact, either monkeys or Pygmies like the one dissected.

Edward Tyson's combined exercise in comparative anatomy, taxonomy, and literary criticism relocated a figure of myth in the discourse of science (cf. Nash 1995, Thijssen 1995). The Pygmie was a being intermediate between human and monkey, a crucial link in the Chain of Being, but still an animal, despite the fact that it resembled humans more than any other animal. Tyson admitted many similarities, among which the form of the brain, the structure of the larynx, and the erect gait, all of which would generate considerable controversy in the next century. But as a keen reader of René Descartes' *L'Homme* (1664), he stopped short of the rational or spiritual soul, unique to humans, and radically separating humans from the rest of nature, not physically but metaphysically. The dissected ape's larynx and pharynx, though morphologically similar – so Tyson thought – to those of humans, were "mere pipes and vessels" (Tyson 1699: 51), never intended by the Creator to enhance rational speech. These structures, he argued, showed the lack of a higher principle steering their use in the Orang-Outang particularly well. Somewhat ironically perhaps, in our eyes, physical resemblance was thus taken to support the disjunction, not the conjunction of human and beast – an argument regularly used in the eighteenth century as well. As in the case of Tulp's essay, the barrier between humans and animals was thus safeguarded, both in the anatomical treatise and in the philological appendix.

The literary text, *An Essay of the Learned Martinus Scriblerus, Concerning the Origin of Sciences*, satirized Tyson's well-known treatise by systematically reversing his claims. This satire was probably written around 1714 by John Arbuthnot, member of a collective of authors known as the Scriblerus Club who set out to ridicule excesses of erudition and the new sciences (Arbuthnot 1732). In the Scriblerian tract, arts and sciences are derived not from ancient humans but from the ancient apish beings described in Tyson's philological essay. It is not Tyson but his Pygmie who is presented as the great, though mute philosopher, and Tyson who is sent to the fair, where he marries such a monster. Here too, but now in a literary mode, the tension generated by a being uncannily similar to humans was coped with by tentatively challenging, but ultimately reinforcing, the threatened animal–human boundary (see Nash 1995: 59, 60 for a slightly different interpretation, and cf. Janson 1952: 336–339).

In retrospect, it is quite clear how these seventeenth-century anatomists, who set the stage for the eighteenth-century natural history of primates, generally tended to underestimate the morphological differences between humans and tropical apes, in particular with respect to the bipedal character of the former's gait and the human speech organ. In Tyson's case, pedomorphism – retention of juvenile characteristics in the adult – may have contributed to this effect, for he was studying a young ape, more similar to humans with respect to anatomy than the adult of the species. As mentioned previously, most of the tropical apes that reached Europe were juveniles, which together with sex differences complicated their categorization.

The recycling of ancient and medieval names and concomitant lore, as in the case of the Pygmie, persisted well into the twentieth century. *Troglodytes gorilla*, first described and officially named in 1847, borrows the first part of its name from the "cliff dwellers," one of the Plinian or Monstrous Races. Along with their names, the Satyr, Pan, Sphynx, *cynocephalus, cercops*, and Pygmie of Antiquity as well as the *homo sylvestris* or Wild Man of the Middle Ages lent some of their traditional connotations to newly discovered primates, among other things, the purported tendency to rape women (cf. Janson 1952: 74). The bonobo was first described as a separate species in 1933 under the name *Pan paniscus*, little Pan, which turned out to be ironically appropriate when more became known on its rich and varied sexual life in the 1970s.

2.2 The Primate Order

In the eighteenth century, more tropical apes arrived in Europe, not only chimpanzees from Africa, but also, starting in the 1770s, orangutans from Southeast Asia. They kept posing problems, though at this point not so much to medical anatomists, as to natural historians like Linnaeus and Buffon, who set out to pigeonhole them, as they were doing with all living beings, in their systematic overviews of nature. At the same time, Enlightenment philosophers and intellectuals speculating on human nature, a just society, and the history of civilization became interested in the Orang-Outang as yet another clue to the "original" or "natural state" from which civilized humankind was speculated to have developed. It added, they thought, to clues provided by "lower races" such as the American Indians, and "wolf children" like the Irish boy displayed in the Netherlands and described by Tulp in another of his *Observationes medicae* as intermediate between brutish animals and civilized humans (Tulp 1641).

In the various editions of his *Systema naturae*, the first of which appeared in Leyden in 1735, the Swedish naturalist and botanist Carolus Linnaeus undertook to categorize and name all living things. Similarities and differences between organisms were dealt with in terms of certain rules of Aristotelian and Scholastic logic, and visible structure was emphasized: the form, number, proportion, and position of particular animal and plant parts. The enterprise did not stop short of humans, and

Linnaeus, taking the many anatomical similarities seriously, became the first to categorize them emphatically with other animals, more specifically with monkeys and apes.

The gist of Linnaeus' complex, confusing, and, in some respects, confused primate taxonomy and terminology, which was partly based on actual specimens and partly on literary sources and changed somewhat over the years, is, slightly simplified, the following. Because of the considerable anatomical similarities, he ranked humans, *Homo sapiens*, in the authoritative tenth edition of 1758, in the same genus, the genus *Homo*, as the Orang-Outang, *Homo sylvestris Orang Outang*, and several other apelike creatures, real or imaginary, or a mixture of both, described in the literature of the day. This genus *Homo* was placed in an overarching "order" (*ordo*) of living beings showing more general anatomical similarities, that of the Primates, literally the first on highest in rank, together with three other genera of monkeys, monkey-like creatures, and bats. Some anthropoid apes formerly described as Orang-Outangs ended up in the same genus as monkeys. The order of the Primates was part of the class of the *Mammalia* or mammals, which in turn was part of the kingdom of animals (Linnaeus 1758: 16 ff.).

If anything, Linnaeus' natural history was Judaeo–Christian science, a *scientia divina*, as he called it in one of his first publications, demonstrating the glory of God, and honouring Him by naming as many creatures as possible (Broberg 1980: 32). Ultimately, the *Systema naturae* described eternal ideas in the Creator's mind, corresponding to the unchanging essences of all creatures – although Linnaeus started to challenge the idea of the fixity of species to some degree in the 1740s. The rise of the natural sciences in general has long been seen as going against the grain of the Judaeo–Christian world-view, but historians of science have recently come to stress the latter's constitutive role in the "scientific revolution." It certainly had a formative role to play in eighteenth-century natural history, to which it provided a metaphysical framework and guiding conceptualizations (Broberg 1980). Linnaeus' scientific work is a case in point.

He was an orthodox Lutheran, and very probably may have agreed when Albrecht von Haller stated in 1746, in a review of his *Fauna Suecica*, and referring to *Genesis* 2: 19, that Linnaeus was a second Adam naming the animals (von Haller 1787: 201).

Taking *Genesis* quite literally, Linnaeus saw nature as God's creation, a strictly ordered whole showing up a harmonious *oeconomia naturae* (Linnaeus 1972 [1749]). It was his sacred mission, he believed, to explore and codify this immensely diverse hierarchy of beings, in which Man, created in God's own image, stood at the apex and the centre. Humans, however, turned out to be very similar to other primates as far as visible, anatomical features were concerned. "It is remarkable that the stupidest ape differs so little from the wisest man, that the surveyor of nature still has to be found who can draw the line between them," Linnaeus wrote in the 12th edition of *Systema naturae* (Linnaeus 1766: 84). He then immediately stressed human dignity, which, he wrote (*ibid.*), was not so much the natural historian's as the theologian's concern. That dignity had to do with something *in*visible in us from which our self-knowledge arises: reason, the noblest of all our features, which makes us immeasurably superior to all other animals, as the preface to his *Fauna suecica* states (Linnaeus 1746: "Praefatio").

Despite his sincere allegiance to the Judeo–Christian world-view, Linnaeus' classification of humans in the zoological class of quadrupeds ("mammals" in the 1758 edition) and in the zoological order of Primates caused an uproar. As it made humans part of natural history and blurred the boundary between them and the animal world, it was perceived as a threat to the unique dignity of humans and their special place in nature. In a letter to Linnaeus dated 19 December 1746, Johann Georg Gmelin of Petersburg immediately challenged the inclusion of man among the Primates, pointing to *Genesis* 1: 26 ff: man is *imago Dei*, the only living being created in the image of God (in Linnaeus 1976: 41–42). In the previously mentioned review, von Haller complained that Linnaeus could "hardly refrain from making man into an ape, or an ape into man" (von Haller 1787, II: 201; cf. Dougherty 1996: 96). The English natural-ist Thomas Pennant stated: "I reject his first division, which he calls Primates, or foremost in Creation, because my vanity will not suffer me to rank mankind with apes, monkeys, maucaucos, and bats" (Pennant 1768–1770, I: iii–iv). Johann Georg Gmelin, Albrecht von Haller, Thomas Pennant, Johan Frederick Gronovius, Johan Gottschalk Wallerius, and Theodor Klein all objected to Linnaeus' violation of the animal–human boundary, while most of these naturalists admired his work (cf. Broberg 1983, 170 ff.).

A letter Linnaeus wrote to Gmelin on January 14, 1747 in response to the latter's criticism shows that he was well aware of the implications of his taxonomy of the human primate, and that he had even considered, however briefly, calling man an ape: "It matters little to me what names we use; but I demand of you, and of the whole world, that you show me a generic character, one that is according to generally accepted principles of classification, by which to distinguish between man and ape. . . . I myself most assuredly know of none. I wish somebody would indicate one to me. But, if I had called man an ape, or vice-versa, I should have fallen under the ban of all the ecclesiastics. It may be that as a naturalist I ought to have done so" (Plieninger 1861: 55; quoted in Broberg 1983: 172). Wisely, however, he did not.

Between 1650 and 1780, some 650 men – ordinary peasants, farm ser-vants, soldiers, craftsmen, and the like – were convicted of bestiality and executed in Sweden, together with hundreds of cows, mares, and other animals (Liliequist 1990). Similar trials took place in other European countries. What today might likely be seen as rather innocent exper-imentation with youthful sexuality in the context of a rural adolescent subculture was, in those days, perceived as a capital offence – a sin against the natural, sacred order of God's creation, and a vile and demonic trans-gression of the sacrosanct animal–human boundary. The public and the authorities reacted with bewilderment and horror. The adolescents were likened to brute beasts, and associated with the devil.

In a less extreme but basically comparable fashion Linnaeus violated the same boundary, when he classified humans together with apes in the same anatomical order, and included a non-human primate in the genus *Homo*. He was, of course, not put to death or even officially tried, but the reaction of many to his daring move, although less severe, was basically similar to the response to these cases of bestiality. Human dignity was in danger, in the Christian sense of the intrinsic worth, excellence, and high rank of a being created in the image of God, in the more secular sense of humanist or Cartesian philosophy, and in the sense of the moral world-view of eighteenth-century urban citizens. Many took offence at the unprecedented rapprochement of man and beast in the numerous editions of *Systema naturae*, although the Uppsala natural historian repeatedly stressed that their invisible, reasonable soul put humans high above animals, despite any number of morphological similarities.

A "second Adam," as von Haller termed Linnaeus, naming the animals, was not an inappropriate description after all. Taxonomy or systematics is the branch of biology that deals with the naming and classifying of organisms, and Linnaeus may indeed have thought of himself as carrying out a divine command. Adam appears here in a more positive role than that of the original sinner. In a miniature entitled *Adam naming the animals*, which served as the frontispiece of an English medieval bestiary kept in Petersburg, he is typically mocked by a monkey holding an apple, anticipating the act which will cause Adam and Eve's fall (Janson 1952: 107 ff.). By the nineteenth century, apes had begun to take over Adam's ancestral role.

By naming the animals at the request of God, the first humans assumed divinely authorized mastery over them. In human societies, names identify individuals as relative, potential marriage partner, or stranger, and situate them in the social hierarchy. Giving a name to a newborn child or bestowing a title is constitutive of the personal identity of the giver and the receiver, and of the relationship between them; it establishes the receiver as a member of a group (cf. below, p. 176). Naming animals, as ape or human or "Primates," had similar aspects, and establishing a hierarchy was certainly one of them.

2.3 Separate Again

The leading French natural historian of the period, Georges-Louis Leclerc de Buffon, superintendant of the Jardin du Roi in Paris from 1739 until 1788, was among those who felt that Linnaeus had underestimated humans. When he and his co-author Louis Daubenton dealt with the natural history of humans in the second volume of their monumental, and widely read, fifteen-volume compendium of natural history (de Buffon and Daubenton 1766–1799), an ape was defined as "a beast without tail, with a flat face, whose teeth, hands and fingers resemble those of man, and who like him walks erect, on two feet" (de Buffon and Daubenton 1749, etc., VIII: 42). Until late in his career, Buffon did not distinguish between the African chimpanzee and the Southeast-Asian orang-utan. He took them to be one species, the Orang-Outang.

Buffon argued that, similarities between Orang-Outang and human notwithstanding, including a similar speech organ, humans were to be separated from the ape lest the former be debased. Like Tyson, whose work he knew and quoted, he pointed to the divine breath that the Creator had infused into the human body and, following Descartes, conceived of man as *homo duplex*, consisting of a body similar to that of the brute apes, but also of reason, a unique feature, connected with the faculty of speech. Cartesian dualism, "a millstone around the neck of biology," according to Ernst Mayr (1982: 97), is a pervasive presence in the whole history of the human and life sciences and, as will be seen, still has a certain role to play today.

In an essay on the "Nomenclature of the apes," which appears in volume XIV of the *Histoire naturelle*, Buffon wrote that the Creator "did not want to make the human body according to a model that was entirely different from that of the animal; . . . at the same time as he bestowed that material form, similar to that of the ape, upon him [i.e., man] he infused His divine breath into this animal body" (de Buffon and Daubenton 1766, XIV: 32). Thus, man was "vassal du Ciel, Roi de la Terre" – vassal of Heaven, King of the Earth (de Buffon 1954 [1764]: 33). His reasonable soul, thought, and speech "do not depend on the form or the organization of the body; nothing shows better that this is an exclusive gift to man alone, for the Orang-Outang, which does not speak, nor think, nevertheless has a body, arms and legs, senses, a brain and tongue entirely similar to those of man" (de Buffon and Daubenton 1766, XIV: 30). If one were only to look at the Orang-Outang's physical shape, "one could easily think of it as the first among the monkeys or the lowest among men" (*ibid.*).

While generally adhering to the concept of the Chain of Being and operating within the framework of the Christian master narrative, Buffon was a declared adversary of Linnaean natural history. In his eyes, it stressed structural morphology and the reality of higher taxonomic categories too much at the expense of the functioning of individual organisms, fulfilling their role in the universal economy of nature according to Divine intention. Focusing strictly on physical reality and taking a nominalistic stance, Buffon undermined any realistic interpretation of Linnaeus' scholastic definitions – in his view mere speculative constructs of human thought. It was not the structural resemblance between human and ape which was important, but the exercise of functions such as thought and speech. Buffon called Linnaeus' system "a humiliating truth for humans"; to confuse man with a beast, as Linnaeus did, you must be as poorly enlightened as a beast, he sneered (de Buffon and Daubenton 1749 etc., II: 437). He concluded that, all in all, the Orang-Outang, "which the Philosophers . . . found difficult to define, whose nature is ambiguous at least and intermediary between that of man and that of the animals, in truth is but a pure animal, wearing a human mask" (de Buffon and Daubenton 1766 etc., XIV: 41). Its morphological resemblance to humans did not put it "closer to the nature of man, nor elevate it above that of animals" (*ibid.*: 70).

In the 1770s, Johann Friedrich Blumenbach, professor of medicine in Göttingen, Germany, split the order of the Primates established by Linnaeus in two, thus ridding the system of the uncomfortable closeness of human and ape. In *De generis humani varietate nativa* (Blumenbach 1775: 152), a treatise on the races of mankind, and subsequently in his *Handbuch der Naturgeschichte* ("Handbook of Natural History," Blumenbach 1779), he situated humans in the biological order of two-handed *Inermis*, literally defenseless, later renamed *Bimanus*, "two-handed." African and Asian apes, together with other non-human primates, were lodged in another order, that of the four-handed *Quadrumana*. The order of the Inermis was exclusively for man; it contained just one genus, *Homo*, and one species, *Homo sapiens*. To Tulp, Tyson, Buffon, and others who had held that the tropical apes walked erect, he submitted that this was just occasionally the case. Only the stick they were leaning on in many of the pictures kept them upright.

Blumenbach's separation of human and ape at the ordinal level had to do with his approach to classification. Following Buffon, he looked more at habits and functions and the functional morphology involved than, as Linnaeus did, at the structural morphology. Their grasping hands and upright gait, he argued, set humans apart from the simians, which were confined to an arboreal life and walking on all fours. Humans were designed to stand and walk upright, as suited their dignity. Their functioning hands, with their versatile thumbs, expressed their intelligent, free will.

This functional–morphological argument was not only connected with the idea of an economy of nature, upheld by the habits of living creatures, but also with Blumenbach's preoccupation with human unicity. As he wrote in a letter to Albrecht von Haller in February 1775 (in Dougherty 1984: 64–66), Blumenbach was determined "to defend the rights of mankind and to contest the ridiculous association with the true ape, the orang-utan." This was a guiding principle of his natural history of humans from the outset, and a decisive factor in the establishment of a separate order for them. Von Haller and others who had criticized Linnaeus along the same lines wholeheartedly agreed.

In addition, Blumenbach rejected some of the entries in Linnaeus' primate taxonomy as imaginary creatures, and was one of the first to distinguish clearly between the African chimpanzee (which he called *Simia troglodytes*) and the Southeast-Asian orang-utan (*Simia satyrus*). He rejected the concept of the Great Chain. If used at all, that concept could only refer to how adjacent links fitted into one another by their complementary functions, as designed by God, and not by anatomical similarity (Blumenbach 1779: 10 ff.; cf. Zacharias 1980). The various human races he took to be degenerations of one single, perfect primordial type, the "Caucasians," who lived near the Caspian Sea.

Edward Tyson had been the first to dissect a chimpanzee in 1698. The Dutch anatomist and university professor Petrus Camper had the opportunity to systematically dissect several infant orang-utans from the Dutch East Indies in the 1770s, as well as various other non-human primates. Camper pointed out a number of differences between the "Orang-Outangs" from Southeast Asia, true orang-utans, and the "Orang-Outangs" from Central Africa, which were, in fact, chimpanzees. The differences, he argued, were so considerable that the two had to be different species (Camper 1782; cf. Vosmaer 1778). As noted previously, part of the earlier confusion between the African chimpanzee, the Southeast-Asian orang-utan, and the African gorilla, the latter not described as such until the 1840s, was due to the earliest specimens studied in Europe being juveniles. Even Camper himself took the skull of an adult orang-utan, which he had obtained after previously dissecting younger individuals, to be of a different species. By the end of the eighteenth century, many more orang-utans and chimpanzees were reaching Europe than ever before, including adults, and this contributed to a clearer picture. A number of more-or-less fictitious apelike beings disappeared from the scene.

Other results of Camper's dissections had to do with the differences between orang-utan and human. The orang-utans he examined lacked the anatomical features that enabled speech in humans. By dissecting the vocal tract of an orang-utan, he showed that this living being was not capable of reasonable speech, as some influential authors had claimed (see below), thus restoring this privilege to humans and sundering them from the apes. The latter also lacked the anatomy for erect stance and gait, Camper argued in concurrence with Blumenbach. Both scientists, therefore, criticized the widespread habit of picturing "Orang-Outangs" standing upright with a stick. Another feature distinguishing humans from Orang-Outangs and other animals – or so Camper thought – was the absence of an *os intermaxillare*, the intermaxillary bone which is clearly present in non-human primates, in the upper human jaw. In fact, it is present in humans, but has fused with the rest of the jaw, as was discovered soon afterwards.

Erect gait in particular, associated as it was with the high position of the human head, was traditionally associated with the divine origin and dignity of humans. In a treatise on the creation of man, the fourth-century Church Father Gregory of Nyssa typically saw the human erect gait as directed towards heaven (Gregory of Nyssa 1944: 103, 106; cf. Stoczkowski 1995). This posture made man suited to command, pointed to his royal perfectness, power, and dignity, and distinguished him from the beasts who were bent towards the soil under that power. Stoczkowski analysed the persistence of this anthropological trope in the history of Western anthropology and its role in eighteenth-century and early nineteenth-century natural history in some detail. Very consistently, he commented, "erect gait signifies a connection to the divine world, while the bent position of animals stands for an attachment to matter . . . [bipedality is a] sign of the intermediary place of man . . . between earth and heaven, matter and spirit, gods and beasts, constantly threatened – as Aristotle says and his learned exegetes repeat – by the weight of the corporeal element which draws it towards the earth and enlarges its distance from heaven" (Stoczkowski 1995: 25).

Camper concluded that the orang-utan clearly was an animal and that man was unique. As was also true of Blumenbach and other naturalists, a distinctly theological–metaphysical agenda steered his research and interpretations. As an exponent of eighteenth-century physicotheology, he was convinced that the empirical study of creation yielded knowledge of the Creator (Meijer 1999: 11 ff., 52 ff.). "[With] the exception of the school of theology," he remarked in 1764 during an anatomical lecture, "where does one give stronger, more solemn evidence of the great wisdom, providence and unlimited power of God than in this lecture hall, where the beauty and perfection of our ingenious and excellent constitution are researched and displayed through the art of dissection?" (in Meijer 1999: 183). Humans stood apart from the animals, and functions such as the human bipedal gait corresponded to God's infinitely wise intentions.

Camper was convinced that all human "races" embodied the same metaphysical prototype and descended from one ancestral pair. In this respect, as well, he concurred with Blumenbach. Variations in skin colour and physical characteristics were attributed to influences of climate and geography. As a comparative anatomist, Camper was especially interested in craniofacial morphology and developed a method for precisely measuring the degree to which the jaw protruded – a feature which was later termed prognathism. The measure he proposed was the "facial angle," formed by a line from upper teeth to forehead (the *linea facialis*) and one from nose base to ear hole (Camper 1791; see below, Figure 3 on p. 64). Thus, he quite literally drew the line between human and ape.

The idea of the facial angle was eagerly adopted by proponents of polygenism, an alternative approach to human biological variation that had been gaining ground since the seventeenth century. It became the dominant theory in the first half of the nineteenth century, when the focus of debate shifted from the human–ape relationship to craniometry and the relationship between "races" (Blanckaert 1987). The wide differences in facial angle in the animal world and presumed differences between the various human "races" were interpreted as physical evidence of gradation in nature: the smaller the facial angle, the lower the creature stood in the hierarchy of creation. Applying this criterion, the dog was lower than the orang-utan, the orang-utan lower than the African, the African lower than the European. In this particular interpretation of the animal–human boundary, derived from the metaphysics of the Great Chain, the "races" constituted gradual steps or links between Caucasians as true humans and the brute great apes.

Unlike monogenists like Camper, who explicitly took an egalitarian stance on "races," or Blumenbach and Buffon, nineteenth-century poly-genists like Samuel Morton in the United States and Paul Broca in France stressed differences between "races" over similarities and explained those differences not in terms of environmental influences, but of fixed essences which formed a hierarchical scale. The genetic variability of humankind, conceived as one species by the monogenists, came to be seen in terms of "races" as separate species. These were ranked from very human to very apish, and in this context the animal–human boundary came to be drawn not between humankind and the apes, but between Europeans and other, "lower," "apish" humans.

2.4 Speaking Apes

"Speak and I shall baptize thee," the Bishop of Polignac is reported to have said to a chimpanzee in the Jardin du Roi in Paris, probably in the 1730s (Diderot 1975 etc., XVII: 206). There was probably too much irony in these words for it to be viewed as a real invitation. More likely, they were meant to fend off a perceived threat: this creature should and would never speak, and would, therefore, never be admitted to the community of rational, God-like persons by the ritual of baptism and naming. Per-haps the phrase was even meant to exorcize an intruder from the sacred space of the human. Speech betrayed reason, and reason humanness, as many argued along the lines of Cartesian rationalism or, more likely in the case of the Bishop of Polignac, scholastic Aristotelianism. *Homo sapiens* is *homo loquens*; speech is the outward appearance of mind. This pivotal nexus in the traditional European view of humans focussed the attention of the naturalists on the speech organs of the Orang-Outang, as did the unorthodox views taken by two widely read Enlightenment philosophers and writers, Jean-Jacques Rousseau and James Burnett, alias Lord Monboddo.

Rousseau disagreed with the optimistic belief of most Enlightenment thinkers in the power of human reason, stressing sympathy and compassion instead, and saw no evidence of inevitable progress but decadence in human history. Tropical apes figured in his political philosophy and cultural critique. In the famous Note X to his *Discours sur l'origine et les fondements de l'inégalité parmi les hommes* ("Discourse on the Origins and Foundations of Inequality among Humans") Rousseau suggested that the so strikingly human-like Orang-Outangs reported by travellers might well not be brute animals, but human beings in their natural state, *l'homme sauvage*, "a race of genuine wild men, dispersed in the woods in ancient times without the possibility of developing any of its virtual faculties, without having acquired any degree of perfection, still living in the primitive state of nature" (Rousseau 1755: 212). These beings represented the golden age of the history of humans. Their existence was not a miserable state of war of all against all, as Thomas Hobbes had suggested, but peaceful, healthy, happy, and free.

It was also solitary, he contended against such seventeenth-century natural law theorists as Hugo Grotius and Samuel Pufendorf, who held sociality to be the natural condition of man. Speech and thought were not natural features of the primeval humans, but were acquired by these malleable, "perfectible" – a concept Rousseau coined – creatures during a long history of living in societies and through cumulative change that did, however, have a corrupting influence upon them and led to selfishness, inequality, slavery, war, and misery, instead of progress.

Such wild humans living in *l'état de nature*, Rousseau argued, situating himself in an old primitivist tradition, provided an adequate normative standard for humans with respect to a good and natural way of living. It was not the artificial, unnatural, and decadent life of *l'homme civil*, but the natural, uncorrupted life of *l'homme sauvage* – the Orang-Outang – which was the true measure of man. In Rousseau's view, the speechless Orang-Outang was on the human side of the animal–human boundary. It was virtually capable of speech and reason, and certainly not spiritually incapable of using its speech organ, as Buffon and others had claimed.

Two decades later, the possible humanness of the Orang-Outang was also defended by the Scottish judge and writer James Burnett, alias Lord Monboddo, a representative of the Scottish Enlightenment, proponent of the Great Chain of Being, and Aristotelian critic of the empiricists. This matter, he commented, "is a very curious question of natural philosophy, and more interesting to us than perhaps any other, for it not only greatly concerns the dignity of our species, as some persons imagine, but if it be true that the Orang-Outang truly belongs to us, it exhibits a scene of human nature utterly unknown, and presents us with a period of the history of our species which it's believed nobody dreamt of before" (Monboddo, unpublished ms., quoted by Barnard 1995: 78–79). This prolific and controversial writer subscribed to Rousseau's uncustomary view that full-blown language was not natural to man but had been acquired in the course of the history of humankind. The Orang-Outang, although speechless, was a rational human in the sense of Aristotle, able to make weapons and tools (Monboddo 1779–1799, IV: 28–30), and, at least in principle, capable of language.

"The Orang-Outangs," Monboddo wrote in his *Of the Origin and Progress of Language*, ". . . are of our species, and though they have made some progress in the arts of life, they have not advanced so far as to invent language" (Monboddo 1773–1792, I: 188; cf. Monboddo 1779–1799, III: 250, 335–378). This took issue with the Cartesian denial of reason among Orang-Outangs by Tyson and Buffon. He saw the vocal organs of the Orang-Outangs, the "primal" or "primeval" humans, as clearly designed for speech. Other examples of the natural state of humankind, starting-point of the progress to civilization, were the speechless so-called feral or wolf children, abandoned or lost in the vast European woodlands and supposed to have been reared by animals – such as an Irish boy displayed in Holland and described by Tulp, and the famous Wild Peter of Hanover discussed by Linnaeus and Blumenbach. "[If] Mr Buffon's Orang-Outang was not a man, because he had not learned to speak at the age of two, it is impossible to believe that Peter, who, at the age of seventy, and, after having been above fifty years in England, has learned to articulate but a few words, is a man" (Monboddo 1779–1799, III: 367).

The rapprochement of human and Orang-Outang by Rousseau and Monboddo went against the grain of the predominant Christian and/or rationalist metaphysics of the day and the scientific agendas that took their cues from these world-views, for example, that of Camper, who by his dissections restored the privilege of speech to humans. "Let Camper's memory be blessed," Martinus Stuart, a Dutch Protestant parson and publicist wrote in 1802, "whose comparative dissections have liberated you from the unbearable humiliation to which a Monboddo intended to bring you – that you should have to call the disgusting Orang-Outang your brother" (Stuart 1802, I: 3).

The concern with the status of apes and apish ancestors and their encroaching upon the purity of humans has run through the history of emerging scientific anthropological disciplines like a thread ever since, as the following chapters will make clear. More specifically, a number of themes from the eighteenth-century ape debate persisted or have resurfaced more recently. The negative image of apes, apish early hominids, animal or apish human nature, and the "natural state" of humankind prevailed until a few decades ago, when more positive views reappeared, for example, as will be seen in Chapter 6, in and through the work of such primatologists as Jane Goodall, Roger Fouts, Sue Savage-Rumbaugh, and Frans de Waal. The linguistic abilities of great apes have returned to scientific agendas and become the subject of renewed fierce controversy since the 1950s. The taxonomical and ethical humanness of apes has also become an issue again. Toolmaking as a human marker, stressed by Monboddo, has been continually present in human origins research since the nineteenth century and has provoked much renewed discussion since the 1960s, when chimpanzee toolmaking was discovered.

The traditional metaphysics of the hierarchical scale of nature reappeared in temporalized form in the notion of evolution as an ascent or progress to civilization. Elements of it have been at play ever since, often implicitly. The most radical materialist stance on humans and souls of the Enlightenment, that of physician and *philosophe* Julien Jean Offray de La Mettrie in his *Histoire naturelle de l'âme* (1745) and *L'Homme machine* (1748), on the other hand, prefigured materialist currents in nineteenth-century anthropology and, to some extent, the evolutionism of Charles Darwin and Thomas Huxley. La Mettrie (1745, 1748) extrapolated Descartes' thesis of the *bête-machine* – the animal as a purely causal–mechanical constellation – to humans. The physiologist von Haller, one of the critics of Linnaeus' bringing together of human and ape, was horrified by de La Mettrie's dedication of *L'Homme machine* to him as his mentor, and publicly distanced himself from it. Linnaeus, likewise, thought little of the Cartesian mechanistic view of animals, let alone La Mettrie's mechanistic view of humans: "Carthesius certe non vidit simias," he remarked in a note – Descartes has certainly never seen monkeys (quoted by Broberg 1983: 166).

The primate order, humankind's place in nature, and the idea of a natural history of humans were thus conceived and contested in the context of a steady increase in empirical knowledge on the great apes, entangled with metaphysical articulations of human identity which were typically European and eighteenth-century. The same goes for the ape debate provoked by evolutionary theory a number of decades later, when the Linnaean primate order, torn asunder by Blumenbach and others, was reinstated by Thomas Huxley with new arguments. This provoked a new, painful intimacy between human and ape which is the subject of the next chapter.

THREE

Up from the Ape

Never use the word higher and lower.

        Charles Darwin (1903, I: 114)

While earlier discussions had been dominated by the theme of simian kinship, in the nineteenth century the problem of simian descent moved to the foreground. In the preceding centuries, new great ape species had been discovered in the context of the worldwide expansion of European nation–states and had come to be distinguished one from the other. In the course of the nineteenth century the first of a long series of early hominid species were discovered. Intricate connections developed between images of apish early hominids, apish "lower races," interpreted as "contemporary ancestors," and apes. Such elements of the key Western cosmological framework of the Great Chain of Being as the notions of fixed types or essences, a hierarchical ordering, and the pre-eminence of humans persisted, but were increasingly applied in the context of the living world developing in time, over much longer periods than the biblical account implied. All three sorts of apish beings came to be perceived as wild and ferocious, in contrast with the peaceful Orang-Outang of the Enlightenment that had been hailed by some influential writers as an uncorrupted "natural man."

The backdrop for these developments was a new conception of life as a harsh and desperate struggle for survival leading to the transmutation of species, rather than a peaceful, harmonious creation of relatively unchanging essences. From the beginning, this new conception was connected to the assumption of the Enlightenment thinkers that cosmic and human history exhibited progress of some form or other, either unidirectional or cyclical. Historical development as the maturing of an organism was another common metaphor of the period. Thus, while in the preceding two centuries European scientists had been confronted with humanlike, yet beastly apes, apish ancestors proved as disturbing in the nineteenth century – intellectually, emotionally, and culturally. In the eyes of many, they posed a similar threat, and challenge, to widely cherished notions of human specialty. For those scientists and writers who, in the wake of Enlightenment materialism and under the influence of Newtonian physics, cherished materialist assumptions, however, the encroaching apemen and apes were much less offensive. They believed that the ultimate constituents of reality were physical bodies and processes.

How the guarding against contaminations of human purity continued in the context of the new view of human origins is traced in the writings of Charles Darwin, Charles Lyell, and Thomas Huxley in Section 3.1. In Section 3.2 it will be shown how in the early twentieth century Sigmund Freud, with his idea of the brutish ape deep within humans, was strongly influenced by the nineteenth-century evolutionists, and how the contemporary German philosopher, Max Scheler provided one of the most explicit metaphysics and rebuffs of apes in the history of continental-European philosophy.

In addition to outright denial of ape ancestry, a common reaction was the distancing of human descendants from their wild animal ancestors by postulating a long evolutionary progress, an ascent to Civilization, exemplified by European culture, thus saving human dignity. By the end of the century, apish ancestors had become firmly established characters in such narrative articulations of North-Atlantic cultural identity. The concluding Section 3.3 addresses the germane role of narratives – as a way of coping with paradoxes – in the views on the human past analysed in this chapter and in constructions of the animal–human boundary in general.

3.1 "A grim and grotesque procession"

The idea of the transmutation of an ape into man had its advent in the late eighteenth century. It was present in the work of Jean-Claude Delamétherie (1778; cf. Stoczkowski 1995b) and was defended by Jean-Baptiste de Lamarck (1809; cf. Barsanti 1995), Julien-Joseph Virey, and other French transmutationists, most of whom were staunch materialists, and postulated a direct descent of humans from apes (Blanckaert, Ducros & Hublin 1989). Lamarck proposed the chimpanzee as the ancestor of man, while Etienne Geoffroy St. Hilaire (1798), who defended a unitary composition for all life forms, including humans, had already pointed to the orang-utan. There were certainly differences between humans and orang-utans, the latter wrote in 1836, but these should not be exaggerated "for the sole purpose of saving the moral dignity of our species" (Geoffroy St. Hilaire 1836; cf. Blanckaert 1991: 126).

"If we consider the progress of organization in the scale of creatures philosophically," the French naturalist and anthropologist Julien-Joseph Virey wrote in 1819, "the apes would seem to be the root of the human genus. From the orang-utan to the Hottentot Bushman, through to the most intelligent negroes, and finally to white man, one passes indeed by almost imperceptible nuances. Whether all beings were created progressively, with the most perfected ones derived from less noble and less accomplished ones, during the early eras of our planet, or every species was formed independently from the others with its actual degree of perfectness, in any case we observe a scale from white to negro, to Hottentot, to orang-utan, and from the latter to other apes. . . . However humiliating it seems to bring together monkeys and mankind, according to the most manifest connections between the construction of the organs, it is impossible to avoid this move in anatomy" (Virey 1819: 385). With the help of Camper's facial angle (cf. p. 53), Virey divided humankind into two species: one consisting of Africans and other dark-skinned peoples with a relatively sharp angle of 75 to 80 degrees, which situated them closer to the apes, the other of Europeans, American Indians, and other lighter-skinned peoples, with angles of about 85 degrees (Figure 3).

Christian authors such as D. Frayssinous, bishop and minister of state, on the other hand, combated the materialist evolutionism of Lamarck – who refused to discuss the human soul because it lacked anatomical features – and other "weird doctors who, tracing the genealogy of beings, honour us by making us descend from the race of monkeys, a disgusting doctrine, which one has tried to found on similarities in physical organization." Let us leave, he continues, "this abject philosophy to the materialists, let them enjoy it if that's what they want; as to us, let us remain humans, as God has created us, rational, free, immortal as He is, and, by all these gifts, a real image, though undoubtedly imperfect, of Him who is our creator" (Frayssinous 1853, I: 349).

In Britain, where these French anthropologists were eagerly studied, Charles Darwin replaced the idea of fixed essences of species with that of transmutation by random variation and selective retention of fit characteristics. This implied that humans descended from apelike ancestors, an idea that even to transmutationist biologists was bizarre in terms of their cultural experience, philosophical views, and moral attitudes. Early hominids were also referred to as the "missing link" between human descendants and ancestral apes. This metaphor, derived from that of the Great Chain of Being, served to establish a connection, but at the same time created distance.

Under the influence of Darwin's ideas, the German biologist Ernst Haeckel postulated the *Pithecanthropus* or "ape-man," combining ape and human features in 1866, and the first fossils believed to qualify for this status, found on Java in 1891, were indeed given this name. Haeckel lent the name *Pithecanthropus* "to the 'speechless primeval men (*Alali*),' who in their general morphology . . . already were 'men' in the ordinary

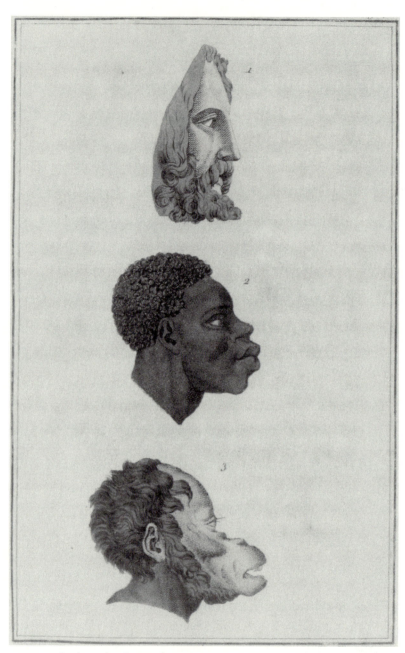

FIGURE 3. In the early nineteenth century, many scientists ranked primate species and human "races" on the "scale of creatures." Africans were believed to be closer to apes and less advanced in the progress towards the perfection believed to be exhibited by Europeans. It was assumed that the extent to which the face exhibited a snout, as measured by Camper's facial angle, illustrated a creature's hierarchical position in nature. From Virey 1834. Courtesy of the Leiden University Library.

sense, but still lacked one of the most important human characteristics: articulate speech and the formation of higher concepts connected therewith. Only the higher differentiation of the speech organ and the brain, determined by those characteristics, constituted true 'man'" (Haeckel 1874: 491). Speech betrayed a human mind. The *homo loquens* topos and animal–human boundary marker was, and has continued to be, pervasively present in the history of the anthropological disciplines, from the seventeenth- and eighteenth-century natural history of primates to the twentieth-century taxonomy of early hominids and recent research on ape linguistic capacities.

In Charles Darwin's bottom-up approach, the traditional view of nature as a hierarchy, created and ruled by divine providence, was replaced by that of nature as random competition, red in tooth and claw. Design was substituted by chance, meaning by matter, and the traditional metaphor of a scale or ladder of nature by that of the branching tree of life.

The more Darwin became persuaded intellectually of the theory of transmutation by natural selection, however, the more he grew uncomfortable with it emotionally. "I am almost convinced (quite contrary to the opinion I started with)," he wrote in 1844, "that species are not (it is like confessing a murder) immutable" (Darwin 1985–1991, Vol.3: 2). The intellectually radical but socially conservative naturalist was concerned about human dignity. He feared that his ideas would endanger his reputation as a God-fearing and law-abiding citizen. "What a book a Devil's Chaplain might write," he wrote to his friend Joseph Hooker on 13 July 1856, "on the clumsy, wasteful, blundering low & horridly cruel works of nature!" (Darwin Archive, Cambridge University; quoted by Desmond and Moore 1991: 449).

"Plato says in *Phaedo* that our 'necessary ideas' arise from the preexistence of the soul, are not derivable from experience – read monkeys for pre-existence," Darwin (1987: 551) had jotted down in one of his notebooks when he still was in his late twenties, prefiguring the rise of evolutionary epistemology in twentieth-century philosophy, but he postponed dealing with human descent until 1871, when his *The Descent of Man* appeared. The postulated genealogical link brought human and ape in even closer association than in Linnaeus' time, and Darwin himself was the first to find this worrisome. He was afraid of being labelled an atheist, a materialist, and a radical (cf. Desmond 1989: 408 ff.).

Traditionally, in the context of questions regarding the origin of man and the world, the term "descent" referred to the demotion of the devil from the realm of angels. According to the *Physiologus*, the most authoritative medieval compendium of Christian zoology, the devil was *simia Dei*, "the Lord's monkey," because of his unceasing ambition to imitate God. The monkey was thus associated with the first humans' fall, and has continued to represent the sinful aspect of human nature ever since. The lack of a tail of some monkeys was interpreted as *hybris*, a desire to rise above their station, and a sign of Divine disfavour towards any being – monkey, angel, or human – trying to do so (Janson 1952: 18–19). The presence of a tail in most other monkeys, again, was interpreted as a phallic indication of their preoccupation with lust. These connections lingered in the Western imagination, and, apparently, in young Darwin's mind. "The Devil under form of Baboon is our grandfather," he wrote in his *Notebook M*, commenting upon the instinctual origin of mankind's evil passions (Darwin 1987: 128).

The traditional pattern of descent was reversed, and the concept was soon partially superseded by that of an "ascent," up from the ape instead of down from the angels. The newly discovered evolutionary process was now cast as a progress towards humanness, epitomized by European middle-class culture as the presumed apex and natural goal of that process. The question whether humans were fallen angels or risen apes soon came to be generally decided in favour of apes, but again the latter were successfully kept at a distance, this time by the long march of progress sundering humans from them. Shame with regard to origins and pride with regard to progress went hand in hand.

On the one hand, Darwin developed a theory of transmutation by blind, strictly accidental variation and selective retention of features which are advantageous for survival, rather than seeing nature as an unfolding of a predetermined structure and hierarchy. "Never use the word higher and lower" (Darwin 1903, I: 114), he pencilled in the margin of his copy of Robert Chambers' *Vestiges of the Natural History of Creation* (Chambers 1844). In early 1838, less than two years after returning from the voyage of the *Beagle*, he saw a female orang-utan in the London Zoo, and a few weeks later he commented: "Let man visit the ouran-outang in domestication . . . see its intelligence. . . . Man in his arrogance thinks himself a great work worthy the interposition of a deity . . . more humble and I believe truer to consider him created from animals." (Darwin 1987: 300).

On the other hand, however, there are quite a few passages in his writings where he uses high/low metaphors himself, and speaks of progress and human worthiness. On the last two pages of *Origin of Species*, it is stated that "[as] natural selection works solely by and for the good of each being, all corporeal and mental endowments will tend to progress towards perfection," and the book ends with the remark that "there is grandeur in this view of life" (Darwin 1859: 489, 490). At the end of *The Descent of Man*, he states that "[man] may be excused for feeling some pride at having risen . . . to the very summit of the organic scale; and the fact of his having thus risen, instead of having been aboriginally placed there, may give him hopes for a still higher destiny in the distant future" (Darwin 1871, II: 405). Despite his "god-like intellect" (*ibid.*) – the *imago Dei* topos again – and other noble qualities, "man still bears in his bodily frame the indelible stamp of his lowly origin" (*ibid.*).

There is no clear consensus among Darwin scholars on how such passages are to be interpreted. There is probably some purposive rhetoric involved, an effort to sugar-coat a bitter pill, but at the same time they betray the implicit persistence of a teleological metaphysical idiom which is not entirely consistent with the role attributed to pure coincidence at the heart of Darwin's theory of evolution by natural selection. In any case, such passages show how intensely he wrestled with the problem of humanity's place in nature, not just biologically but also metaphysically, morally, and politically (cf. Desmond and Moore 1991).

The idea of ape descent was experienced by many as a threat to human dignity. Charles Lyell, the leading geologist of the day and a close friend and former teacher of Darwin's, for one, feared that the spiritual status of humans would be compromised by a close relation to brute apes. Despite his plea for an explanation of nature and its history in terms of natural causes in his standard work *Principles of Geology, Being an Attempt to Explain the Former Changes of the Earth's Surface, by Reference to Causes now in Operation*, he wished to preserve the "high genealogy of his [own] species" (Lyell 1830–1833, II: 21). It took many years before he more or less accepted transmutationism, though his acceptance was of an ambivalent nature, as was shown by Bartholomew, whose detailed analysis is generally followed here (Bartholomew 1973; cf. Desmond 1989: 327 ff.). Three decades later, Lyell still considered the close affinity of humans with the lower animals in all essential points, corporeal and motivational, as "a cause of disquiet and alarm . . . derogatory to our dignity . . . a rude shock to many traditional beliefs" (Lyell, 1867–1868: 492–493).

"[If] Sir Charles could have avoided the inevitable corollary of the pithecoid [ape] origin of man for which, to the end of his life, he entertained a profound antipathy," Thomas Huxley wrote to Darwin, "he would have advocated the efficiency of causes now in operation to bring about the condition of the organic world, as stoutly as he championed that doctrine in reference to inorganic nature" (Darwin 1887, II: 193). As a geologist, Lyell claimed that not one or more catastrophes but the same gradual, natural processes of formation such as those we can currently observe had shaped the earth's surface. How well-taken Huxley's observation was is clear from Lyell's following consideration, which records his spiritualist concerns and his personal struggle with two conflicting approaches to the place of humans in nature: "If the geologist . . . [arrives] at conclusions derogating from the elevate position previously assigned by him to Man, if he blends him inseparably with the inferior animals & considers him as belonging to the earth solely, & as doomed to pass away like them . . . he may feel dissatisfied with his labours & doubt whether he would not have been happier had he never entered upon them & whether he ought to impart the result to others" (Lyell 1970: 196).

During the 1860s, in the substantially revised tenth edition of *Principles of Geology*, Lyell, having been influenced by Darwin, admitted natural causes for the rest of life, but he kept making an exception for humans as the subject of God's unique creative attention. In his view, they represented a sudden leap (Lyell, 1867/1868: 167–173). "You will think me rather impudent," Darwin, upon reading the proofs, reacted, "but the discussion at the end of Chapter IX on man, who thinks so much of his fine self, seems to me too long, or rather superfluous, and too orthodox, except for the beneficed clergy" (Darwin 1903, I: 272). Darwin also wrote to Lyell: "I feel sorry to say that I have no 'consolatory view' on the dignity of man. I am content that man will probably advance, and care not much whether we are looked at as mere savages in a remotely distant future" (Darwin 1887, II: 262). But Lyell never gave up the idea of Divine intention, however remote, behind nature. "[In] whatever direction we pursue our researches, whether in time or space, we discover everywhere the clear proofs of a Creative Intelligence, and of His foresight, wisdom and power" (Lyell 1833, III: 384) is a remark made in all of the editions of *Principles of Geology* he himself saw to print, until 1872 (Bartholomew 1973: 266).

Adrian Desmond exposed a wider social and political dimension to Lyell's – or, for that matter, Richard Owen's (see below), and even Charles Darwin's – fear regarding the bestialization of humans. Lyell was a lawyer and member of the ruling elite who worked on his *Principles* on his father's Scottish estate. He feared social degradation, the abolishment of rank and privilege by political radicals undermining the church and demoralizing society by "a social Lamarckian science of progressivism, materialism, and environmental determinism" (Desmond 1989: 329).

The most astute Darwinian next to Darwin himself was probably Thomas Huxley. Eight years before Darwin's *Descent of Man*, this distinguished zoologist weighed in with the *Evidence as to Man's Place in Nature* (Huxley 1863). This was primarily an anatomical and taxonomical treatise, but Huxley was well aware that he was dealing with "[the] question of questions for mankind – the problem which underlies all others, and is more deeply interesting than any others – the ascertainment of the place which Man occupies in nature and of his relations to the universe of things" (1863: 57).

He shifted the attention back from eighteenth-century functional morphology and the *oeconomia naturae* to structural features and their evolutionary meaning. In Blumenbach's functionalist approach, the Linnaean primate order had been split up into two-handed *Bimana* and four-handed *Quadrumana*, but Huxley did not see structural differences between paws and hands which were great enough to justify that move. What mattered was not that certain body parts functioned differently, but that their structure was similar. Because of the structural, evolutionary unity of all primates, including humans, he reinstated the primate order.

"[Let] us imagine ourselves scientific Saturnians," Huxley wrote, "... fairly acquainted with such animals as now inhabit the Earth, and employed in discussing the relations they bear to a new and singular 'erect and featherless biped,' which some enterprising traveller, overcoming the difficulties of space and gravitation, has brought from that distant planet for ... inspection" (Huxley 1863: 69). The outcome of the thirty pages of analysis of morphological resemblances and differences between humans and other animals is that "the sagacious foresight of the great lawgiver of systematic zoology, Linnaeus, becomes justified, and a century of anatomical research brings us back to his conclusion, that man is a member of the same order (for which the Linnaean term Primates ought to be retained) as the Apes and Lemurs.... These are the chief facts, this the immediate conclusion from them to which I adverted in the commencement of this Essay. The facts, I believe, cannot be disputed; and if so, the conclusion appears to me inevitable" (*ibid.*: 104–105). No observer outside of humankind would have invented a special category for humans as opposed to other primates.

Huxley illustrated the strong anatomical homologies between gibbon, chimpanzee, orang-utan, gorilla, and human in a frontispiece showing a sequence of skeletons of these species, suggesting an evolutionary succession. To the Duke of Argyll, a biblically inspired degenerationist who preferred to lodge humankind not just in a separate order but in a separate class, the picture showed "a grim and grotesque procession" (Argyll 1868: 265; cf. Argyll 1863). Whatever structural similarities there were with apes, Argyll objected, humans had real distinctive characteristics, not only the capacity of language, numbers, or generalization, but also that of conceiving the relation of man to his Creator and the power of knowing good from evil (Argyll 1869: 74–75).

Huxley insisted that the scientific fact that humans shared anatomical features and instincts with certain animals should not degrade them from a humanist point of view: "[Our] reverence for the nobility of manhood will not be lessened by the knowledge that Man is, in substance and structure, one with the brutes" (1863: 112). Linnaeus the believer had pointed to the invisible soul humans possessed, which elevated them above living beings of similar anatomy. Huxley the agnostic, in a Cartesian spirit, pointed to reason, and to the associated "marvellous endowment of intelligible and rational speech, whereby ... [man] has slowly accumulated and organized the experience which is almost wholly lost with the cessation of every individual life in other animals; so that now he stands raised upon it as on a mountain top, far above the level of his humbler fellows, and transfigured from his grosser nature by reflecting, here and there, a ray from the infinite source of truth" (Huxley 1863: 112).

Out of "the darkness of prehistoric ages man emerges with the marks of his lowly origin strong upon him. He is a brute, only more intelligent than the other brutes; a blind prey to impulses, which as often as not lead him to destruction; . . . [he is] attended by infinite wickedness, bloodshed and misery" (Huxley 1889: 191). But a Hobbesian nature can be reconciled, Huxley argued in his Romanes lecture, delivered at the Sheldonian Theatre in Oxford in 1893, with a humane society by the triumph of ethics, a human invention (Huxley 1893). On this point, he diverged from Darwin and prefigured Sigmund Freud's views (see below). A man has no reason to be ashamed of having an ape for his grandfather, he had already argued in his memorable confrontation with Samuel Wilberforce, bishop of Oxford, at a meeting of the British Association in Oxford on 30 June 1860 (Lucas 1979). Dignity was not inherited but was to be won. The fact that humans descended from apes does not "diminish man's divine right of kingship over nature; nor lower the great and princely dignity of perfect manhood which is an order of nobility, not inherited, but won by each of us, so far as he consciously seeks good and avoids evil" (Huxley 1861: 68).

Huxley tore down the fence between humans and apes using anatomical arguments, but at the same time he replaced it with a new one, between the human mind and the human anatomy, using philosophical arguments and metaphors – sacred kingship, princely dignity, nobility – taken from European feudalism. In Huxley's perspective, there was "no absolute structural line of demarcation" between humans and animals wider than any line between animals, and "even the highest faculties of feeling and of intellect begin to germinate in lower forms of life." But "at the same time, no one is more strongly convinced than I am of the vastness of the gulf between civilized man and the brutes; or is more certain that whether *from* them or not, he is assuredly not *of* them." The belief in the "unity of origin of man and the brutes" did not imply "the brutalisation and degradation of the former" (Huxley 1863: 109–110). Only a fool would "base Man's dignity upon his great toe, or insinuate that we are lost if an Ape has a hippocampus minor. . . . I have done my best to sweep away this vanity" (Huxley 1863: 109).

The hippocampus minor, a portion of the temporal lobe of the brain, is one of the many structural features that, in the history of the anthropological disciplines, have been deployed to prove human metaphysical specialty, in addition to such features as erect gait, the intermaxillary bone, the speech organ, bipedality, a large brain, or a flat, snoutless face. It became the subject of a controversy between Huxley and the anatomist Richard Owen, who saw evolution as governed not by coincidence, but by divinely implanted laws, controlling the development – "orthogenesis" – of anatomical structure. Such laws, to him, were apparent in the archetypeal blueprints of groups of organisms such as the vertebrates. This approach took its cues from German holistic, teleological, and idealist *Naturphilosophie* as defended by, among others, Friedrich Schelling and Rudolf Oken. In Richard Owen's view, contrary to Huxley but similar to Blumenbach and Camper, it was not just the spiritual but also the morphological separation of human and ape which was a moral and metaphysical imperative during the whole of his career (cf. Desmond 1989: 288 ff.). Thus, he stressed anatomical features that helped in classifying humans as a separate category.

"In Man, the brain presents an ascensive step in development, higher and more strongly marked than that by which the preceding subclass was distinguished from the one below it," Owen stated in the *Proceedings of the Linnaean Society* of 1857. "The superficial grey matter of the cerebrum, through the number and depth of the convolutions, attains its maximum extent in man. Peculiar mental powers are associated with this highest form of the brain, and their consequences wonderfully illustrate the value of the cerebral character; according to my estimate of which, I am led to regard the genus Homo, as not merely representative of a distinct order, but of a distinct subclass of the Mammalia" (Owen 1857: 19–20). "I wonder what a chimpanzee would say to this?" Darwin wrote to J. D. Hooker on July 5, 1857, when he heard Owen wanted to place man in a separate subclass at the head of creation (Darwin 1903, I: 237).

One feature unique to man, Owen claimed, was the hippocampus minor. In the course of the controversy that developed, Huxley and others proved him wrong with detailed anatomical analysis. The hippocampus minor and two other features of the human brain, Huxley concluded, were not structures peculiar to and characteristic of humans but cerebral characters they had in common with the apes (Huxley 1861; 1863: 95–118).

Caricatures of Owen and Huxley – the latter as the naturalist Professor Pttmilnsprts of necrobioneopaleonthydrochtho anthropopithekology – appeared in the satirical novel *The Waterbabies: A Fairy Tale for a Land-Baby*, originally a serial in MacMillan's Magazine, by Huxley's friend Charles Kingsley (1863). Wit, parody, and ridicule were as much part of the reception of the idea of simian descent as of the idea of simian kin in the case of the Scriblerians and Tyson's Pygmie, or Monboddo and the Orang-Outang. Few of the earliest scientists connecting humans with their extant or extinct non-human kin escaped being caricaturized as an ape. The old hideous or ridiculous monkey icon resurfaced in countless cartoons of Darwin and the Darwinians as monkeys. In a meeting of the Red Lions, a learned society in Edinburgh, in 1871, the members growled and swung the tails of their coats while one of them recited the following lines: "An Ape with a pliable thumb and big brain/When the gift of gab he had managed to gain/As Lord of Creation established his reign/Which nobody can deny" (Wallace 1905, II: 48).

Such symbolic inversion, "far from being a residual category of experience, is its very opposite. What is socially peripheral is often symbolically central, and if we ignore or minimize inversion and other forms of cultural negation, we often fail to understand the dynamics of symbolic processes generally" (Babcock 1978: 32). The established rules, hierarchies, and structures are corroborated by occasionally playful but often bitter parody, which reflects, but also reflects on, and plays with, dominant cultural codes. Nicknames, as Anton Blok points out, like symbolic inversion, in addition to "helping to define social groups, marking bound-aries, expressing and fostering a sense of belonging, and reflecting the norms of the community," also comment on "the existing order of things, challenging, inverting or subverting prevailing moral standards" (Blok 2001: 156).

The ugliness of the monkey was the opposite of classical beauty, and this latter anthropocentric and Eurocentric aesthetic standard – as a canon of disgust – was widely applied to "apish" non-European "races" and early hominids as well. The ape's body is the grotesque form anal-ysed by Stallybrass and White, following Mikhail Bakhtin; it is the op-posite of the classical statuary of the Renaissance, elevated on a pedestal and monumental. Grotesque bodies are hairy and disproportionate, have protuberant faces, bellies, buttocks and feet, visible genitals, and an open mouth. They appear in carnivalesque inversions as parodies of what is deemed to be proper and fair. Such inversions are dangerous and pow-erful signifiers (Stallybrass & White 1986: 21 ff.). Nicknames often allude to physical abnormalities of the human body too.

How the various parts of the body are associated with human dignity is demonstrated by the French modernist writer Georges Bataille's parody and inversion of European *bourgeois* culture in the 1930s, in the wake of Friedrich Nietzsche. To the citizens' noble head and heart, Bataille playfully opposed the ignoble anus and toe, traditionally as infamous as monkeys being compared with humans (Corbey 1994). Such avant-gardist violations of prevailing conventions unveil the structure of the latter, just as the Darwinian intrusion of apishness did – although it must be admitted that Huxley did not think human dignity depended on the structure of the great toe, as the citation given above illustrates.

3.2 The Monstrous Other Within

Apish others loom large not only in scientific, but, under the influence of evolutionism in biology and ethnology, also in literary and political writings in the late nineteenth and much of the twentieth century. Early hominids, great apes, humans from colonially dominated foraging and tribal societies, or indeed one's political opponents were quite consistently depicted as unable to restrain themselves, as prone to violence, rape, incest, and cannibalism. The Darwinian perception of nature as competition provided new support to the age-old icon of a beastly, humanlike, and now preferably apish Other.

One influential channel through which the beast-in-man stereotype spread from nineteenth- into twentieth-century scientific and cultural discourse was Sigmund Feud's psychoanalysis, as shall be seen in this section. Freud's version of the beast-in-man can be compared to that of the philosopher and metaphysician Max Scheler, whose ideas are typical of the fashion in which most traditional continental-European philosophy approached the animal–human boundary. While Freud, philosophically speaking, was a naturalist, Scheler presents an up-from-the-ape scenario which, despite its spiritualist character, is similar to Freud's. In the foregoing, the term "naturalist" was used a number of times in the eighteenth- and nineteenth-century sense of one who makes a special study of animals and plants. In the present context, the term "naturalist" refers to one who regards observable natural causes – as opposed to, for example, souls, or God – as a sufficient explanation of the world and its phenomena.

The image of early hominids as monsters wielding heavy clubs was very common at the beginning of the twentieth century. According to Gabriel de Mortillet, who held the first chair in prehistoric archaeology in France, palaeolithic human ancestors were "violent, irascible and pugnacious . . . [they] could not speak . . . [and] probably walked about totally naked" (de Mortillet 1883: 248–251). These "intelligent animals" who could make fire and stone tools "were not humans in the normal geological and paleontological sense of that word, but animals of a different kind . . . precursors of man in the scale of beings" (1883: 104, 126; cf. 99). De Mortillet called them *Anthropopithecus,* "man-ape," a term also used for the chimpanzee in the nineteenth century. There is a "great law of progress in humanity", he held, and the *anthropopithèque-précurseur* stood half-way between the beast and full humanness (de Mortillet 1883: 393).

Monstrous apemen can also be found in the many editions of the authoritative *Les hommes fossiles*, first published in 1921, by the leading French palaeoanthropologist Marcellin Boule, who looked upon Neanderthals – in his view, not direct ancestors but an evolutionary dead end – as simian in anatomy and behaviour: "The utilisation of a limited number of raw materials, the simplicity of his stone tools, the probable absence of any trace of aesthetic or moral preoccupation correspond well to the brutal aspect of this strong and heavy body, the thick bones of this head, the robust jaws, where the predominance of purely vegetative or bestial functions over cerebral ones still manifests itself" (Boule 1946: 262).

While the examples given are from France, analogous ideas were present in British and German anthropology, as well. Often, such ideas were tied to highly specific, conservative or liberal, religious or anti-religious political programs and propaganda, as in the case of de Mortillet, who subscribed to a radical, anti-religious political agenda. They were also, obviously, subject to fine-grained shifts and developments in the course of the scientific and intellectual careers of the anthropologists involved – for example, in the case of Huxley. While such specifics are important, they are not our primary concern in the present context. What is sketched out in this monograph is a reconstruction of overall patterns in, and constraints on, negotiations of the ape–human boundary in anthropological disciplines since the mid-seventeenth century – the intricately intertwined network of assumptions, topoi, arguments, metaphors, and narratives which have been have drawn upon.

The following comment on developments in Germany was written in Paris in 1934 by an anonymous German intellectual in exile who was probably drawing upon nineteenth-century sources. It situates a stereotypical primeval wild other deep within civilized humans themselves: "It is true that the wild, the bestial, the wild colours of the drives have evened

FIGURE 4. "Gorilla carrying off an African woman" by the French sculptor Emmanuel Frémiet, presented at the Salon de Paris in 1859. This scene corresponds to the stereotype of the ferocious, lustful ape – and apelike primeval man – which was widespread until the second half of the twentieth century, and to the age-old Beauty-and-the-Beast topos. Bronze, 45 cm. Courtesy of the Musée des Beaux-Arts de Dijon.

out, worn off, and have been polished up and subdued in the course of the centuries, in which society has quelled age-old urges and impulses. It is true that increasing refinement has made [man] more serene and noble, but all the time the animal spirit sleeps at the bottom of his being. There is still a lot of animal in him. . . . When the graph of life curves downward to the red line of the primitive, the mask drops; naked as in the old days he breaks loose, primeval man, the cave-dweller, in the total profligacy of his unleashed drives" (quoted by Theweleit 1987, II: 25).

The "beast in man," usually depicted as apelike and an avatar of earlier, Platonic, Pauline, and Protestant dualistic views of human nature, is a forceful, omnipresent metaphor in the late nineteenth and early twentieth century. It depicts human nature before, or deprived of, civilization. King Kong, the fierce rapist–ape who appeared on the white screen in 1933, thrilling audiences worldwide, is close to what the beastly Other was imagined to look like. Similar apelike monsters (see Figure 4) popped up in fascist anti-communist propaganda and communist anti-fascist propaganda. Many pictorial and literary descriptions of early hominids and great apes were similar. They were inspired by the pervasive narrative of an ascent towards humanity that even governed its occasional negations, and a still-widespread Victorian hierarchy of disgust and pollution which organized races, classes, manners, bodily parts, city topography, and political metaphors in terms of high and low and acceptable and unacceptable. The dominant physical anthropology textbook of the 1930s, for example, was called *Up from the Ape* (Hooton 1931).

One of the most influential views of human behaviour, psychology, and culture of the twentieth century was developed by Sigmund Freud. At the same time, he was probably the most influential advocate of the idea of a wild primeval other within of the time. Freud was widely read not only in ethnology, but also in archaeology and cultural history, and was a collector of antiquities. He was also a great admirer of Heinrich Schliemann, who delved into what he believed to be the debris of ancient Troy, and often compared the analyst's work to the archaeologist's laborious interpretation of excavated prehistoric layers. Archaeological metaphors are pervasive in psychoanalysis: the archaeology of the soul, structuring its discourse, and the inner space constructed by it. They suggestively communicate authoritative core distinctions as that between surface and depth, manifest and latent, adult and infantile, civilized and uncivilized, historic and prehistoric, and fact and fantasy as being less and more fundamental, respectively (Kuspit 1989: 135).

In a Lamarckian vein, Freud held that everything once formed in the mind, in particular that which befell our prehistoric ancestors in their harsh struggle for survival during the ice ages, would survive or leave traces in one way or another in deep "layers" of the psyche. The concepts "archaic," "primitive," and "prehistoric," abound in *The Interpretation of Dreams* (1900), as well as in his *Three Essays on the Theory of Sexuality* (1905), and in what is probably his most important publication on cultural history, *Totem and Tabu: Some Points of Agreement between the Mental Lives of Savages and Neurotics* (1913). In fact, Freud was convinced that an impulsive ancestral apeman still roamed the depths of the human psyche in a quite literal sense.

Many of the building blocks of *Totem and Tabu*, Wallace concludes from a careful investigation of Freud's early writings, were present as early as 1900 (Wallace 1983: 51). Here, Freud launched his famous thesis of the primal patricide. In prehistoric hordes, fathers dominated their sons and monopolized the women of the group. The sons then murdered and ate their fathers, thus gaining access to these women, their sisters and mothers. But remorse over this terrible deed troubled them, for they had not only hated but also loved their fathers. Therefore, they refrained from intercourse with the women of their group and totem, and from killing that totem, which was the substitute or surrogate of the dead father (Freud, *Standard Edition*, 1953 etc., Vol. XIII: 141–143). What became taboo here corresponded to the two crimes of Oedipus, and to the two primal wishes of the present-day male child: to kill the father and to marry the mother. Thus originated social order, law and religion.

In addition to being influenced by Haeckel's biogenetic law – which states that the development of the individual mirrors the evolution of the species, in other words, ontogeny recapitulates phylogeny – Freud was a staunch Lamarckian. He believed that the memories of this tragedy, acquired characteristics, were inheritable, and had become part and parcel of everybody's psychological make-up. In his view, contemporary "primitives" or "savages" represented an early phase in the development of humanity – they were contemporary ancestors. As such, they were comparable to the early phase of individual development: the child, with its characteristic sexual inclinations and world-view. In addition, primitives, prehistoric or contemporary, were comparable to another case of arrested development: the neurotic. Neurosis was an atavism, a case of regression, not only ontogenetically, but also phylogenetically. All three, the primitive, the child, and the neurotic, Freud held, are characterized by a deficient sense of reality and by belief in the omnipotence of thought (Corbey 1991).

In 1983, an unknown manuscript by Sigmund Freud was found among the papers of his friend Sandor Ferenczi. It concerned a sketch for an *Overview of the Transference Neuroses*, as it was entitled, written in 1915, two years after the publication of *Totem and Tabu*. The second part of this manuscript, never intended for publication, is of interest in the present context. In a letter to Ferenczi, dated July 18, 1915, he called it his "phylogenetic fantasy" (Freud 1987). Here, specific causal connections are postulated between the experiences of humankind during the harsh, anxiety-provoking ice ages which put an end to its paradisiacal existence and several types of contemporary neurosis. Problems in the psychosexual development of the individual reflect what happened in correlating phases in the development of prehistoric humanity. Many of the characteristic emotional reactions, sexual peculiarities, and coping strategies of neurotics were once effective adaptations to the severe, traumatizing living conditions, natural and social, of primal times: the cold, scarcity of food, persecution and castration by fathers, and the killing of fathers.

In Freud's later publications, this Lamarckian point of view surfaces time and again. In his *Introductory Lectures to Psycho-Analysis*, published in 1916/17, for instance, he remarks that it is very well possible that everything which is related as a fantasy during analysis today – to wit child seduction, the awakening of sexual excitement by watching parental intercourse, castration – was once, in the earliest days of humankind, reality. In his 1921 *Group Psychology and the Analysis of the Ego*, mass movements are interpreted as a revival of the power struggle in the primal horde, with the father and leader with whom all the group members identify as the key to social cohesion. "Just like primitive man survives potentially in every individual," Freud held, "so the primal horde may arise once more out of any random collection; insofar as men are habitually under the sway of group formation, we recognize in it the survival of the primal horde" (Freud 1953, etc., XVIII: 123).

In *The Future of an Illusion*, published in 1927, he tried to understand the institution of religion in terms of neurotic remorse over the murder of the primal father. In 1930, *Civilization and its Discontents* stressed the importance of the aggressive instinct and interpreted culture as a struggle to control it. It explains the excessively strong aggressive reactions of children to their first heavy instinctual frustrations and their correspondingly strong super-ego by postulating that they are "following a phylogenetic model and (are) going beyond the response that would currently be justified" (Freud 1953, etc., XXI: 131).

But it is his final work, in particular, his "psychoanalytic novel" as he once called it, *Moses and Monotheism: Three Essays* (1939), which represents a last and firm recapture of the phylogenetic plot of *Totem and Tabu*. "The behaviour of neurotic children towards their parents in the Oedipus and castration complex," Freud writes here, "abounds in . . . reactions . . . which seem unjustified in the individual case and only become intelligible phylogenetically – by their connection with the experience of earlier generations" (XXIII: 99). The essential point, however, is "that we attribute the same emotional attributes to these primitive men that we establish by analytic investigation in the primitives of the present day – in our children" (XXIII: 81–82). Among the instinctual wishes, "born afresh with every child," he had stated earlier, in *The Future of an Illusion*, "are those of incest, cannibalism and lust for killing" (XXI: 10).

A major influence on Freud was the evolutionist anthropology of such Victorian authors as Edward Tylor, John Lubbock, and John McLennan, as well as the work of Herbert Spencer. McLennan, in his *Primitive Marriage* (1865), held promiscuity, even to the point of incest, to be normal during the first stage of the evolution of humanity. As men were aggressive and violent, and women usually depraved, primitive marriage had been – and still was among contemporary pre-state peoples – no more than a kind of rape. What is punished in civilized countries as a crime had been and still was customary among savages. This constituted a received view of the period. A similar perception of early hominids guided Cesare Lombroso and others when they interpreted prostitution and criminal behaviour as atavisms: pathological regressions of modern individuals to the savagery and apishness which once were the normal characteristics of our earliest ancestors (Lombroso 1876; cf. Gould 1981, Verwey 1995).

To Freud, in line with these ideas, the predicament of primitive man was one of impulsiveness and a lack of self-control, of passing directly from impulse to gratification. Intellectually, the situation was no better: the primitive mind was inconsistent, childish, confused, deficient in foresight, and inclined to embroider facts with fantasies. Civilization was only possible on the basis of steering, regulating and even repressing man's crude primary impulses. Evolutionary progress implied the domestication of man's bestial nature, the taming of the beast within, the triumph of reason in the transcending of brute creation.

In Freud's writing, the animal–human boundary is thus drawn within humans themselves. A stereotypical primeval other, now internalized, roams the inner landscape of the human psyche, the wilderness within, as he once roamed the wilderness outside. His aggressive and promiscuous nature may have contributed considerably to Freud's Hobbesian view of man: "After all, we assume that in the course of man's development from a primitive state to a civilized one his aggressiveness undergoes a very considerable degree of internalisation or turning inwards; if so, his internal conflicts would certainly be the proper equivalent for the external struggles which have then ceased" (Freud 1953, etc., XXIII: 244).

There is some irony in the psychoanalytic paradigm, which has so often been deployed to explain images of other and self – e.g., the perspectives of the common citizen on peasants, criminals, and prostitutes, or European images of "primitives" – itself being a typical articulation of such structures of alterity and identity. Instead of helping to explain such images it needs explanation itself (cf. Corbey 1991). Furthermore, Freud's archaeological metaphors have been criticized as unparsimonious, deceptive, unsupported by clinical evidence, and hermeneutically naïve in suggesting the possibility of reconstructing historical truth from context-free, unequivocal data (Spence 1987).

Freud's contemporary and critic Max Scheler, a metaphysician who applied the so-called phenomenological method, was a prominent representative of a broad reaction in German philosophy to the thriving of new forms of philosophical naturalism, materialism, and positivism and the implied obliteration of the animal–human boundary. "At a time when a world that had been shaped by Christianity and Antiquity is falling apart," his disciple and later colleague Helmuth Plessner wrote of this reaction, "man, now completely abandoned by God, in opposition to the threat of sinking away into animality, again examines the essence and purpose of being human" (Plessner 1983: 35). These two thinkers had the same philosophical agenda and pursued analogous lines of argument, though Plessner had a stronger inclination towards empirical biology and was skeptical of Scheler's metaphysics. The title of Scheler's best-known work, a rather short but influential essay first published in 1928, was *Man's Place in Nature* (Scheler 1961). Plessner published his *Die Stufen des Organischen und der Mensch: Einleitung in die philosophische Anthropologie* ("The Stages of Organic Life and Man: An Introduction to Philosophical Anthropology") in the same year (Plessner 1928). The fact that quite a few books with similar titles had appeared since Huxley's *Evidence as to Man's Place in Nature* (Huxley 1863) was no coincidence.

Like Plessner and Martin Heidegger (1983), Scheler tried to make sense of the first experiments on the cognitive abilities of chimpanzees, conducted by the German biologist Wolfgang Köhler (Köhler 1921; 1925). He argued that although chimpanzees exhibited intelligent problem-solving in such experiments, their behaviours, however flexible, and perceptions were still determined directly and fully by their instinctive impulses and needs. Therefore, they were not yet "open to the world" – *weltoffen*. They had not yet crossed the animal–human boundary into that dimension of existence in which it is possible to know the (things of the) world as such – divorced from definitions lent by instincts, such as the significance of a specific object in its being edible or dangerous or providing shelter – and, concurrently, in the same movement of mind, to know oneself as such (Scheler 1961 [1928]: 31 ff., 37 ff.; see Corbey 1988).

Toolmaking, usually seen as a human marker, was now dissociated from humanness. In the perspective of Scheler, Heidegger, and also Henri Bergson, all critics of philosophical naturalism, mere technological behaviours, even if executed intelligently, were not enough for a being to qualify as human. Only intuition, an intuitive grasp of reality as it truly is, indicated transgression into the human sphere. One is reminded of Saint Thomas Aquinas, who, in the context of his scholastic metaphysics, admitted a *vis aestimativa* in animals, a capacity of calculated behaviour, without allotting them the truly rational deeds that in humans testified to a rational soul.

Apes, in Scheler's view, were conscious, but not self-aware; they could choose, but not freely. Their behaviour was a predictable outcome of inborn and learned tendencies, and keyed to their species-specific milieu or *Umwelt*. They did not have minds of the human type. Mind – *Geist* – was what made us human. Naturalistic thinkers like Ernst Haeckel and, indeed, Sigmund Freud did not comprehend, Scheler, the phenomenologist, complained time and again, that this was something completely new, "not a stage of life, especially not a stage of the particular mode of life we call psyche, but a principle opposed to life as such, even to life in man . . . a genuinely new phenomenon which cannot be derived from the natural evolution of life" (*ibid.*: 36; cf. 59 ff.). Humans "can exhibit, to an unlimited degree, behaviour which is open to the world," while "the" animal, on the contrary, "lives, as it were, ecstatically immersed in its environment, which it carries along as a snail carries its shell. It cannot transform the environment into an object. It cannot perform the peculiar act of detachment and distance by which man transforms an 'environment' into the 'world,' or into a symbol of the world" (*ibid.*: 39).

Yet, remarkably, despite his criticism of Freud, the conceptual structure of Scheler's own thought, especially in later writings in the 1920s, is analogous to that of psychoanalysis. Both authors analysed human behaviour in terms of conflict and compromise between spontaneous, uncontrolled impulses, associated with animality, and civilized, rational control. In their view of human motivation, they are both indebted to, and representatives of, a tradition in German philosophy, the so-called *Metaphysik des Lebens* (metaphysics of life) to which both Arthur Schopenhauer and Friedrich Nietzsche made important contributions.

Scheler's *philosophische Anthropologie,* as he called it, was a rearguard action of continental-European philosophy, by one of the last of its great thinkers and a proponent of an absolute, rather than a relative, distinction between human and animal – a distinction that is of *essentia*, essential nature, and can be found in the rational soul or mind of humans, and not a distinction of gradual differences. These thinkers, concomitantly, regarded animals as "low," dull and brutish beings. In the present, early twenty-first-century climate of opinion, the presupposition that there are no essential differences between humans and animals, that humans are as natural as animals, that they *are* animals may seem plausible at first sight, perhaps even self-evident, but still is in fact contested and controversial, especially among philosophers drawing upon the continental-European tradition.

The latter usually do not underwrite the continuity of beast and man. They operate in the wake of Aristotle or Descartes rather than that of Locke or Dewey; engage in Kantian rather than evolutionary epistemology; in phenomenology or hermeneutics rather than a naturalistic philosophy of mind. They tend to take their cues from literature, the arts, religion, politics, or the everyday lifeworld – not from biology or physics. As different as these various European philosophical outlooks may be, they do have one thing in common: they all, in one way or another, draw a strict boundary line between animals and humans, and assume that in at least one essential respect the gap between the two is unbridgeably wide.

They do so because, in the process of philosophical analysis according to their specific methods, they encounter a characteristic which they define as uniquely human, denote as reason, mind, rationality, or self-consciousness, and associate with a truly free will and moral responsibility. They all, like Max Scheler, see no possibility of fully accounting for this characteristic in terms of gradual differences or continuity with animal cognition, the central nervous system, organic processes in general, or indeed anything three-dimensional and physical. In their eyes, the human rational, self-conscious mind is a qualitatively different, irreducible phenomenon which gives to the being which possesses it a very special place in nature compared to those which do not. Sometimes this is defended with sophisticated and elaborate argumentation, sometimes assumed implicitly, as if the matter is too self-evident to pursue further. Such positions are basic to the moral and legal status of animals in Western societies, where they are available for and exploitable by humans in many ways, as objects rather than persons, properties rather than proprietors.

3.3 Narrative and Paradox

Dichotomies such as high/low, civilized/natural, human/animal, and controlled/wild are as omnipresent in Scheler's and Freud's writings as in the history of scientific dealings with primates. Such dichotomies have always, more or less explicitly, been an element of narrative scenarios with human and non-human primates as narrative characters. The storied or narrative nature of scientific and philosophical views of the development of humankind deserves, therefore, some further attention at this point.

The backdrop of several centuries of scientific dealings with primates was a shift from an explicitly metaphysical cosmos, founded in and structured by a transcendent beyond, to a secular or secularized one. Basically, three master narratives have been involved here, as varied as their historical articulations may have been. All three posited a natural order which implied, more or less explicitly, a social, moral, religious, political, and economic order, as well as an alimentary regime. The first narrative was that of a transcendent Creator and a single privileged category of creatures in particular. It informed the views of Linnaeus and other eighteenth-century natural historians. The second – a secular successor, and, arguably, to some extent heir to the first – was the story of an ascent or progress from bestiality to civilisation and reason. It constitutes the master scheme of Freud's view of the human psyche and of most late nineteenth- and early twentieth-century interpretations of human evolution. The third scenario involves evolutionary approaches in terms of strictly contingent blind variation and selective retention.

The first two narratives, each in its own way, explicitly posited a hierarchical, teleological natural order of unworthy beasts and unique humans, edible and inedible beings, lower and higher "races." They have continued to guide evolutionary perspectives, surfacing in the very core of such technical scientific viewpoints as Camper's facial angle and cranial capacity as studied by nineteenth-century craniometrists. Occasionally, they have even influenced recent versions of the third type of master narrative: evolutionary scenarios in terms of pure contingency. The March of Progress, from crouching apish ancestor to erect civilized human (see Figure 4 on page 78), persists as an apparently ineradicably popular image in cartoons, advertisements, and other current popular imagery.

Narration, the telling of stories of who did, gave, told what to whom, why, when, and where is a basic human and anthropomorphist way of making sense of, and communicating on, things human, the rest of nature, and reality as such. Apes and apish ancestors were dealt with by Linnaeus, Huxley, Freud, Scheler, and others in terms of master narratives which identified the protagonists, their particular competence, their goals, their helpers and adversaries, tests to which they were put, difficulties they had to overcome, space they moved through, boundaries they had to cross, and transformations they underwent – their quest, and their success or failure. The chief protagonists in the anthropocentric stories looked at here were always humans or apish humans-to-be. Because stories are basically about agents, however abstract, trying to accomplish something, every story posits a teleology, a purpose, as the characteristic hero tale of becoming human, encountered in its several guises, clearly illustrates. In this case, inevitably, humanness was the goal. To reach that goal, the animal–human boundary had to be transgressed, usually heroically, by a primeval apish being questing for humanness.

Landau (1991a; cf. Bowler 2001; cf. Latour & Strum 1986) has shown the pervasive presence of narrative frameworks, the hero tale from folklore and myth as analysed by the Russian folklorist Vladimir Propp in particular, in a number of theories of human evolution since the nineteenth century. In these theories, a humble primate typically departs on a journey by leaving its native arboreal habitat, is put to the test of competition, change of climate, and predators, and is finally rewarded with humanness. Landau shows how the interpretation of anthropological data differs according to what the palaeoanthropologist believes is the primary evolutionary agent: bipedalism, encephalization, toolmaking, or language. In folktales and myth, a donor figure or guiding force usually appears in animal or human form and provokes, helps and rewards the protagonist, thus moving the story forward. In scenarios of human evolution, the donor is often an abstract force such as natural selection or neo-Lamarckian principles, and the reward may be intelligence, tools, or a moral sense (Landau 1991a: 11; cf. Caporael 1994).

Structuralist narratology, concurring with structuralist myth analysis, conceives of the story as basically a way of dealing with the paradoxes, the cognitive dissonance, of human experience and existence. People tend to make sense of elusive, frightening, ambiguous, incompatible things or events – natural disasters, the prohibition of incest, sickness and death, an evil world and a good creator, or indeed the simian ancestry of humans – by relating them to one another through a *mise-en-intrigue*, a narrative plot. This makes such events more comprehensible and manageable. Without dissonance, strains, and shifts in the power balance between acting subjects, entities, or values, there is no story line to mediate between the incongruent parties (Greimas 1990; Corbey 1991). This line of argument, interestingly, also suggests that some incongruence is always necessary to keep the story going. The ambiguity of and the threat of pollution by apish beings, as analysed in Section 1.3, time and again provoked narrative manoeuvres which had to ward off the danger and confirm the cherished presupposition of human unicity and dignity.

In many cultures, as a massive ethnographic literature shows, humans conceive of their identity in terms of exclusive but complimentary opposites, of which the relationship to one another is articulated by the story line. Europeans saw themselves as human, but experienced their bodies and bodily functions as animal; they were part of nature, yet transcended it; their God was of infinite goodness, but the world was full of misery and evil; they loved animals, yet ate them; they conceived of themselves as civilized beings, but had to admit they descended from brutish apes. In modern Western culture, the question "who are we?" was and still is typically understood to mean: "are we (essentially) human *or* animal?" Apart from folk perceptions and materialist currents in philosophy, there was usually not much space for graduation and continuity, either in Aristotelian or Cartesian ontology, or in narratives – that is not how stories work.

The methodological point here is that one must always look for the story. All kinds of human "others" have been categorized and labelled as wild, brutish, childish, irrational, and impulsive, with the opposite, inverse qualities usually being ascribed to one's own group. In the end, however, such anthropocentric categorizations are – and should, therefore, be analysed as – embedded in narratives, in a storyline which articulates how such opposites are related and specifies the boundary between them. The ape–human categorial distinction defined one such boundary. Narrative plots dealt with the paradox and anxiety provoked by the polluting encroachment of categorially ambiguous apelike beings upon the exclusionary human space. Human evolution scenarios, "up from the ape," inspired by an even more fundamental narrative on natural order, articulated human identity (who we are) in terms of apish origins (where we come from). Metaphysically and morally authoritative stories were told and naturalized, helping to ward off threats and deal with what was emotionally disturbing and cognitively confusing.

FOUR

Homo's Humanness

Art thou a man? Thy form cries out thou art. . . . Thy wild acts
denote the unreasonable fury of a beast.

Shakespeare, *Romeo and Juliet*

The series of discoveries of fossil material of early hominids, starting in
the mid-nineteenth century and summarized in Section 1.2, was accompanied by a steady growth of archaeological data on hominid behaviour: the Oldowan (flake and core/chopper), Acheulean (handaxe), and
Levalloisian (prepared core) stone tool technologies; the transport of
raw materials; the use of fire; subsistence strategies; the use of space, on
several levels; and, in the late Palaeolithic, the burial of the dead and
ritual art.

Colloquial and philosophical notions of "humanness" have continued
to guide scientific interpretations of such palaeoanthropological data.
This happened not only in the context of more general views of natural and human history, but also in that of detailed technical issues of
zoological classification and archaeological interpretation, for example
in palaeoanthropologist Philip Tobias' work on *Homo habilis*, dealt with
in Section 4.1. More generally speaking, there has been a certain preoccupation in biological anthropology with human unicity, to the extent
that quantitative criteria have been revised when new data on (other)
animals situated them too close to humans. Analogously, archaeologists

have struggled with the boundary between animal-like "ancient" and "fully human" modern hominid behaviour (Section 4.2). They, too, have been prone to dichotomizing and the wielding of all-too-flexible human-specific, and often double, standards in their interpretations of behavioural data.

That such features of present-day humans as erect gait, large brains, toolmaking, and language did not appear simultaneously in hominid evolution was mystifying in the light of traditional all-or-nothing views of humanity and animality. Colloquial and philosophical definitions of the term "human" in Western cultures turned out not to correspond exactly to the biological genus *Homo* and its behaviours. *Homo*'s humanness was at stake.

Witness the publicity surrounding the discovery of the first fossils of *Australopithecus afarensis*, in the Autumn of 1974 in Hadar, Ethiopia (Johanson, White and Coppens 1978). In the press coverage, this hominid was also known as "Lucy," and hailed as the mythical "mother of mankind" and the beginning of "the human family." The latter expression was not used here in the taxonomical sense, but as part of a post-World War II anti-racist cultural and political discourse on the unity of humankind (cf. below, p. 170 ff.). In secularized societies with origin myths decreasingly derived from religion and increasingly tied to science, this little hominid took over the roles of the biblical characters Eve and the Holy Virgin. Its ecological setting, a late Tertiary East-African savannah, popularly called the "African Eden," replaced the biblical Garden of Eden. In the late 1980s, the term "African Eve" appeared explicitly in the context of a theory, based on the analysis of mitochondrial DNA, of an African ancestor common to all modern humans some 200,000 years ago.

The humanized *Australopithecus afarensis* was, in fact, much more like an upright walking ape than a present-day human. From about 1980 onwards, even the Neanderthals were increasingly being excluded from humanness again, although they had lived three million years later, and immediately preceded present-day humans, in addition to being much closer to humans both anatomically and behaviourally.

Elements of the predominant European world-view – such as nature as a hierarchy of essential types, teleology in natural history as well as history, and the unicity of humans – have influenced the attribution of fossils to the genus *Homo* as well as the identification of the earliest traces of behaviour, cognition, and language of the present-day type (cf. Bowler 1986). In many cases, *hominitas* (being human in the sense of belonging to the biological genus *Homo*) and *humanitas* (being human in the colloquial, moral, and philosophical sense) have not coincided. In contemporary anthropological literature, "human" is still a remarkably random term and a continuing source of confusion.

In fact, most of the hominid finds – from *Australopithecus africanus* through *Homo habilis* and *Homo erectus* up to *Homo neanderthalensis* – are ambiguous with respect to "human" and "animal" as mutually exclusive folk and metaphysical categories. They combine features of recent humans with "apelike" ones, anatomically as well as behaviourally. Philip Tobias, a leading palaeoanthropologist, referred to *Homo habilis* as "twilight creatures" (Tobias 1979: 29), and "the dawn of mankind" was a widespread metaphor. The earliest known hominids, small-brained australopithecines, walked erect and at least some of them made tools; both features are traditional markers of humanness. Bipedality had been associated with human dignity and unicity in Christian thought and in the eighteenth-century taxonomy of Blumenbach and others. Now it came to be seen as just another adaptation to a specific ecological niche, no different from that of horses using four legs. Its role as a traditional marker of human dignity was taken over by such features as manual dexterity and large brains.

Homo habilis and even *Homo erectus*, toolmakers with relatively large brains, did not, in the view of many experts, possess the ability to use full-blown language, another marker of humanness. As such, exhibiting some and lacking other "essentially human" features, they were "betwixt and between," profoundly ambiguous with respect to the animal–human distinction which is so germane to the world-view of those societies where the anthropological disciplines burgeoned. The names conferred upon newly found fossils are telling in this respect: *Pithecanthropus erectus*, literally "upright ape-man" (Dubois 1894); *Plesioanthropus transvaalensis* (Broom 1936), "near-human from Transvaal"; *Paranthropus robustus* (Broom 1938), "robust almost-human;" *Praeanthropus*, "before-man" (Wood and Collard 1999); and so on. Even *Homo sapiens*, the Linnaean species modern-looking fossils were assigned to, was ambiguous because of the necessity of the pleonastic adjective *sapiens*, paradoxically implying the existence of non- or less sapient representatives of the genus *Homo*.

Palaeoanthropologists Alan Walker and Pat Shipman expressed themselves in a vein similar to that of Tobias – quoted above – on the *Homo erectus* boy discovered at Nariokotome near Lake Turkana, Kenya, in 1984: "He was an extraordinary combination of the familiar and the strange, an animal that looked and walked and sweated as we do, yet one who could not talk and whose ability to make mental maps of his world was extremely limited." His physical and physiological adaptations seemed "so sophisticated and uniquely human," but "[at] some deep level, being fully human is predicated upon being linguate," and in many ways, this being, therefore, was "an animal in a human body" (Walker and Shipman 1996: 296–298).

This chapter deals with the negotiation of the diachronous boundary between anatomically and behaviourally more and less modern hominids – "archaics" and "ancients" are both terms that have been used for the latter. I will start with the taxonomic boundary between the *Australopithecus* and the *Homo* genus, with *Homo habilis* fossils as the contested item, the major palaeoanthropological debate during the 1960s. The idea of "man the toolmaker" – the *homo faber* topos – has been one important criterion in the determination of this boundary. The Neanderthals (*Homo neanderthalensis*), *Homo heidelbergensis*, and *Pithecanthropus/Homo erectus*, as earlier interesting cases of accomodation of fossil species within the genus *Homo*, are touched upon only briefly in this context. Anthropocentric standards in palaeolithic archaeology are subsequently examined. The affinities and differences between extant human and non-human primates, especially the great apes, again both behaviourally and taxonomically, are the subject matter of Chapter 6. There, too, tool use looms large.

4.1 The Earliest *Homo*

Archaeologist Louis Leakey, digging in East Africa in the 1950s with Mary Leakey, felt that the ability to make stone tools was a necessary feature for early hominids to qualify as human ancestors, in addition to, and associated with, a large brain as a crucial and defining characteristic leading the way in hominid evolution. Like his British teachers, Leakey believed in a long direct line of yet undiscovered human ancestors belonging to the genus *Homo*. The assumption that there were "predetermined trends of development" (Le Gros Clark 1934: 288; cf. Cartmill 1993: 191) – which resulted in bipedality, big brains, and manual dexterity of humans as pre-ordained, self-explanatory features – still lurked in the background. The then-known hominids – *Homo heidelbergensis* and Neanderthals from Europe, *Pithecanthropus* from China and Java, and australopithecines from South Africa – were thought of as primitive, small-brained, aberrant evolutionary dead-ends. The large-brained Piltdown skull, found in the 1910s and for decades believed to be a missing link between apelike ancestors and human descendants, had been revealed to be a hoax in 1953.

In 1959, Mary and Louis Leakey found the first East-African australopithecine in Olduvai Gorge. In a publication in *Nature*, Louis assigned it to a newly created genus, *Zinjanthropus*, literally East African man and also known as "nutcracker man," playing down obvious anatomical similarities to the South African australopithecines, and exaggerating similarities to modern humans because the find was associated with stone tools (Leakey 1959). The australopithecines had, until then, generally been believed to be incapable of tool manufacture. However, when the Leakeys subsequently discovered remains of a new, more lightly-built hominid in Olduvai Gorge, with a larger brain and also associated with stone tools, "Zinj" was demoted to the status of an aberrant. Leakey now hailed the gracile new fossils as the large-brained, toolmaking, and, therefore, human ancestor for which he had been searching so long, despite a number of australopithecine characteristics and a brain that was, in fact, considerably smaller than that of the then-accepted *Homo* species.

The preconception of toolmaking as a pivotal event, introducing humanness and a unique human adaptation, carried a great deal of weight in the question of whether the new species, which it obviously was, should be assigned to either the genus *Australopithecus* or the more recent genus *Homo*. In Leakey's opinion, it was more likely to be of the *Homo* genus as it was capable of toolmaking. More fossils of this type were found, and in an April 1964 paper in *Nature*, Louis Leakey, John Napier, and Philip Tobias assigned the material to the genus *Homo* and a new species which they named *Homo habilis*, literally "handy man," a "more advanced toolmaker" (Leakey *et al.* 1964: 9) – but only after sustained resistance by Tobias and Napier. Leakey's two co-authors initially believed the fossils could be accommodated within *Australopithecus*, but they changed their minds after further specimens had been found. The paper pointed out consistent *Homo*-like departures from australopithecine morphology in at least five individuals. One of those features was a brain volume of about 640 cc, which was significantly more than the average of about 500 cc for *Australopithecus africanus*. Other features were the proportions of the front teeth and premolars, and the morphology of hand and foot.

In a letter to *The Times* responding to criticism of their interpretation, Tobias and Napier argued that the association with stone tools was a decisive indication that *Homo habilis*, anatomically "midway between . . . *Australopithecus* . . . and *Homo erectus*," between "the most advanced *Australopithecus* [and] the lowliest *Homo*" was "the more advanced man . . . the maker of tools of a definite culture and with a definite

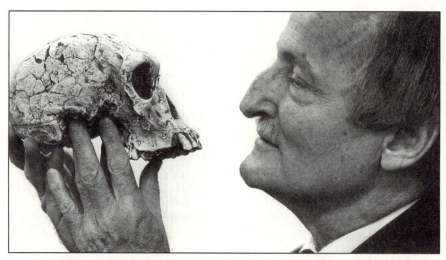

FIGURE 5. The South African palaeoanthropologist Philip Tobias in 1990 with a skull of *Homo habilis*, the first truly human being in his view, marking the appearance of humankind on earth. The fossil, KNM-ER 1813, found in Koobi Fora in Kenya in 1973, is approximately 1.9 million years old. Photograph by David Sandison, republished with permission of *The Star* and *Independent* newspapers.

trend of progressive development" (Tobias and Napier 1964). Australopithecus "had not attained to the crucial stage of stone toolmaking to a set and regular pattern" (*ibid.*).

For the young South African palaeoanthropologist Philip Tobias, tool use – let alone toolmaking – was already a "great step forward of the australopithecines over the apes," on the basis of cultural and manipulative capacities "which even apes possess" (Tobias 1965a: 189) (see Figure 5). With *Homo habilis*, however, "a new major breakthrough occurred. Stone tool-making of the complexity of an Oldowan culture became feasible; new, virtually limitless possibilities opened up. A new kind of man was born – *Homo habilis* – with a new set of implemental capacities, achievements and frontiers" (*ibid.*). The breakthrough occurred when some of the many *Australopithecus* groups "did acquire the right quantity and/or quality of brain to be able to use a tool to make a tool" (*ibid.*).

Tobias has stuck to the quite dualistic basic assumptions feeding into his early scientific work ever since. Time and again, he has sharply distinguished between the "hominid ecological adjustments" of the australopithecines and the "human cultural behaviour" of the genus *Homo* (Tobias 1994: 71). The former "animal hominids" were "essentially biological and social in character" and, although they had some degree of tool behaviour and culture, they lacked the linguistically based cultural dependence of the latter "human hominid" (*ibid.*: 71, 72).

Man the Tool-Maker, a catalogue of the prehistory exhibits of the British Museum by curator–archaeologist Kenneth Oakley, appeared in six large editions between 1949 and 1972. It is one of the clearest and most influential articulations of the widely held view that toolmaking indicates humanness. The subtitle of an American edition from the 1960s is very explicit: *Man the Tool-Maker: An Up-to-date and Authoritative Account of the Early History of Man's Distinguishing Trait, his Ability to Make Tools* (Oakley 1968). Oakley found it questionable whether the definition of man as "the tool-making primate" as such got to the core of what he was searching for, to wit "the heart of the difference between man and the higher apes" (Oakley 1972: 1). He considered "the possession of a great capacity for conceptual thought, in contrast to the mainly perceptual thinking of apes and other primates . . . as distinctive of man. The systematic making of tools of varied types required not only for immediate but for future use, implies a marked capacity for conceptual thought" (Oakley 1972: 3). The use of termite-fishing tools by chimpanzees as observed by Jane Goodall was disqualified as "a far cry from the systematic making of stone tools, the earliest known examples of which . . . evidently require much premeditation, a high order of skill and an established tradition implying some means of communication" (Oakley 1972: 2–3). Therefore, this behaviour by chimpanzees was no threat to human distinctiveness. Recent primatology, as we shall see in Section 6.2, takes the opposite view, stressing what humans and chimpanzees share in this respect and opposing the tendency to set humans apart by applying human-centered standards.

In addition to archaeological indications of complex implemental behaviour, there was another feature of *Homo habilis* which Tobias saw as a confirmation of his construction of the animal–human boundary: Broca and Wernicke's speech areas were found to be already present, as the inner structure of the skull revealed. In this respect, Tobias argued, *habilis* resembled modern humans more closely than it resembled *Australopithecus africanus* or extant apes. This led him to propose that *habilis* very probably had possessed speech (Tobias 1983), which, in combination with its large brain and tool use, indicated its humanness. Tobias thought it highly unlikely that so complex and intricate a cultural adaptation could have been passed on to future generations without some form of speech as a mechanism of transmission, cooperation, and social cohesion (e.g., Tobias 1995: 26, 31, 32).

Tobias' general view of *Homo habilis* concurred with archaeologist Glynn Isaac's (e.g., Isaac 1972, 1977; see below, p. 105 ff.) interpretation of archaeological remains in terms of home bases, food sharing, delayed consumption, division of labour, and pair bonding. Both Tobias and Isaac were influenced by the introduction of the New Synthesis of evolutionary theory and population genetics into physical anthropology by Sherwood Washburn in the 1950s. In this New Physical Anthropology, the typological species concept was abandoned. Hunting and toolmaking by bipedal hominids of the *Homo* genus, into which most then-known species were grouped (Mayr 1950), came to be seen as a key adaptational complex, a "grade." The evolution towards modern humans was presumed to be unilinear, and no two hominid species could live in the same ecological niche (cf. Delisle 2001: 107 ff.). In addition to such theoretical considerations, there were ideological pressures towards assuming the unity of mankind, in the wake of the racist excesses of World War II (see below, Section 6.3). Gradations within "humanity," synchronically as well as diachronically, were suspect – which is yet another example of a *humanitas*-ideal influencing the taxonomy of hominids.

As a taxonomist, Tobias has adhered to the same basic assumptions quite consistently throughout his career. When he looked back upon his research in the *1st Abbie Memorial Lecture*, in Adelaide, Australia, in 1979, the concept "human" clearly carried philosophical connotations. He spoke of "[the] stages in man's ascent" and the "cerebral explosion" which is "one of the hallmarks of mankind" (Tobias, 1979: 29). *Homo habilis* was "essentially an African manifestation of humanity" (*ibid.*). There had been a "humanizing reorganization in the little brains of the australopithecines," while *Homo habilis* showed "further reorganisation and advancement" (*ibid.*: 41, 44). In the human lineage, "thought [had] expressed itself uniquely by the development of a culture," archaeologically visible through "the material products of man's genius and craftsmanship" which pointed to "the dawning of Man's technology" (*ibid.*: 45, 46). The small australopithecine brain, on the other hand, had "not left an unequivocal mark as the wielder of a man-like material culture," but *Homo erectus* subsequently "carried culture towards a new pinnacle with the first glimmerings of ritual," and was "poised on the brink of one more great step forward" which was represented by *Homo sapiens* (*ibid.*: 49). "Through these stages . . . the graph of human cultural versatility and progress [rose] ever more steeply" (*ibid.*).

His publications from the 1990s, including his authoritative monograph on *Homo habilis* (Tobias 1991), are in line with this paradigm. The living great apes, and perhaps *Australopithecus*, had "carried non-verbalised, learned behaviour to its *highest pinnacle* (unless it be that the giant marine mammals have gone *as far or further*)" (*ibid.*: 836; italics in this and the following citations added). The brain volume of *Homo habilis* represented "a real *advance* in encephalisation over the small-brained australopithecines" and was "the most *dramatic* change to have occurred in hominid evolution in the last three million years" (Tobias 1995: 15). Speech represented the attainment of "a new *level* of organization . . . in the evolution of life on earth" (*ibid.*: 42). A "diagram of the *degrees of hominisation* shown by various parts of the evolving hominid bodily structure and by phases of material cultural *advancement*" (*ibid.*: 69) plots physical and behavioural features attaining "100% at the top of the vertical axis with the appearance of various species of *Homo* plotted on the horizontal axis." Toolmaking as a cultural tradition "might have catalysed the further great step which brought the genus *Homo*, true human beings, into existence" (Tobias 1991: 832).

For a palaeoanthropological work, the last chapter of Tobias' monograph on *Homo habilis* is unusually explicit as to the book's philosophical premises. He sees "[the] coming of the genus *Homo*," as the first part of the chapter's title reads, as "[the] attainment of a new level of organization on planet earth," as its second part states. Tobias' view of culture and humanness is holistic. Tangible expressions such as stone tools, he writes, referring to R. H. Lowie and the Boasian tradition, are "only a part of the whole," in addition to socially transmitted beliefs, habits, and norms, with spoken language as the mechanism of transmission and key organizing feature. Language is "the indispensable prerequisite for the development of all these things that, from a behavioural point of view, have made some hominids human." It is "the cardinal factor in the evolution of the human brain, intellect and spirit" (*ibid.*: 841, 842).

Language was connected to the differential enlargement of the brain in a positive feedback relationship, which "made over an animal hominid into a human hominid" (*ibid.*: 842). Again, the term "human" carries much more weight than membership in the biological genus *Homo*. For Tobias, it refers to a novel organizational level in progressive cosmic development, transcending and "not comparable in degree or kind with the . . . lower levels" (*ibid.*: 844), as Tobias maintains, citing the concept of *scala naturae* used by, among others, Theodosius Dobzhansky, Joseph Needham, Herbert Spencer, and Scholastic metaphysics itself. Hominids which preceded "articulate, language-bound, and culture dependent" *Homo habilis* "were essentially upright-walking apes [which] behaviourally . . . had distanced themselves but little from their animality" (*ibid.*:

845). *Homo habilis* "was the first culture-bound and language-dependent primate. That duality marked the beginnings of humanity as we comprehend it today" (*ibid.*: 840).

Tobias' problem with his "enigmatic stranger" (*ibid.*: 20), *Homo habilis*, was similar to the one Tyson (1699) had with his stranger, the Pygmie. Tobias wondered whether his fossils were australopithecine or human, Tyson whether the Pygmie was a monkey or a human. For Tobias, cultural behaviour tipped the scale in favour of *Homo*. Subscribing to an evolutionary taxonomy, which takes adaptive features into account, he saw *Homo* as a large-brained, unilinear, culturally adapted lineage, with *Homo habilis, Homo erectus,* and *Homo sapiens* as three consecutive chronospecies representing "grades" or adaptive stages. Competitive exclusion was thought to prevent the sharing of the same ecological niche by two similarly adapted species, and speciation was believed to be "allopatric" – to occur through adaptive radiation to other niches.

The cladist perspective in taxonomy, on the other hand, which has been gaining ground since about 1970, takes a different approach. It aims at ascertaining evolutionary relationships by looking at genetically based features contemporary organisms share with others irrespective of the adaptive value of those features. These features must be derived, that is, newly evolved, and not shared with ancestors. The cladist approach looks at "clades," not (adaptive) "grades," and replaces adaptationist and gradualist unilinear approaches which tend to lump species – as does Tobias – with multilinear, bushlike patterns and, often, punctuational, abrupt speciation or "cladogenesis." A clade, literally "branch," then, is a valid group with a common ancestor unique to that group.

Cladists have criticized evolutionary taxonomy in terms of "grades" for its tendency towards anthropocentrism, essentialism, and a teleology of progress (e.g., Cartmill 2001, Wildman *et al.* 2003: 7181). The New Synthesis, writes Ian Tattersall (2000: 8), "has imparted a sense almost of inevitability to the arrival of *Homo sapiens,* for under the dictates of the Synthesis the story of human evolution has been effectively that of a long, dogged, single-minded, trudge from primitiveness to perfection." The australopithecines, for example, "were not simply a monotonous early 'stage' in the ascent to humanity. Rather, while maintaining a basic body plan, they represent a period of intense speciation and evolutionary experimentation in early hominid history. It is from this ferment that the human ancestor ultimately emerged" (*ibid.*: 11). The analysis of Tobias' views given above supports this criticism (as does Landau 1991: 161 ff.).

In the foreword to a reprint of Willi Hennig's revolutionary *Phylogenetic Systematics* of 1966, three cladists wrote: "Hennig established a criterion of demarcation between science and metaphysics at a time when neo-Darwinism had attained a sort of metaphysical pinnacle by imposing a burden of subjectivity and tautology on nature's observable hierarchy. Encumbered with vague and slippery ideas about adaptation, fitness, biological species, and natural selection, neo-Darwinism (summed up in the evolutionary systematics of Mayr and Simpson) not only lacked a definable investigatory method, but came to depend, both for evolutionary interpretation and classification, on consensus and authority" (Rosen, Nelson and Patterson 1979: ix; cf. Delisle 2001: 114 ff.). However, the last chapter of the present analysis argues against such stereotypical and slightly self-congratulatory dichotomizing between ("hard") science and (speculative) metaphysics.

In the eyes of "gradist" palaeoanthropologist C. Loring Brace, on the other hand, "a cladistic view amounts to typological essentialism, or mind-made categories, which have nothing to do with the adaptive aspects of evolution" (interview with Ferrie 1997: 855). He refutes the endless "splitting" – proliferation of specific names – by cladists. Only major adaptive changes such as a significant increase in brain size warrant formal taxonomic recognition: "The teeming profusion of formal specific names that have been spawned over the last decade or so has been an intellectual and pedagogical disaster ... there should be a systematic reassessment of hominid taxonomy with due attention paid to the difference between traits and trait configurations that indicate genetic relationships only and those that have major adaptive significance" (Brace 1993: 162–163).

Here again, there is a parallel with eighteenth-century natural history. Linnaeus, like the cladists, classified strictly according to *structural* morphology. Blumenbach, on the other hand, and more in line with a grade approach, preferred to look at *functional* morphology, for instance, the grasping hand, in relation to how an organism fitted into the "economy of nature." Of course, neither had an evolutionary point of view.

4.2 "Ancients" and "Moderns"

Physical anthropologists like Tobias looked primarily at the skeletal material of early hominids in order to reconstruct what they were like physically and how they relate taxonomically. Archaeologists, on the other hand, focus on stones, bones, and spatial patterning with a view to reconstructing behaviour. While Tobias was the foremost specialist on early hominid fossils of his generation, Glynn Isaac, another South-African, was one of the most influential and original specialists on their behaviour, and drew upon palaeontology, ethnology, ecology, primatology, nutritional studies, and geology in his interdisciplinary approach. The major fieldwork he did was at Lake Natron in Tanzania, and Olorgesailie, Naivasha/Nakuru, and Koobi Fora in Kenya. In Isaac's research, too, the question loomed large of when, how, and why hominids became modern, like us, though not primarily in the sense of anatomical modernity but from the perspective of behavioural and cognitive modernity. What, in this sense, was the earliest human?

Isaac argued that "hunting, food sharing, division of labour, pair bonding, and operation from a home base or camp, form a functional complex, the components of which are more likely to have developed in concert than in succession. It is easy to see that tools, language, and social cooperation would fit into the functional complex as well" (Isaac 1972: 174). In line with Tobias' views and the "Man the Hunter" paradigm of

Sherwood Washburn and his pupils, the idea was that *Homo habilis* and *Homo erectus* were full-fledged humans. They were thought to display an adaptation of the modern type, with bipedalism, toolmaking, a ranging around home bases, hunting, food carrying, language, cultural traditions, complex sociality with cooperation, and a division of labour between the sexes. Present-day hunter–gatherers such as the !Kung Bushmen were looked upon as exemplars of the deep past.

Lewis Binford and other New (or Processual) Archaeologists, however, resented what they viewed as too idealist an approach to the material record of the past. What they saw when looking at the very same archaeological patterns was not so much the condensation of one single past society as an accumulation of many activities over large spans of time, combined with the effects of natural processes. They did not see a Pompeii, lying as it once was, but a hard if not impossible to disentangle palimpsest. They called for a more objective examination of the physical processes which had contributed to the archaeological record, which, they felt, should not be approached in the fashion in which historians dealt with documents and archives, left behind in a distant past and now ready to be read and interpreted.

Such East African sites as Olorgesaillie and Koobi Fora were re-analysed. Associations between stone tools and remains of fauna were re-interpreted as the result of many unrelated visits to the same spot, combined with post-depositional processes such the action of running water and the impact of carnivores. The New Archaeologists saw no evidence of "base camps" in the Isaac sense, nor of food sharing, big-game hunting, or much planning depth. They objected to what in their eyes was the uncritical projecting of knowledge concerning present-day foragers into a deep past that may well have been very different. What they saw was scavenging, not hunting (Binford 1981, 1989). The verdict was that Isaac's interpretations had been given uncritically, in terms of an assumption of modernity and a fallacious projection of survival strategies of recent foragers into the early Pleistocene. *Homo habilis* and *Homo erectus*, the first humans and mighty hunters according to Tobias and Isaac, among others, were demoted to the status of beastly marginal scavengers and, thus, again dehumanized.

In the course of the 1970s, Isaac reconsidered and to some extent revised his model. While sticking to the idea of home bases, or at least, in a more cautious formula, "central place foraging," he came to place more stress on food sharing and less on hunting as unique human adaptations. The bipedal, toolmaking hominids of one million years ago seemed to have lived in cooperating groups, sharing food and hunting, "but the archaeological record suggests," he now wrote, "that by our standards their capacity for culture was slight. Very probably they lacked effective language and did not have the mind–brain configuration that we regard as human. By the end of the Middle Pleistocene, some fifty to one hundred thousand years ago, both the archaeological and osteological evidence attest the emergence of hominids with fully human capabilities" (Isaac and Isaac 1977: 219). Despite these concessions, Binford still opined that Isaac told "just-so" stories about "a kind of middle-class genteel proto-human who shared his food, took care of his family, and was on his way to being emotionally and intellectually human" (Binford, 1981: 295).

From the status of modern and human hunters in the sense that they were defined by Washburn, Isaac, and Tobias, early hominids were de-moted to that of "ancient" animal-like scroungers, up to and includ-ing Neanderthals. During most of the twentieth century, many, but not all, authors had viewed the Neanderthals as a separate subhuman side branch of the ascent to *Homo sapiens* – the pre-sapient lineage which had inspired and was supported by the Piltdown fraud. By 1960, *Homo neanderthalensis* – along with *Pithecanthropus* – had been incorporated into the human species and into modern-human ancestry as the sub-species *Homo sapiens neanderthalensis* and gained humanness in recon-structions of behaviour and appearance. Subsequently, cladist taxonomy, combined with a stress on punctuational branching and critical read-ings of the Neanderthal archaeological record in the style of the New

Archaeology, led to the resurrection of Neanderthals as a separate, not too human, biologically and behaviorally distinct species. In that view, still vividly disputed at present, the Cro-Magnons are the earliest humans of the present-day type, cognitively and behaviorally speaking.

This implied that the animal–human boundary be repositioned from about two million years ago, where Tobias and Isaac had situated it, to just 40,000 years ago. The archaeologist Clive Gamble, for example, has set up a dichotomy between ecological and cultural adaptations similar to that constructed by Tobias, but while the latter saw humanness appearing two millions years ago, Gamble situated the transition to humanness almost two million years later. He claimed a sharply punctuated transition from animal-like "ancients" to fully human "moderns" at the beginning of the Upper Palaeolithic, with the arrival of the Cro-Magnons. "[The] notion of a paleoculture with a reduced level of symbolic content," Gamble wrote, "[is] untenable. Symbolism is not a quality of social life that can be turned up and down. Either all behaviour is symbolically constructed, or none of it can be. The transition would be punctuated, rather than a gradual process" (Gamble 1994: 101). Because Neanderthal material culture "was not symbolically organized . . . [and Neanderthals] did not have culture in the sense we understand it today and recognize it over the last 40,000 years," it is claimed that "[just] as birds are assisted in their survival by the nests they build, so too . . . were Neanderthals as tool-assisted hominids" (Stringer and Gamble 1993: 212). Both Chris Stringer and Clive Gamble have moderated their views on this matter somewhat since.

In a number of co-authored publications, archaeologist Iain Davidson and psychologist Bill Noble have explored theoretical, empirical, and methodological grounds for a relatively late emergence of full-blown syntactic language, dating it at less than one hundred thousand years ago. One of their arguments is the finished-artefact fallacy. This entails seeing the final form of an artefact as having been intended by a clever stone knapper, while, in fact, it is but the unintended residue of repeated resharpening, a cognitively much simpler *ad hoc* behavioural routine.

Envisioning the end-product and continuously testing each step of the action sequence against it, they argue, was not a necessary requirement. Handaxe or other tool types which provide evidence of a considerable degree of standardization over vast expanses of time and space, therefore, do not necessarily reflect the self-consciously articulated mental categories and cultural standards of their makers, usually associated, explicitly or implicitly, with linguistic capacities. Davidson and Noble presuppose "that 'the mental' equates to language in human life, hence make for the unicity of human mentality" (Noble and Davidson 1996: 226; cf. Noble and Davidson 1993, as well as Davidson and Noble 1993). *Homo sapiens*, thinking man, in other words, is *homo loquens*, speaking man.

An interesting implication of scenarios like those of Gamble and the Davidson and Noble duo, assuming a very recent crossing of the animal–human, "ancient"–"modern" boundary, is the uncoupling of modern anatomy from modern behaviour. These two were still welded firmly together in the idea of a typically human adaptive grade in the work of Tobias and others. Noble and Davidson (1996: 216) think that the archaeological evidence "allows the proposition that for some time subsequent to the evolution of morphologies approximating the form of modern human beings, behaviours expressed by them had crucial similarities to those observed among other modern primates." The implication is that humanness may come in mozaically configurating constituents instead of being an integral essence which is either completely present or completely absent.

The dichotomizing by Davidson and Noble as well as many others when it comes to the emergence of humanness has been criticized on methodological grounds by Barbara King, an anthropologist whose works centre on communication in baboons and apes. What these archaeologists do, she claims, is assume that the human form of a particular characteristic, say vocal communication, is the main defining feature of that characteristic. When one defines language, as they do, in terms of the wielding of arbitrary signs and an awareness of their meaning or reference, non-human primates as well as most early hominids fall below the mark (King 1994a; 1994b: 133 ff.). The definition is so narrow that it excludes non-human behaviour altogether. Researchers on the linguistic skills of apes have uttered the same complaint, as is made clear in Section 6.2. They have refused to take the grammatical competence of human, especially American, children as the – species-specific, anthropocentric – standard against which the abilities of apes are judged. King herself proposes a broader, non–species-specific approach which looks at what apes, or early hominids, actually do or did, without a narrow focus on the human form of the feature under study.

King draws on an argument developed by Matt Cartmill regarding anthropocentrism in physical anthropology. Measuring and comparing is the physical anthropologist's trade. The yardsticks wielded to assess distances between species, Cartmill argues, have often been human-oriented, under the influence of traditional European metaphysics, which sets humans apart from the rest of nature. Anthropologists kept searching for unique human characteristics such as upright bipedalism, a large brain, or, indeed, syntactic language. Cartmill criticizes the "persistent anthropological focus on human unicity as the phenomenon to be explained." Supposedly unique human features "are uniquely human by definition rather than as a matter of empirical fact. Much scientific effort and ingenuity has gone into redefining such characteristics whenever discoveries about other animals have posed a threat to human uniqueness" (Cartmill 1990: 173; cf. Cartmill 2001).

A clear case is the large brain that features prominently in the history of palaeoanthropology as a marker of humanness, serving to separate the hominid family from the ape family, and humans from animals. The notions of human intellectual superiority and evolution as progress endorsed the assumption that the relative enlargement and differentiation of brains reflected a progressive evolutionary trend towards greater intelligence. Many researchers are preoccupied with ranking the brains of different species along a linear scale. However, the anthropocentric definition of a uniquely large human brain – "bigger is better is smarter" – has come under attack several times. Elephants and whales have turned out to have much larger brains than humans. These were dealt with by shifting the criterion to brain size relative to body size. Unfortunately, according to that criterion, humans are surpassed by squirrel mice and other small animals, so it was corrected for allometry – relative increases in organs, physiology, or behaviour in relation to scale and size, such as in mice, which unlike horses can jump several times their own height. This move again brought porpoises uncomfortably close, but these animals were neutralized by taking metabolic rates into account. The diagnostic traits were revised whenever they proved not to produce the desired result, which was human specialty (Cartmill 1990: 11, 12).

In addition, the effects of brain size on differentiation and complexity are poorly understood, and correlating brain size or brain complexity with intelligence or information-processing capacity is problematic because of allometric effects at various levels of the anatomical structure. As Terrence Deacon (1990) has shown in detail, much research in this field fails to take these effects into account and is fraught with methodological problems. This contributes to fallacies of progression in interpretations of the evolution of brain size, brain complexity, and intelligence. "The single most pervasive issue behind most of [the] preconceptions [in this type of research]," he writes, "is the notion of human intellectual superiority. The almost ubiquitous assumption that human intelligence and human relative brain size together represent an unassailable datum for the start of all comparative analyses of other species' mental abilities, has remained at the centre of this problem for over a century, despite numerous articulate critiques of methodological assumptions used to demonstrate an intellectual *scala naturae*" (*ibid*.: 194). The implied view of evolving organisms is that of a linear progression instead of a diversely and accidentally branching bush.

In line with Cartmill's critique of anthropocentrism, palaeontologists John de Vos *et al.* (1998) argue against a tendency they see in the work of palaeoanthropologists to treat the hominid – bipedal – locomotion pattern as a unique phenomenon which needs a special explanation. In their view, the evolution of locomotion in hominids follows patterns similar to those seen in other animals, especially in horse species when, like hominids, they entered more open landscapes. They analyse concomitant and comparable changes – from an all-round to a striding gait with stretched legs – in the functional morphology of the feet of both horses and hominids, and point to the occurrence of selection favouring larger and more complicated brains in both groups in a comparable fashion. Their argument is illustrated elegantly by the 3.5 million-year-old footprints of australopithecines in volcanic ash found at Laetolil, Tanzania, and mentioned in Chapter 1. The hominid footprints were, characteristically, highly publicized, but two *Hipparion* – an early horse – trails intersecting them scarcely received attention.

"In one way or another," Cartmill concludes his argument, "policing and maintaining the [human–animal] boundary has been a tacit objective of most palaeoanthropological model-building since the late 1940s. The theoretical content of palaeoanthropology has suffered accordingly" (*ibid.*: 178). Human unicity was axiomatic, and was protected from any threats posed by new empirical data. Although Cartmill does not go that far back in time, his argument can easily be extended to Tyson tallying differences and similarities between human and Pygmie, Camper comparing facial angles between species and human "races," and nineteenth-century craniometrists investigating the cranial capacities of "races." In all of these cases, the standard of measurement was European humans.

Another example of gate-keeping by moving the markers is provided by *Homo habilis*, with its 670 cc brain volume. When the new species was discovered, the minimal brain volume of *Homo* – the so-called cerebral Rubicon – was generally set at 750 cc, following Arthur Keith (1948). Leakey, Tobias and Napier (1964) lowered that generally accepted criterion for appurtenance to the human genus to 600 cc in order to be able to accommodate the fossils they proposed calling *Homo habilis* in the *Homo* genus instead of the *Australopithecus* genus. With this move, which did not go uncriticized, they safeguarded toolmaking as an essentially human characteristic, preventing the undesirable consequence of a non-human being behaving in a presumably typically human fashion.

The notion of Man the Toolmaker which was so important to Philip Tobias is of interest in the present context, as well. Whenever undesirable candidates for humanness in the sense of the toolmaker criterion surfaced, that criterion was quickly revised or amended in such a manner that the hominids, primates, or other animals it concerned no longer qualified for humanness. Amendments which have been proposed since the late fifties, in line with discoveries regarding tool behaviours in non-human species are making-tools-with-tools, continuous dependence on tools, and association of tool behaviour with language, role complementarity, or purposeful training. Tobias safeguarded his toolmaking criterion for humanness by assuming that the australopithecines fell short of "one intricate conceptual and technological mechanism: the ability to use a tool to make a tool" (Tobias 1965b: 30). "It is enlightening," Adrian Desmond observes, "to watch anthropologists manoeuvring as the first reports of regular chimp tool-making trickled in." Scanning the literature of the years after 1964, when Jane Goodall reported toolmaking in East African chimpanzees, he found "a veritable spate of ad hoc amendments" to the notion of "man the toolmaker," designed "to readjust the wording, while leaving its *intent* unchanged" (Desmond 1979: 148).

Periodizations of the Palaeolithic are often binary and constructed with the help of a double, recent-humans–oriented standard. Usually two periods are distinguished, an earlier one of "ancient" and a more recent one of "modern" behaviour. An example – in addition to those already given – is the treatment of lithic assemblages from the Lower and Middle Palaeolithic as opposed to those from the Upper Palaeolithic. In the case of the earlier periods, uniformity through various ecological zones is seen as a manifestation of a lack of flexibility, as "ancient" rather primitive tool-assisted behaviour. Upper Palaeolithic lithic assemblages exhibit a great deal of uniformity through time and space as well, but here that characteristic is seen as suggesting considerable flexibility and adaptive capacity – for example, by Chilardi *et al.*, writing on the Aurignacian site Fontana Nuova in Sicily (Chilardi *et al.* 1996; cf. Corbey and Roebroeks 2001b).

Similarly, behavioural associations between faunal remains and lithics from earlier periods are expected to be proven explicitly and elaborately, but are assumed implicitly and routinely for recent periods. For the earlier periods, the default explanation of configurations of stones and bones tends to be in terms of geological processes; for the more recent ones, human butchering is assumed. Such concepts as "hearth" and "dwelling structure" are to be applied to early sites only on the basis of elaborate argument, while at Upper Palaeolithic sites they are assumed almost automatically (Corbey and Roebroeks 2001a: 71–72). The effect is a "spatiotemporal collapse" (Conkey 1985: 301). Each of the two periods is homogenized. Differences between the two periods are overvalued; differences within each period undervalued.

In fact, the European palaeolithic archaeological record, for one, is much too ambiguous and varied for rigid dichotomizing in terms of Ancients and Moderns, despite some striking differences between the Upper Palaeolithic and the earlier periods. These differences would seem to have been blown out of proportion as a result of different treatment of the archaeological record depending on which side of the cognitive and behavioural Rubicon – the figurative river separating symbolic "moderns" from presymbolic "pre-moderns" – it is assumed to be located. The preoccupation of researchers with human unicity and characteristics considered typical of, and exclusive to, "modern humans" serves as a self-fulfilling prophecy when they deal with empirical data, in particular scarce, gap-ridden and ambiguous data.

Take five meters of sediment in an *abri*, a shallow cave in Southern France, consisting of a few score of perturbated layers, some of which contain knapped flint, fragments of animal bones, and traces of fire. The layers may represent some two hundred thousand years of hominid activities. Now take one of those layers with archaeological material, approximately five centimeters thick. It may not be clear whether this is the sedimentation of weeks, months, or centuries of occupation; of one continuous period of use of the cave or of a number of visits to the spot. Nor may it be clear whether that layer is 80,000 years old, 120,000 years, or a mixture of remains from several periods. Such data provide rich playing fields for archaeological interpretation, not unlike the inkblots in the Rohrschach projection test used by psychologists. There are various preconceptions with respect to what a "camp site," "language," a "ritual deposition," or a sequence of technological acts are and how these phenomena should be conceptualized. Such preconceptions, together with the ambiguous data, make up our reconstructions of the past.

The Neanderthals, in particular, have moved to-and-fro between animality and humanness. Major specialists on Neanderthal structural and functional anatomy believe that morphological differences with modern humans must reflect significant differences in behavioural and evolutionary adaptations. Like Gamble (1994, 1998) or Noble and Davidson (1996), they see Neanderthal cultural behaviour as "ancient." In the eyes of others, this implies a serious underestimation of the many ingenious behaviours of these Pleistocene foragers. Brian Haydn inventoried interpretations of Neanderthals in 1993 and found a widespread tendency to dehumanize them, denying them language, anticipation, hunting, alliances, ethnic identities, artistic expression, intentional burial, aggregation sites, and even home bases. In some cases, he concludes, "the trend to dehumanize Neanderthals has gone to such extremes that it constitutes a betrayal of data, common sense and good theorizing. . . . [The] esteem accorded to Neanderthals is at its lowest nadir since Marcellin Boule's . . . early portrayals of them as semi-simian brutes" (Haydn 1993: 114; cf. Moser 1998, Trinkaus and Shipman 1993). More recently, in the context of a massive debate on the replacement of Neanderthals by Cro-Magnons in Europe,

João Zilhão has criticized the image of Neanderthals as a biologically and culturally "inferior, doomed-from-the-beginning side-branch or dead-end of human evolution," lacking language (Zilhão 2001: 72). Along similar lines, Gaudzinski and Roebroeks (2000) have argued that the sophistication and complexity of archaeologically reconstructable hunting behaviours of Neanderthals on a number of Western European sites was conspicuously "modern."

In the second half of the nineteenth century, the Cro-Magnons of the Upper Palaeolithic, currently perceived as the paragon of behavioural modernity, were still interpreted as a kind of animal that had not yet crossed the threshold to humanness – a view not unlike that accorded the Neanderthals in recent times. Upper Palaeolithic figurative art was interpreted as an expression of an "archaic," "primitive" style of cognitive functioning. It was believed to reproduce nature mechanically as perceived by the senses, without composition, perspective, or indeed any trace of symbolism or abstract thought: the product of shallow minds capable only of imitation, not of reflection, anticipaton, or symbolization (Richard 1993). Around 1900, this began to change. Rich graves and complex cave paintings were discovered, and the Upper Palaeolithics were promoted to humans like us, or at least like contemporary pre-state peoples. The animal–human boundary between "ancients" and "moderns," basically unaltered, was moved back in time, not unlike what Zilhão and others have done with respect to the Neanderthals.

The sundering of natural history and cultural history, setting up a nature–culture boundary, is a recurrent conceptual structure in a number of the disciplines contributing to the intensely, and often confusingly, interdisciplinary field of human origin studies. Titles like, on the one hand, *The Information Continuum: Evolution of Social Information Transfer in Monkeys, Apes, and Hominids* (King 1994a) and, on the other hand, *Uniquely Human: The Evolution of Speech, Thought and Speechless Behavior* (Lieberman 1991) demarcate where minds part in studies on the evolution of language. Thomas Wynn has pointed out the existence of two incompatible intellectual orientations in studies of early hominid technology: a "natural history tradition," and a "sociocultural tradition." The former deals with changes in tools and tool use in terms of biological adaptation, while the latter tends to see such changes rather exclusively in terms of cultural processes which are autonomous vis-à-vis those which are biological, and provide evidence of progress (Wynn 1994; cf. Ingold 1994b). An example of the latter view is Oakley's "man-the-toolmaker." Another is French prehistorian's André Leroi-Gourhan's diagram of increasing mean length of the cutting edges of stone tools of the same weight in the course of human evolution as an index of technological progress – for example, when Acheulean handaxes are compared to earlier Oldowan chopping tools of the same size (Leroi-Gourhan 1964: 192).

The interpretation of five million years of hominid behaviour, from apelike ancestors to extant humans, is complicated considerably by theoretical divergences between as well as within relevant disciplines, in particular along the axis of natural sciences versus human sciences. There is a certain consensus that the African bipedal australopithecines, generally speaking at least, were within the range of extant non-human primates behaviourally and cognitively. There is also a consensus that most European Upper Palaeolithics from about twelve to forty thousand years ago were "people like us," not only anatomically, but also behaviourally and cognitively, burying their dead ceremonially and creating the beautiful, intriguing cave paintings found mainly in Southwest Europe. Opinions diverge sharply, however, regarding the large grey era in between, when, in the course of the Pleistocene, "anatomically modern" hominids, physically at least similar to extant humans, appeared more or less gradually. Some see a continuous development from animal to human behaviour; others see a sudden shift when language came into play, whenever they think that was.

Many Anglophone archaeologists assume a sharp break between Ancients and Moderns. At the same time, by analysing cultural and social organization as survival strategies, they treat Australopithecines in the same manner as Upper Palaeolithic hunter–gatherers with complex symbolism, extant foragers such as the Inuit, or even extant non-human primates. Even myth and ritual are studied as natural phenomena, for example, as repositories of ecological knowledge. British "post-processual" archaeologists, on the other hand, tend to look at interpretive cultural anthropology for guidance when dealing with relatively recent small-scale, but symbolically complex, prehistoric societies of fully linguistic humans. In their view, culture has to do with the symbolic meaning infusing kinship and exchange, and they have criticized processual archaeologists for their neglect of matters of cultural meaning.

In recent years, a number of authors from different disciplinary backgrounds have postulated an intermediate phase of functioning which differs from both modern human as well as non-human primate modes of behaviour. The postulated behavioural modes may have been specific to early *Homo*, and different from how its apelike Australopithecine ancestors as well as its human-like descendants behaved. Linguist Derek Bickerton (1990, 1995), for instance, has proposed a stage characterized by a semantically rich but syntactically poor protolanguage. Merlin Donald, a psychologist, points to mimetic imitation as a flexible and creative, non-linguistic (*sic*) mode of representation and communication (Donald 1991). While necessarily somewhat speculative, such approaches are useful not only for the criticism and research they provoke, but also as an attempt to provide a more differentiated picture of the so-called Ancients. Donald's theory of mimesis has the additional merit of shifting attention away from the ever-present "Cartesian" and anthropocentric stress on human language.

But even in hard-boiled natural science approaches such as the one found in Donald's monograph or the book on the spectacular early *Homo erectus* skeleton from Nariokotome by palaeoanthropologists Pat

Shipman and Alan Walker, intriguing remarks on the verge of, or even slipping into, a different discourse do occur. Or is it still the same discourse, with a remnant of the traditional European world-view? Shipman and Walker conclude that, basically, the Nariokotome boy was "not one of us" (Walker and Shipman 1996: 294). Merlin Donald ends his book with the remark that, because of the modern human cognitive architecture, "we must conclude that the Darwinian universe is too small to contain humanity. We are a different order. We are not just another family within the superfamily of Hominidae ... [but] unlike any [creatures] that went before us. ... [This] much is not speculation: humans are utterly different." He adds that nineteenth-century biology was "absurdly, grotesquely wrong in its classification scheme," positioning humans so close to apes because it "had no adequate vocabulary for assessing the cognitive dimension of human evolution. It was a specialist's error, a classification scheme that glorified anatomy and devalued mind" (Donald 1991: 382).

In this chapter, it has become clear that the tendency towards the all-or-nothing conceptualizations which characterized the early days of the anthropological disciplines persists in recent scientific practice. Archaeologists have constructed boundaries between animal-like ancient and "fully human" modern hominid behaviour using methods and tactics similar to those applied by Tobias and other palaeoanthropologists looking at morphology. Like the latter, they have been prone to dichotomizing and the wielding of flexible, human-specific, and often double, standards in their interpretations of archaeological data and reconstructions of cognition and language. In hindsight, features humans happen to have ended up with – bipedality, large brains, tools, and symbols – were sought after in the fossil record while significant other traits not considered essential were given less attention. An alternative view is that cultural developments were gradual or at least mosaical and cannot be conceptualized simply in terms of the presence or absence of "essentially human" minds and behaviours typical of the present-day human primate.

In the following chapter, it will be seen that cultural anthropology is, likewise, not immune to the same anthropocentric metaphysic of humanness, which has profoundly influenced not only its scientific conceptualizations but even its disciplinary identity. The same goes for primatology, as will be argued in some detail in Chapter 6.

FIVE

"Symbolic Man" in Ethnology

[The] distinctive quality of man [is] not that he must live in a
material world, a circumstance he shares with all organisms, but
that he does so according to a meaningful scheme of his own
devising, in which capacity mankind is unique. . . .

Marshall Sahlins (1976a: vii)

Eighteenth-century anthropology was steered by a metaphysical discourse on creation and souls. For most natural historians, speech as the
direct outward manifestation of the human rational soul was a crucial,
essential difference with animals. For many, probably most twentieth-
century cultural anthropologists, it was a token of the uniquely human
capacity to confer meaning upon the world with the help of arbitrary
symbols and to transcend the here and now. The animal–human boundary reappeared at the heart of cultural anthropology or ethnology – in
the following, the latter, shorter term will generally be used – in the form
of its disciplinary demarcation vis-à-vis the natural sciences, including
biological anthropology.

In the Boasian tradition of American cultural anthropology and in the
French Durkheimian tradition, in particular, there has been a tendency to
construct the discipline's field of study in terms of an opposition between
acquired culture and nature, between meanings and laws (Section 5.1).
To some extent, this tendency persists to this day. It is assumed that

humans became such only by entering a different order of existence: the intellectually, spiritually, and morally superior world of society, language, and culture. This basic assumption is an indirect corollary of the view of human identity, rationality, dignity, and unicity that, in various guises, has imbued three centuries of research on humans, early hominids, and other primates.

In Section 5.2, it will be shown how the disciplinary identities of neo-Darwinian behavioural socioecology and similar approaches in biology are the precise opposite of that of cultural anthropology. These disciplines set out to analyse human behaviour in exactly the same fashion as the behaviour of other animals, which provoked fierce reactions from anthropologists who saw their basic premises threatened. The anthropology of conflict and violence is a salient example of this polarity.

5.1 A Discipline's Identity

The present monograph is about kinship, more precisely on the convolutions of biological kinship and culturally constructed kinship between humans and other primates. Biologically speaking, simian kinship and simian descent are about genes. As conceived culturally, by anthropologists as North Atlantic natives, it is about self and other, totemic animals as "good to think with," to use Claude Lévi-Strauss' wording (see above, p. 6), values and obligations, and even, as in the case of the baboon slaughterhouses described in Chapter 1, edibility.

Kinship as a subject of anthropological research provides a telling example of conflicting conceptions of anthropology. In one of two chapters on this subject in an ethnological handbook from the 1990s, Robin Dunbar, a primatologist, presented human kinship and sociality as natural biological phenomena, to be studied mainly by such disciplines as comparative biology and behavioural ecology (Dunbar 1994). Another influential representative of the biological approach is Robin Fox, who has characterized his "biosocial anthropology" as follows: "I have held, contrary to the mainstream of social/behavioural science, that the subject matter (society, culture, behaviour, action) must be a 'natural' phenomenon: as much a product of natural selection as our brains and bodies. Thus it follows that its study is an empirical one whose methods should be those appropriate to the study of all forms of life" (Fox 1989: 1; cf. Fox 1994, and Quiatt and Reynolds 1993: 212 ff.).

In the same handbook, ethnologist Alan Barnard took a diametrically opposed approach, giving voice to a majority view in ethnology. In this view, kinship is not primarily a biological phenomenon, but has to do with the meanings people give *to* the biological. It is a matter of language and symbols, of how relatives and non-relatives are classified socially. Approaches such as Dunbar's, Barnard argues, "hold only if we accede to the premiss that human society is to be comprehended in behavioural rather than cultural terms." But kinship in humans is "fundamentally different from that of other species in that it is characterized by culturally articulated sets of rules which may operate to a great extent independently of observable behaviour . . . [it is] a cultural and social construction, whatever facts of reproduction may lie behind the variety of kinship systems to be found" (Barnard 1994: 786).

Not all of one's biological cousins are always treated as such to the same degree, but only those, for example, who live nearby, or come in handy in terms of trading, land claims, or prestige. A biologically distant relative can be quite close socially speaking. Analogously, in many societies one's mother's brother, the bride-giver, is more important than one's uncles on the father's side, or even one's biological father. Certain biologically very edible animals may be inedible even in ecotypes where protein is scarce because they are considered to be kin, or taboo. The point is that it is not so much the biology as such that matters, but how it is dealt with in terms of meanings and values. Seen from the perspective of Dunbar and Fox, however, views of kinship and other cultural phenomena such as those held by Barnard are, in Fox's words, part of "the dominance of neo-relativist, hermeneutic, critical, symbolic, deconstructionist, and

interpretive versions of the social science enterprise [which involve] a retreat from science and the very idea of objective knowledge" (Fox 1989: 4).
The issue is the continuity and discontinuity between nature and culture,
and the extent to which cultural anthropology is dependent on the biological sciences or is a relatively autonomous discipline.

Two influential publications from the 1970s giving voice to the "cultur-
ological" or "culturalist" standpoint attacked so vigorously by Fox were
Clifford Geertz' collection of essays *The Interpretation of Cultures* (1973)
and Marshall Sahlins' *Culture and Practical Reason* (1976b). "Believing,
with Max Weber, that man is an animal suspended in webs of significance he himself has spun," Geertz wrote, "I take culture to be those
webs" (Geertz 1973: 5). Sahlins argued against "the idea that human cultures are formulated out of practical activity and, behind that, utilitarian
interest," as in Marvin Harris' so-called cultural materialism for example, or in Napoleon Chagnon's several decades of research among the
Yanomami Indians in Amazonia (see below). The alternative Sahlins –
Geertz's close competitor in terms of standing within the discipline –
offers, is, characteristically, "a reason of another kind, the symbolic or
meaningful [which] takes as the *distinctive* quality of man not that he
must live in a material world, a circumstance he shares with all organisms, but that he does so according to a meaningful scheme of his
own devising, in which capacity mankind is *unique*. It therefore takes
as the *decisive* quality of culture . . . not that this culture must conform
to material constraints but that it does so according to a definite symbolic scheme which is never the only one possible. Hence it is culture which constitutes utility" (Sahlins 1976a: vii, viii; italics added).
In this camp, ethnology is a human, humane, humanistic science, and
those who, like Fox, refuse to see this tend to be viewed as right-wing
reductionists, positivists, objectivists, or materialists. Either explicitly
or more implicitly, this opposition surfaces time and again in various
guises in the rich and theoretically diverse landscape of contemporary
anthropology.

The symbolic capacity was thought to imply a rupture with nature, organic life, and genes, both diachronically, in the course of hominid evolution, and synchronically, at every moment of human existence. Consequently, ethnology, as a discipline dealing with cultural meaning, tended to be conceived as autonomous with respect to the biological and other natural sciences. Its disciplinary identity was, thus, an indirect corollary of a specific western conception of human identity. Efforts to draw human cultural behaviour within the reach of such natural science perspectives as behavioural ecology were rebutted. Of course, the culturalists did not deny the role of biological and material constraints, but they saw symbolic meaning as decisive. More ecologically or biologically minded anthropologists, conversely, did not completely ignore ideas and values as subjects of study, but they did not think they mattered much.

The discontinuity stance in American ethnology goes back to Franz Boas and exhibits similarities with the climate of opinion in late nineteenth-century Germany, where Wilhelm Dilthey and others pleaded for the relative autonomy of hermeneutical or interpretive human sciences vis-à-vis the natural sciences. The latter, it was contended, explained objects in terms of laws, but were not suitable to understanding acting subjects in terms of intentions and meanings. Boas, who trained in Germany, was well aware of this line of argument, which inspired his historically particularistic critique of evolutionism in Victorian anthropology. While the latter speculated on the evolutionary stages and universal characteristics of humankind, Boas and his pupils favoured fieldwork over speculation, the study of individual present-day societies over that of their evolutionary origins, and interpretation in terms of specific local meanings over explanation in the style of the natural and life sciences.

Anthropologists in the Boasian tradition like Edward Sapir, Alfred Kroeber, and Ruth Benedict mostly saw culture as an extremely variable, relatively autonomous layer superimposed upon humankind's uniform biology, and demanding of a methodology different from, and irreducible to, that of the biological sciences. "For culture," Benedict declared in 1943, "is . . . learned behaviour: behaviour which in man is not given at birth, which is not determined by his germ cells as is the behaviour of wasps or the social ants, but must be learned anew from grown people by every generation. The degree to which human achievements are dependent on this kind of learned behaviour is man's great claim to superiority over all the rest of creation; he has been properly called 'the culture-bearing animal' " (1943: 9–10). David Schneider's more recent culturalist and relativist separation of the study of kinship from its biological foundations, questioning the universality of the family and the possibility of universally translatable elementary kin terms, was of Boasian inspiration as well (Schneider 1984).

The so-called "interpretive approach" in cultural anthropology is the most radical avatar of this tradition, and one that is taken to its utmost consequence. "I [became] . . . deeply engaged, entangled is perhaps a better word," Clifford Geertz wrote on this development, " . . . in what turned out, after a while, to be an extremely influential – and extremely controversial – effort to redefine the ethnographical enterprise whole and entire. . . . [This] redefinition consisted in placing the systematic study of meaning, the vehicles of meaning, and the understanding of meaning at the very centre of research and analysis: to make of anthropology, or anyway cultural anthropology, a hermeneutical discipline" (Geertz 1995: 114). It was this paradigm shift in particular which Robin Fox attacked as a retreat from science and the very idea of objective knowledge (Fox 1989: 4). Yet Geertz has always been well aware of the evolutionary and biological basis of human symbolism.

Even for Leslie White, the influential protagonist of an evolutionary–materialist and ecologically, economically, and technologically determinist approach to culture, symbolic culture was autonomous. The difference between humans and animals was "one of kind, not of degree: a creature can either 'arbitrarily impose signification,' can either create and bestow values, or he cannot. There are no intermediate stages . . . ," and because human behaviour "is symbol behaviour and since the behaviour of infra-human species is non-symbolic, it follows that we can learn nothing about human behaviour from observations upon or experiments with the lower animals" (White 1949: 29, 35; cf. *ibid*.: 79, 141, 406). To White "[man] is unique; he is the only living species that has a culture . . . an extrasomatic, temporal continuum of things and events dependent upon symboling. . . . All peoples in all times and places have possessed culture; no other species has or has had culture" (White 1959: 3). This antireductionist strain in his approach, clearly of Boasian inspiration, sat uneasy with the nomothetic utilitarian materialism that dominated his evolutionary writings and for which he is now remembered and respected. It was only towards the end of his career that he became acutely aware of the fact that he adhered to two incompatible philosophies, and he then abrogated significant aspects of his utilitarianism (Barrett 1989; cf. Sahlins 1976a: 103).

Kindred spirits have since repeatedly taken equally ambiguous stances, thinking ecologically or biologically but stopping short of those human features traditionally deemed to be higher or special (for example, Holloway 1969). The two positions – "culture shapes nature" versus "nature shapes culture," interpretation versus explanation, idealism versus materialism – were most sharply articulated in the United States. British social (*sic*) anthropology – in the wake of B. Malinowski, A. R. Radcliffe-Brown, and E. E. Evans-Pritchard – traditionally concentrated more on social structure. It was less polarized than American cultural anthropology, and generally found the "culturalist" stress on meaning that characterized much of American cultural (*sic*) anthropology exaggerated, until, in the 1970s, the latter gained more influence in Britain. The simultaneous British reception of French, Durkheimian ethnology added to this effect.

A strict boundary between the realm of nature and human society was, and still is, as important to much of French *ethnologie* as it is to American cultural anthropologists, though not entirely in the same way. French Durkheimian (and British neo-Durkheimian) ethnology tends to see nature as a projection of social categories and analogous to society. One of the most influential French ethnologists, Marcel Mauss, disciple and close associate of Emile Durkheim, offers a convenient starting-point with his approach to exchange in what is probably his best known and most influential publication, *The Gift: The Form and Reason for Exchange in Archaic Societies* (Mauss 1990; first published in French in 1925). A notion of the "natural" or "original" state of humankind and human nature is continually present in Mauss' thinking, guiding his empirical work as an ontological presupposition and linking his approach to that of the great social theorists of the Enlightenment. In his perception, exchange is constitutive of sociality and moral order, for it is the earliest solution, both phylogenetically and ontologically, to the Hobbesian *warre* of all against all that, in his view, ensues from the human individual's selfish animal nature.

"Societies have progressed," Mauss writes in the conclusion to *The Gift*, "in so far as they themselves, their subgroups, and, lastly, the individuals in them, have succeeded in stabilizing relationships, giving, receiving, and finally, giving in return. To trade, the first condition was to be able to lay aside the spear. From then onwards, they succeeded in exchanging goods and persons, no longer only between clans, but between tribes and nations, and, above all, between individuals. Only then did people learn how to create mutual interests, giving mutual satisfaction, and, in the end, to defend themselves without having to resort to arms" (Mauss, 1990: 82). Two lines later, he characterizes the "natural state" (*état naturel*) as one of "war, isolation and stagnation" – which is overcome through "alliances, gift and commerce" and by "opposing reason to emotion." In the natural state, the "fundamental motives for human action: emulation between individuals of the same sex, that 'basic imperialism of human beings' " (*ibid.*: 65) still had free reign in Mauss' socialist, anti-liberalist perspective. Through the gift, humanity progressed from its pristine state of war – a persisting menace – towards reconciliation, reason, and morality.

État naturel refers to *both* humankind before history and civilization in an evolutionary sense – its natural history – *and* a state of "raw nature" that is a constituent element of human society, a condition that must continually be transcended to make humanness possible. Becoming human, in Mauss' analysis, occurred over time, in the course of the evolutionary development of certain primates, but it has also become a permanent, structural feature of humans who, in his view, continually transcend the brutish state of nature – by giving, receiving, and giving-in-return. The "natural state" is seen as primordial, both phylogenetically and ontologically, and social order as discontinuous with nature in both respects.

In a similar vein, neo-Durkheimian ethnologists like Louis Dumont, Daniel de Coppet, and Cécile Barraud take exchange to be constitutive of social order. Time and again they show, using detailed ethnographic analysis, how "in every society, certain "ideas/values" perpetuate themselves beyond the life or death of particular individuals, imposing themselves in all the various sorts of social relations" (Barraud et al. 1994: 110; along the same lines, Platenkamp 1988). The plethora of exchanges going on in a village every day form a value-orientated matrix which is constantly renewed and is constitutive for the persons involved, including the dead and the spirits. "Subjects and objects intertwine ceaselessly," they write, underlining one of the key insights of Mauss' essay on the gift, "in a tissue of relations which make of exchanges the permanent locus where these societies reaffirm, again and again, their highest values" (105). Exchange in this sense – not in a narrow economic sense, but as *symbolic* exchange, as a "total social fact," (*fait social total*), with many non-separated aspects, of a normative, economic, legal, religious nature – is, to use what is probably the most well-known dictum from Mauss' *The Gift*, "one of the *human* foundations on which our societies are built" (Mauss 1990: 4, italics added).

The influential structuralist approach developed by Claude Lévi-Strauss shares the Durkheimian presupposition of social order as a human imposition upon a relatively unstructured, brute state of nature which he presumed to be exemplified by non-human primates: "The social life of monkeys does not lend itself to the formulation of any norm. . . . [The] monkey's behaviour is surprisingly changeable. Not only is the behaviour of a single subset inconsistent, but there is no regular pattern to be discerned in collective behaviour" (Lévi-Strauss 1969: 6–7; cf. Rodseth *et al.* 1991: 222, 233). In Lévi-Strauss' view, animals became human and social organization came into being only through the prohibition of incest. "[Mankind] has understood very early," he stated in an essay on kinship and the family, "that, in order to free itself from a wild struggle for existence, it was confronted with the very simple choice of 'either marrying-out or being killed-out.' The alternative was between biological families living in juxtaposition and endeavouring to remain closed, self-perpetuating units, overridden by their fears, hatreds and ignorances, and the systematic establishment, through the incest prohibition, of links of intermarriage between them, thus succeeding to build, out of the artificial bounds of affinity, a true human society" (Lévi-Strauss 1956: 277–278). Social, political and economic order is achieved through the exchange – giving and receiving, giving and giving-in-return – of women between male-dominated descent groups, whereby the raw "state of nature" is transcended.

As was already seen in Chapter 3, that natural state of humankind had until only shortly before generally been associated not only with apes, but also with small-scale foragers and sedentary non-state peoples, who were perceived to be uncivilized "savages" or "contemporary ancestors," lesser beings lacking social order, logic, and control of impulse. Jean-Nicholas Démeunier, for example, wrote in 1785 that "the savages have no society; they meet by coincidence; they leave each other without ceremony; and the concern for their subsistence splits them up instead of bringing them together" (Démeunier 1785–1786, III: 1–2; cf. Blanckaert 1998: 22). Another French ethnologist, Henri Thulié, stated as recently as 1907 that "there are still races that preserve an almost bestial immobility and are not capable of organizing themselves into a society" (Thulié 1907: 10). This view, widespread in that period of imperialism (cf. Corbey 1993b), was soon afterwards criticized by Durkheim, Mauss, and, indeed, Lévi-Strauss. According to an authoritative mid–nineteenth-century French dictionary, the word "savage" (*sauvage*) meant beastly, dull, and brutish. When applied to a human, it stated, it meant "that the human has the brutalness and callousness of the beast; dull, that he has its awkwardness, its stupidity, its lack of reason; brutish, that he has its blind ruthlessness, its ferocious wildness and its unrestrained licentiousness" (Littré 1872: "sauvage").

The Tasmanians, for instance, were generally treated as exemplars of the quintessential brute savage in the nineteenth-century anthropological disciplines and considered as reliable models for the earliest hominids (Murray 1992). The general view of non-human primates in those days was similar to, and as negative as, contemporaneous views of non-Western peoples, but as a rule persisted much longer, as the citation from Lévi-Strauss shows. The complex social life, high intelligence, and capacity for self-control of non-human primates were discovered only in the 1960s. Early hominids, the third group occupying a similar slot in the Western and scientific imagination, that of apish other or humankind in its "natural state," has also been emancipated only in recent decades from a presumed lack of society, logic, and control, as was made clear in the preceding chapter.

The Durkheimian conceptualization of the relation between society and nature resembles the social contract theory of the seventeenth-century philosopher, Thomas Hobbes. "The final Cause, End or Designe of men," Hobbes writes in the first part of *Leviathan*, " . . . in the introduction of . . . restraint upon themselves, . . . is the foresight of their own preservation, and of a more contented life thereby; that is to say, of getting themselves out from that miserable condition of Warre, which is necessarily consequent to the natural Passions of men, when there is no visible Power to keep them in awe" (Hobbes 1972 [1651]: 223). Social order is not in human's nature, but is installed by a social contract that constrains the pristine natural state of humankind and the solitary individual's natural tendencies. While in Hobbes' thinking the state is primarily an instrument of selfish individuals, to the Durkheimians, the social fabric that comes about through exchange is a moral and religious order. Their approach was pitted critically against the liberal, in their view too individualistic, voluntaristic, and utilitarianist *homo oeconomicus* approach to the foundations of society proposed by Hobbes and other leading social theorists of the Enlightenment. Ironically, the Durkheimians did not escape entirely from this approach themselves. The Maussian gift is "[the] primitive analogue of the social contract . . . the primitive way of achieving the peace that in civil society is secured by the State" (Sahlins 1972: 169).

According to Mauss, it is not only social order but also personal identity, which he calls *personnage*, that is constituted through gifts and exchange (Mauss 1990; 1995: 333–364) in traditional non-state societies. According to this line of analysis, continued by Louis Dumont and his followers, individuals are not primarily particular biological organisms, but are formed and transformed – for instance, from living to dead – through the ritual and intergenerational bestowal upon each other of souls, names, titles, rights, and duties that are part of the family clan. This takes place in birth ceremonies, marriages, funerals, and other important rituals that punctuate the life cycle. It takes place in the context of subsistence activities such as hunting and horticulture, usually conceived of as an exchange with spirits inhabiting the landscape, and in the context of such seemingly trivial everyday activities as greeting, gossiping, and sharing food. In Durkheimian terminology: raw organic nature is incorporated into the sociocosmic hierarchy of *idées-valeurs*. A person is not primarily seen as a living being in the sense of behavioural ecology or ecological anthropology, a part of natural processes, but as a moral subject, constituted through symbolic exchange, and transcending instead of issuing from nature.

The view of humans and nature underlying Mauss' analysis of the gift and the person is the Cartesian perspective of *homo duplex*, previously seen in Buffon's natural history. It was formulated succinctly by Emile Durkheim in a 1914 article: the individual has "a double existence . . . the one purely individual and rooted in our organisms, the other social and nothing but an extension of society" (Durkheim, 1960: 337; cf. Sahlins, 1996: 402). A deep antagonism between the demands of the individual organism and those of the social order is postulated, a conflict in which Durkheim and Mauss are firmly on the side of the *morale de la réciprocité* which triumphs over the *intérêt personnel*. Humans become human phylogenetically (in the course of evolution), ontogenetically (when growing up as an individual), and ontologically (as a structural feature, continuously) through inculcation in a *different* order of existence, the morally and intellectually superior world of society, symbolic language, and culture. Thus, they rise above their naturally selfish animal individuality which is directly rooted in the biological organism. Ethnology, in this French tradition as in the American Boasian strain, is therefore a *human* science.

Ironically, the *homo duplex* view at the foundation of the valuable, though one-sided, Maussian approach to social order and personal identity is at odds with Mauss' own programmatic heuristic of *phénomènes de totalité* and *hommes totaux*. We "hardly ever find man divided into several faculties," he wrote in 1924; we "always come across the whole human body and mentality, given totally and at the same time, and basically, body, soul, society, everything is mixed up here" (Mauss, 1995: 303). One of the best examples of a total social phenomenon – *fait social total, prestation totale* – is the gift.

In the rich and variegated disciplinary playing fields of contemporary American cultural anthropology and French *ethnologie*, the notion of a chasm between symbolic human culture (Boasians) or human societies (Durkheimians) and the biological aspects of existence would more frequently seem to be implicitly reproduced rather than explicitly challenged. The animal–human boundary thus, to some degree at least, continues to feed into ethnology as a discipline, serving to legitimate its autonomy vis-à-vis the biological sciences, including biological anthropology.

5.2 Biological Approaches Rejected

Such biological approaches as human behavioural ecology and human sociobiology are based on an assumption which is diametrically opposed to the *homo symbolicus* view of cultural anthropology: the uniformity of all behaving organisms, including humans. They study the behaviour and sociality of all species, including the human one, in the same vein: in the light of evolution, analysing how individuals maximize their reproductive success and inclusive fitness in the context of optimal foraging, mating tactics, dispersal patterns, life history strategies, rank acquisition, and the like.

Edmund Wilson's influential *Sociobiology: The New Synthesis* (Wilson 1975) dealt with human social behaviour in the same fashion as that of apes and other animals, as did Richard Dawkins' *The Selfish Gene* (Dawkins 1976). Wilson called for a new, genetic anthropology, suggesting a genetic basis not only for aggression and gender roles, but also for morality and religion: "Sociology and the other social sciences as well as the humanities, are the last branches of biology waiting to be included in the Modern Synthesis [of evolutionary theory and genetics]. One of the functions of sociobiology, then, is to reformulate the foundations of the social sciences in a way that draws these subjects into the Modern Synthesis" (Wilson, 1975: 4). He elaborated on this theme in the last chapter of *Sociobiology*, and in a separate book, *On Human Nature* (Wilson 1978).

This provoked a storm of protest of unprecedented dimensions, from ethnologists, other human scientists, and even biologists who saw their basic premises threatened and furthermore recognized an avatar of Malinowskian functionalism thought to have long been repudiated.

They found such approaches too deterministic and too reductionist. Behavioural ecology's stress on individual variation within populations was at odds with the units of analysis and explanation the ethnologists preferred: specific cultural systems of symbolic meanings and values, or specific social systems and their internal dynamics. In addition, they accused sociobiology of immoral and politically incorrect racist and sexist tendencies. At their 1976 meeting, attended by several thousand anthropologists, the members of the American Anthropological Association even considered a motion to formally censure sociobiology and to ban two sessions on the subject, a motion which was defeated by only a very narrow margin.

In a sharp essay entitled *The Use and Abuse of Biology: An Anthropological Critique of Sociobiology*, Marshall Sahlins gave voice to the disapproval of the breed of ideas articulated by Wilson, Dawkins, and many others. "[While] the human world depends on . . . the whole panoply of organic characteristics supplied by biological evolution," he argued, "its freedom from biology consists in just the capacity to give these their own sense. In the symbolic event, a radical discontinuity is introduced between culture and nature. . . . The symbolic system of culture is not just an expression of human nature, but has a form and a dynamic consistent with its properties as meaningful, which make it an invention in nature" (Sahlins, 1976a: 12–13). It was precisely this freedom which created the space for ethnology as a discipline distinct from biology, and aimed at filling in the void left by the latter. The patterning of social relations had no one-to-one relation to genetic, evolutionary, or ecological determinants, but was symbolically and meaningfully organized in terms of how humans conceived of themselves and the world in terms of cultural ideas and values.

Sahlins (1976a: 93 ff.) linked his criticism to the thesis – previously suggested by Karl Marx and Friedrich Engels – that since Hobbes, a liberalist and individualist self-conception of Europeans as competitive, acquisitive individuals – as *homo oeconomicus* and *homo bellicosus* – had been read into the animal kingdom. In a curious dialectic, this conception of a "bourgeoisified" nature was then regularly reapplied to the explanation of human society. He saw this "back and forth between the culturalization of nature and the naturalization of culture" (*ibid.*: 105) as a vicious circle, frustrating our understanding of both human society and living nature. To his opponents, however, the proof of a theory was not the context of discovery, but its empirical justification. Ironically, Sahlins (*ibid.*: 106) invoked the very point of view introduced in Section 1.3 of this book to explain such gestures of rebuttal: the theory of pollution and taboo. He realized that the association with the animal world and the confusion of categories with which he was wrestling was a state of dirt and disorder, but did not conceive of his own positioning as pollution avoidance, in the sense defined by Mary Douglas.

Spin-offs of first generation sociobiology and socioecology are gene–culture co-evolutionism, evolutionary psychology, and cognitive ethology. Like Robin Fox' previously mentioned attempts, starting in the late 1960s, to introduce biology into ethnological human kinship studies, they have so far failed to take hold in mainstream cultural anthropology, not least because of that discipline's commitment to cultural meaning. After the refutation of the grand evolutionary perspectives of Victorian anthropology by early twentieth-century approaches, the evolution of society has until quite recently been unpopular among ethnologists and other human scientists. The anthropologists "largely stuck to their Durkheimian guns and were not interested," as Robin Fox (interview with Walter 1993: 242) commented.

In the introduction to the volume they edited on *Understanding Behavior: What Primate Studies Tell Us About Human Behavior*, James Loy and Calvin Peters (1991) complain about the fundamental reluctance of the human sciences to give serious attention to behavioural data from animals or to take an evolutionary approach – a reluctance which is a direct corollary of their disciplinary identity. Because of a fervent attachment to human unicity, animals are situated on the other side of an unbridgeable gap, excluded from the human sciences and disqualified as models for human behaviour or even as objects of worthwhile study (*ibid.*: 11, 12). Anyone who has worked in an anthropology department has likely experienced to some degree the divergence between cultural anthropologists, on the one hand, and physical anthropologists, palaeoanthropologists, and primatologists, on the other. Most cultural anthropologists do not think primate studies can tell us much about human behaviour. Primatologists do believe this to be the case, with such pioneers of the discipline as Robert Yerkes, C. R. Carpenter, Ernest Hooton, and Sherwood Washburn, but most of them "live a peculiar, resident-alien–like existence among their human-oriented colleagues. They speak a different language – macaques, not Marx – and generally publish in journals seldom read and often unknown outside the primatological community" (*ibid.*: 10).

In current scientific practice, there are baffling divergences both between as well as within disciplines depending on whether one is following a natural science approach or a typically human sciences course of investigation. The study of human violence and warfare, which has become a prominent research field in the last decade, can serve as a case in point. Support has been given to Hobbesian perceptions of human nature primarily by many researchers using evolutionary, sociobiological, or socioecological approaches, in the wake of, among others, Konrad Lorenz, Irenaeus Eibl-Eibesfeld, Edmund Wilson, Richard Alexander, Robin Fox, and Richard Dawkins. Van der Dennen's (1995) monograph on the origin of war, for example, takes a rigorously sociobiological approach, analysing warfare as a highly effective, high-risk/high-gain male-coalitional adaptive and reproductive strategy. Combining biological insights with those of cultural materialists, anthropologist Napoleon Chagnon, in his much-discussed Yanomami research (see Figure 6), stresses the inclusive fitness of male warriors in the complex interrelationship between individuals, groups, and their natural environment. The more women they realize access to, the better the proliferation of their genes (Chagnon 1997).

FIGURE 6. Ethnologist Napoleon Chagnon during fieldwork in the Yanomami village Bisaasi-teri, Venezuela, in February 1985. His uncompromising Darwinian approach as a human scientist, applying the same models and concepts as used for animal species, was severely criticized by other ethnologists. Courtesy of Napoleon A. Chagnon.

Another group of anthropologists, however, see their discipline as a human science and society as a cultural and normative order, not primarily an instinctual or ecological one. They interpret warfare and violence as a predominantly cultural phenomenon, following collective rules and values, rather than directly issuing from individual basic drives, ecological circumstances such as resource scarcity, or historical circumstances such as expanding or disintegrating states. "Indeed," Leslie Sponsel (1996: 909) writes tellingly in a lemma in an anthropological encyclopaedia entitled "Peace and Non-Violence," "in recent decades diverse lines of evidence have converged to strongly suggest, if not to demonstrate, to everyone's satisfaction, that human aggression, including warfare, is overwhelmingly determined by culture."

This contrasts sharply with sociobiologist Van der Dennen's claim that warfare is primarily determined by biology, and only a rigorously neo-Darwinist model can explain it. Sponsel and quite a few other authors have argued that peacefulness, not war, and sociality, not aggression, are the default – the natural and normal condition. When aggression and warfare occur, they do not issue from basic human nature, but are caused by historical and cultural circumstance. The Hobbesian idea of aggression as germane to the human condition, has accordingly been criticized as Social Darwinist ideology. Biologically orientated authors, on the other hand, have retorted that peacefulness is but a romantic utopian dream – a case of primitivist wishful thinking.

Globally speaking, the disagreement between researchers who stress natural determinants and those who favour a culturalist approach has led to characterizations of certain peoples as explicitly aggressive and fierce or, alternatively, unambiguously gentle and peaceful. As a counterpoint to the Maring and Dani of New Guinea, Chagnon's vengeful and abusive Yanomami aggressors, or the traditionally chronically violent Waorani of Ecuador, other peoples have been thrown in the balance as decisively peaceful. The Central-African Pygmies, the Chewong and Semai Senoi from Malaysia, the Sakkudei from Indonesia, and the Kalahari Desert

!Kung Bushmen, among others, were cast as gentle, harmless peoples (Sponsel and Gregor 1994). "The Sakkudei," their ethnographer Reimar Schefold writes, "differ radically in their fundamental stance from the attitude of the Yanomami as described by Chagnon. In the structure they give to the ritual periods, the Sakkudei make it clear that the ideal of partnership, balance and harmony is their own concern and not the projection of a western observer" (Schefold 1988: 669). The considerable role of preconceived ideas in research is evidenced by the fact that most of these claims, on both sides, have been contested (Knauft 1987; Otterbein 2000). Even the image of the Yanomami as a "fierce people" has been criticized, and Chagnon has dropped that phrase from the title of the more recent editions of his book, initially entitled *Yanomamö: The Fierce People* (cf. Chagnon 1968 with his 1997) and has even called another book, for a wider audience, *Yanomamö: The Last Days of Eden* (Chagnon 1992).

Biologically orientated and other researchers have highlighted the bloodthirstiness of the !Kung as well as the Semai Senoi, and in *War before Civilization: The Myth of the Peaceful Savage*, Lawrence Keeley attacks what he sees as a nostalgic and idealized image of pre-state peoples influenced by the trauma of World War II and the Cold War: "The facts recovered by ethnographers and archaeologists indicate unequivocally that primitive and prehistoric warfare was just as terrible and effective as the historic and civilized version. . . . Peaceful pre-state societies were very rare; warfare between them was very frequent, and most adult men in such groups saw combat repeatedly" (Keeley 1997: 174).

A similar issue was at stake when Margaret Mead's fieldwork on Samoa was questioned. In her best-selling classic of anthropology, *Coming of Age in Samoa: A Psychological Study of Primitive Youth for Western Civilization* (1928), she used an image of harmonious lives and easy-going adolescent sexuality there to criticize the restrictive sexual education in the United States of the day and to stress cultural variability. The Australian anthropologist Derek Freeman, who more strongly stresses evolution and biological variables, attacked this image on the basis of his own fieldwork – which lasted decades, not months as in the case of Mead's research on Samoa (Freeman 1983). He argued that Mead had missed the role of jealousy, abuse, rape, violence, and suicide on Samoa, and accused her of too exclusively stressing cultural factors and social conditioning at the expense of biology. He found the image Mead offered unrealistic, and testifying to a culturalist and relativist bias. In the ensuing emotional controversy, which even reached national newspapers and talk shows, the parties opposed each other along the well-known lines. In a symposium at the 82nd annual meeting of the American Anthropological Association in November 1983, Freeman's then recently published book *Margaret Mead and Samoa: The Making and Unmaking of an Anthropological Myth* was condemned. Freeman himself had not been invited by the symposium organizers. At the annual business meeting of the association later that day, a formal motion denouncing his refutation of Mead's fieldwork as "unscientific" and "irresponsible" was put to the vote and passed unanimously (Freeman 1997: 66).

An even more wide-ranging firestorm of controversy developed in the autumn of 2000, when two avowed culturalists launched a vicious attack on, once again, Chagnon's research in a five-page e-mail to the president and president-elect of the American Anthropological Association, an e-mail which was made public on the Internet. They accused Chagnon of having exploited the Yanomami in a number of ways, including medical research, for his own profit, and of a systematic violation of this people's rights which "[in] its scale, ramifications, and sheer criminality and corruption ... is unparalleled in the history of anthropology ... putting the whole discipline on trial" (Turner and Sponsel 2000). The accusation was based on an at that time still unpublished book manuscript by an investigative journalist allegedly substantiating these claims (Tierney 2000). However, a committee set up by the American Anthropological Association to examine these allegations came to the conclusion that although the book raised important ethical questions it contained "numerous unfounded, misrepresented, and sensationalistic accusations about the conduct of anthropology among the Yanomami. These misrepresentations fail to live up to the ethics of responsible journalism even as they pretend to question the ethical conduct of anthropology" (American Anthropological Association 2001: Preface).

While not immediately at issue, the question whether a people's genetic impulses basically control their culture or the other way around ran like a red thread through these debates, and its protagonists tended to cluster according to their theoretical stance on this matter. Of course, these debates in the full glare of the media are lightyears away from the careful ethnographic analysis in which the majority of sociocultural anthropologists are engaged, using a more varied range of often quite implicit theoretical standpoints. Still, such outbursts are telling indices of some of the fundamental assumptions which are at play in the field.

The Durkheimian perception of a Hobbesian primordial condition of humankind, which has to be transcended for real morality and sociality to be possible, is partially supported by biological approaches. But most ethnologists prefer to explain war and violence in terms of cultural history, and the role of aggression is relativized by those who have both strong views and strong feelings on peacefulness as the basic human nature. The earlier part of this debate took place against the backdrop of the Vietnam war. The Durkheimian view analyses social exchange in terms of "real," not basically selfish, altruism, and assumes reciprocity to be elementary morality and a means of maintaining equality within the total moral universe, the "sociocosmos" of ideas and values in Louis Dumont's terminology (Barraud *et al.* 1994). Accordingly, Mauss has criticized Bronislaw Malinowski's work on Melanesia as too utilitarianist. Mauss' own work, in turn, in spite of his eye for agonistic aspects of ritual exchange, has in recent decades been criticized for underestimating this Hobbesian dimension of utility.

Annette Weiner and others have criticized the Maussian camp for neglecting the calculation of outputs and the maximization of returns, preferring themselves to analyse ritual exchanges not so much as adhering to basic values but as strategic activities aimed at increasing power and inequality (Weiner 1992). Weiner is much closer to Malinowski than to the Durkheimians in this respect. Malinowski, while criticizing a too narrow and Western conception of "primitive man" as a *homo oeconomicus*, considered that, among the Trobrianders of Melanesia, "economic elements enter into tribal life in all its aspects – social, customary, legal and magico-religious – and are in turn controlled by these." He pointed to the "constant economic undertow to all public and private activities," a "materialistic streak which runs through all their doings . . . [giving] a special and unexpected colour to the existence of the natives, and [showing] the immense importance to them of the economic aspect of everything" (Malinowski 1921: 15–16, 8).

According to Weiner, social life and the Maussian gift do not eclipse but express Hobbesian selfishness and Machiavellian manoeuvring. Remarkably, and regrettably in the eyes of some (Carrithers 1996, Corbey 2000, and cf. below, Section 7.2), this anthropological viewpoint is largely out of touch with biology, even though it converges considerably with, for example, the idea of inclusive fitness, as the following quote from sociobiologist van der Dennen clearly shows: "I regard human beings as shrewd social strategists, clever manipulators, and conscious, intelligent decision-makers in the service of their inclusive fitness, operating within the constraints of their cultural semantics: the signification and interpretive frameworks . . . provided by the culture they happen to be born in" (van der Dennen 1995, I: 9).

Three avatars of the old philosophical idea of Hobbesian *warre* as the quintessential mark of the human beast and three constructions of the animal–human boundary have now been compared. The first, Durkheimian – and Freudian, see Section 3.2 – sees this boundary as subdued and transcended by cultural ideas and values. A second, biological manifestation of the idea tends to support it in terms of inclusive fitness, in an updated and more subtle version. A third major theoretical stance can be found in individualist and functionalist ethnology, which indirectly supports the idea of *warre* by regarding utility as all-important in social and cultural life.

Of course, fierceness and gentleness do not exclude one another and both have roles to play. Nobody subscribes unequivocally to such simplifying ahistorical essentializations as either war or peacefulness as the basic nature of humankind, or of certain groups. And nobody in either camp would deny that there are biological and environmental as well as cultural and historical aspects to warfare as a social phenomenon which is as complex as it is variable. Still, such ideas are obviously capable of creating considerable theoretical divergence in ethnology.

It has become clear in this chapter how, in recent decades, ethnology, struggling with its methodology and disciplinary identity, has been one of the fields in which the animal–human boundary has been profoundly at stake, in manners analogous to the developments in palaeoanthropology and archaeology which were the subject matter of the previous chapter. In the next chapter it will be shown how similar issues have surfaced, or resurfaced, in research on non-human primates.

SIX

Pan Sapiens?

Shoo-ba dee-do
An ape like me
Shoo-be do-bee do-bee
Can learn to be
Human too.

> Walt Disney, *The
> Jungle Book* (1967)

A third period of intense debate and research on apes and how they compare to humans began around 1960, roughly two hundred years after the discussions provoked by Linnaean systematics, and a hundred years after the ape debate in the context of the Darwinian theory of species change by natural selection. The new developments revolved around a series of freshly discovered ape–human similarities, which again were sobering if not simply embarrassing to Euro–American citizens used to situating themselves at the apex of the natural world, and which provided new challenges to the human urge to set its species apart. In 1962, a leading New Synthesis biologist could still maintain that "*Homo sapiens* is not only the sole tool-making animal and the sole political animal, he is also the sole ethical animal" (Dobzhansky 1962: 339), but these and other presumed human monopolies were soon to be contested. In the following, some of the relevant aspects of field and laboratory studies on primate behaviour, communication, and cognition since 1960 are discussed, as well as related changes in popular primate images, and new ethical views which have been proposed in this period of "emancipation" of the great apes.

Newly discovered molecular resemblances between humans and African apes are leading to a taxonomic rapprochement similar to those of a hundred – the evolutionists – and two hundred years – the natural historians – earlier, still based on gross anatomical similarity. In 1962, it was proposed that gorillas and chimpanzees be classified in the same family as humans, the Hominidae, instead of the separate Pongidae, because of their immunological similarity (Goodman 1962). Subsequent research led biochemists to suggest the same subfamily, tribe, and subtribe. Molecular biologists Allan Wilson and Mary-Claire King reported that humans and chimpanzees were only one percent distinct at the level of proteins (King and Wilson 1975a, 1975b), and suggested sister species status, in line with genetic distances within the genera of *Drosophila* fruit flies, amphibians, reptiles, and mammals. Quite a few biochemists now prefer to categorize chimpanzees and humans in the same genus, as sibling species, because of their genetic near-identity (Goodman *et al.* 1998; Watson, Eastall and Penny 2001; Wildman *et al.* 2003). A genetic identity of more than 99% is less than surprising considering that chimpanzees and humans share 99.9999997% of their evolutionary histories.

Genetic differences between human, chimpanzee, and gorilla are within the range of distances between species within the same genus in the animal world. It is, therefore, no longer defensible, it is argued by adherents of the school of biological systematics known as cladistics, that humans should be in a separate genus while equally or even more distant mammal species of, for example, antelope, seal, or gibbon are in the same genus. Striving for consistency of genetic and taxonomic distance at least within the category of mammals, Watson, Eastall and Penny (2001) proposed one genus, *Homo*, for humans (*Homo sapiens*), chimpanzee (which they termed *Homo niger*), and gorilla (*Homo gorilla*). The name *Homo* has historical precedence because it was the first to have been bestowed, by Linnaeus, on a genus containing both humans and then-known morphologically similar apes. They attribute the refusal of others to make that move – a transgression of the traditional animal–human boundary – and the concomitant neglect of accumulating evidence to uneasiness because of a commitment to human specialty (*ibid.*: 314).

However, there is no consensus on what a genus is or should be. The aforementioned authors are cladists, reconstructing phylogenetic patterns on the basis of morphological and biochemical similarities and differences between organisms irrespective of their adaptive value. Evolutionary systematists, on the other hand, are adaptationists. They take the evolutionary processes taking place within populations of living organisms in their environmental settings into account. Species within the same genus should occupy the same adaptive zone and display overall adaptive similarity. Adaptationists, therefore, refuse to classify crocodiles and birds closely together, as cladists do, or humans and chimpanzees, although in both cases there is a relatively recent common ancestor (cf. above, page 103–105). Some combine elements of both approaches. Palaeoanthropologists Wood and Collard (1999), for example, demand that the *Homo* genus has both phylogenetic and adaptive significance: it should be monophyletic, and its members should share the same adaptive strategy.

Looking at these divergent approaches in systematics from a distance, they would appear to be not so much differing views on what nature is like, but on the most convenient way of classifying organisms given specific scientific agendas. The cladist approach tends to be more attractive to systematists proper, interested in phylogenetic patterns, while palaeoanthropologists and primatologists working on extinct or extant living populations with their adaptive strategies may prefer to speak of (adaptive) grades, not clades, when classifying the organisms they research. Those closely involved, though, may take less detached views. As was seen in Section 4.1, cladists accuse adaptationists of a unilinear, essentialist approach, ideologically tinged by the notion of progress towards humanness.

The title of the present chapter, "Pan Sapiens?," deserves some attention. *Pan* is the genus to which chimpanzees and bonobos (*Pan troglodytes* and *Pan paniscus*) belong. Pan is a theriomorphic figure from Greek myth and lore, part animal, part human, presumed to live a lascivious life in the forests. The name was proposed for the chimpanzee in 1816. Of the two known species of the genus, one, *Pan troglodytes*, was named after one of the Plinian or Monstrous Races from Antiquity. The other was called *Pan paniscus* in 1933, with the diminutive "paniscus," meaning "little pan," refering to its finer general and craniofacial anatomy. New insights into chimpanzee cognition challenge the traditional use of the second word, "sapiens," meaning "thinking," for humans exclusively. *Pan sapiens* has also been suggested as a new name for humans, as a counterpoint both to *Homo sapiens* as a taxonomical category and *homo sapiens* as a philosophical view of humans (cf. Diamond 1993).

Section 6.1 sketches how, since the 1960s, the complexity and subtlety of the social life of non-human primates in general and that of great apes in particular has become clear as a result of studies of free and semi-free living groups, and how the traditional image of the brutish, dull, and ignoble ape has correspondingly changed into more positive views. In the same period, tool use, self-recognition in mirrors and symbolic capacities have been discovered in apes, and these and other markers of humanness that formerly were thought to render humans unique came to be challenged (Section 6.2). Closely connected to these developments was the movement to confer human rights, and with them a certain degree of humanness, to apes. This is one of the most recent – and controversial – negotiations of the ape–human boundary, and it is dealt with in Section 6.3.

6.1 Fierce or Gentle

Research on the behaviour and cognition of captive apes had been going on since the early twentieth century, but serious, long-term field studies of non-human primates on a large scale only began around 1960. They were marked by initiatives by – among many others, and not least of whom a contingent of Japanese primatologists – physical anthropologist Sherwood Washburn and archaeologist Louis Leakey. Both were interested in what monkeys and apes living in the wild could reveal about human evolution.

Washburn's neoDarwinian New Physical Anthropology – touched upon in Section 4.2 in connection with Isaac's archaeology – moved beyond the descriptive and static typological approaches of the first half of the last century towards a populational and functionalist understanding of human biocultural evolution that was dynamic and processual (Washburn 1951). The hunting way of life, in which males, bipedalism, and tool use loomed large, came to be seen as the crucial hominid and humanizing adaptational complex: "Tools, hunting, fire, complex social life, speech, the human way and the brain evolved together to produce ancient man of the genus *Homo*" (Washburn 1960: 63; cf. Washburn and Lancaster 1968). Fieldwork on extant non-human primates and hunter–gatherers as exemplars of earlier stages of human evolution was the logical next move. Stimulated by Washburn, primatologist Irven DeVore began studying male dominance hierarchies in baboons in Kenya in 1959 (Washburn and DeVore 1961), and in 1963, anthropologist Richard Lee turned his attention towards the subsistence ecology of the !Kung San Bushmen of the Kalahari Desert (Lee 1979).

At roughly the same time, in 1960, as part of his efforts to better understand the early hominids he and Mary Leakey were digging up in East Africa, Louis Leakey encouraged young Jane Goodall to study chimpanzees on the eastern shore of Lake Tanganyika. He believed this particular ecological setting to be comparable to that of the early hominids, the remains of which he was excavating in Kenya. Dian Fossey's work on mountain gorillas commenced in 1966, and Birute Galdikas took up her work with orang-utans in Kalimantan in 1971 – both under the patronage of Leakey. These three primatologists, and the publicity surrounding them, did much to change the then predominantly negative image of the generalized apish other to a more Rousseauesque perception of the "natural state" of humankind. The well-known photographs of a young Jane Goodall and a young chimpanzee reaching their fingers towards each other in 1967 summed it up neatly, as did a similar encounter between Fossey and a young adult male mountain gorilla in 1970. The latter event was repeated in Michael Apted's film *Gorillas in the Mist* (1988), with Sigourney Weaver this time facing gentle giants instead of the monstrous aliens she fought in Ridley Scott's 1979 science fiction film *Alien* and its sequels.

The larger audience perceived such gestures by females, the gender deemed to be "closer to nature," as a bridging of the animal–human boundary. A new *mythe d'origine* was constructed, not least in *National Geographic* magazine, of lone women–scientists heroically venturing out into the wild, seeking out sacred knowledge of the origin of humankind, and restoring the broken contract between industrial societies and nature. The rest of the staff and personnel and the complex logistics of such field research were carefully kept out of sight (Callan, 14; Haraway 1989: 148). In this respect, "Leakey's girls" fit in the long strain of Beauty-and-the-Beast stories in western culture (cf. Jensen 2002: 141 ff.). The apes these women studied, however, were cast as happy and noble rather than brutish Caliban- or King Kong–like beasts, and were sketched as living in harmony with their kin in a primordial East-African Eden, as opposed to having to survive in harsh circumstances.

In close correspondence with the new public image of chimpanzees and gorillas as a type of noble savages, a new image of early hominids arose. The monstrous primeval apemen of earlier scientific and popular literature – armed with clubs, struggling violently for survival and epitomized by the widely publicized paintings by Zdenek Burian – began to give way to happy families of early hominids in peaceful, indeed paradisiacal, East-African landscapes. In addition to theoretical considerations, the anti-apartheid political ideals of the Leakey family and Philip Tobias meshed with this portrayal of one ancestor, one hu-mankind. A comparable shift took place in the views held with respect to the Kalahari Bushmen. Once regarded as one of the most primitive and desolate races of humankind, slotted between Caucasian humans and the lowly apes, they were now romanticized as *The Harmless People* (Thomas 1959), quintessentially human noble savages, who, unlike west-ern humans, lived in close harmony with one another and with nature, sharing food in egalitarian groups. As such, they were presumed to be exemplars of early hominids.

The traffic in images of the great apes, early hominids, and extant human foragers during this third era of ape debate has been complex. Like a hundred years earlier, but on a larger scale, scientific research programs, philosophical views, the zeitgeist, political agendas, science writing, and the popular imagination have fed on one another. Symptomatic of the new role of the ape as ideal self instead of despised other, not so much threatening as threatened itself, are the titles of a number of books by primatologists for a wider audience. Goodall's *In the Shadow of Man* (1971) appeared in almost fifty languages. The previously-mentioned picture of Goodall and a young chimpanzee appeared in an article in *National Geographic* in 1967 entitled "My Friends the Wild Chimpanzees," while the similar picture of Fossey with a gorilla was in an article entitled "Making Friends with Mountain Gorillas," in the same journal three years later (Fossey 1970).

One of the articles in which biochemical similarities between humans and chimpanzees were reported was entitled "Our Close Cousin the Chimpanzee" (King and Wilson 1975b). Roger Fouts and his co-writer, or their market-oriented publishers, called their book on the symbolic capacities of chimpanzees, Fouts' advocacy of captured individuals, and his thirty-year friendship with Washoe *Next of Kin: What Chimpanzees Have Taught Me About Who We Are* (Fouts & Mills 1997). Sue Savage-Rumbaugh's book, co-authored by Roger Lewin, on a bonobo's successes at communicating with humans with the help of symbols was called

Kanzi: The Ape at the Brink of the Human Mind. Shirley Strum's *Almost Human* (1987) is on baboons; Birute Galdikas' *Reflections of Eden* (1995) on the orang-utans of Borneo.

The semantic field such titles draw upon is that of kinship, friendship, and respect. Dian Fossey's attitude towards the mountain gorillas she studied and tried to protect is characteristic: "<Kweli nudugu yangu!> These words in Swahili, whispered by the awestruck Manuel, who was also seeing his first gorilla, summed up exactly what I was feeling. <Surely, God, these are my kin>." (Fossey, quoted by Mowat 1987: 14). While traditionally the beastliness of non-human primates had been prominent, they now moved across the animal–human boundary towards individuality, proper names, and near-humanness. "Equality beyond Humanity" was the subtitle of an edited volume, discussed below, on ape ethics and proposing a Declaration of the Rights of the Great Apes (Cavalieri and Singer 1993). The new attitude was one of sympathy and admiration for the harmonious, natural life of the great apes. This particular cultural role bears some similarity to, for instance, that played by the little birds portrayed in nineteenth-century European middle- and upper-class children's books, in which they form pairs, build cosy nests, and carefully rear their children together – the ideal of the family. Every era, every generation, in its own specific way, has its favourite and vilified animals, its ideals of living in harmony, its positive and negative ethical models for human action. There are ignoble and noble savages, demonized and noble wolves, man-eating sharks and friendly dolphins.

However, negative perceptions of primates persisted alongside the new positive ones. Concurring with Washburn's hunting hypothesis, Richard Lee, in his work on the !Kung San Bushmen, and Glynn Isaac, on early *Homo*, stressed food sharing. Irven DeVore, however, saw male dominance and aggression as the key to baboon socioecological adaptation, and the baboon as a model for the simian substrate of human evolution and the earliest hominids (cf. Van Reybrouck 2000: 219 ff.). While in other settings or periods it was either the chimpanzee, or the gorilla, or, more recently, the bonobo that primarily determined the image of the apish other, here the baboon moved to the fore. A grim view of primate nature, in general, and human nature and ancestry, in particular, was presented by playwright and science writer Robert Ardrey in such best-sellers as *African Genesis* (1961), *The Territorial Imperative* (1966), and *The Hunting Hypothesis* (1976). In addition to selectively read and tendentiously presented baboon primatology (cf. Strum 1987), Ardrey found inspiration in the interpretation of the South African australopithecines as carnivorous and even cannibalistic "killer (man-)apes," developed by Raymond Dart, the discoverer of the first australopithecine fossil. Ardrey was also influenced by the theory of innate aggression formulated by Nobel Prize-winning ethologist, Konrad Lorenz. In the period of Cold War pessimism and its aftermath, such authors as Ardrey, or Lionel Tiger and Robin Fox with their *The Imperial Animal* (1971), found a wide readership.

Dart's scenario in "The Predatory Transition from Ape to Man," his 1953 article, had the earliest humans "slaking their ravenous thirst with the hot blood of victims and greedily devouring live writhing flesh" (1953: 209). It found expression in the opening scene of Stanley Kubrick's 1968 film *2001- A Space Odyssey*, where tools are weapons used by ferocious early hominids to kill, the opposite of the images of Goodall and Fossey reaching out to the apish other. In the 1970s, Dart's scenario was refuted by a new scrutiny of the archaeological remains of australopithecines which showed that they had not been not predators but prey. Proponents of the methodologically rigid New Archaeology even doubted their very capability to undertake such a complex activity as hunting. At the same time, Marxists criticized the blaming of human nature for war and other social ills instead of economic history, and suspected an ideological justification for militarism.

But the main criticism of the predation model of human genesis came from feminist primatologists and anthropologists who launched a gynocentric "woman-the-gatherer" paradigm (Tanner and Zihlman 1976), critically pitted against the androcentric "man-the-hunter" perspective of Washburn, DeVore, and others, as well as the influential conference of the same name (Lee and Devore 1968). This particular research tradition moved the focus away from aggressive and dominating hunting males to peaceful-and-caring gathering mothers as the driving force behind the humanization of hominids. Chimpanzee and baboon mother–offspring bonds were now shifted to the core of social and economic life and considered to be better exemplars of early hominids than baboon male bonds. The "woman-the-gatherer" paradigm converged with the stress on foraging and sharing among Kalahari Bushmen articulated by Richard Lee at the famous *Man the Hunter* conference in 1966, undermining the intention suggested by its title. The new paradigm added to the positive effect of Jane Goodall's research. At the same time, it refuelled conflicts and tensions between primatology and the human disciplines, the latter remaining wary of any rapprochement between humans and animals (Gilmore 1981; Sperling 1991).

The images of both chimpanzees and Bushmen became more ambiguous and probably more realistic when, in the mid-1970s, it was discovered that neither the Gombe reserve nor the Kalahari desert were idyllic Shangri La's after all: in both cases, murder and violence turned out to be just as much a part of the behavioural fabric as gentleness and cooperation. The noble savage turned out to be as mythical as the noble ape. "[The] brutal killings, observed among the chimpanzees ... changed forever my view of the chimpanzee nature," Goodall wrote in retrospect on the cannibalistic feasts and systematic lethal gang raids she encountered. "During the first ten years of the study I had believed ... that the Gombe chimpanzees were, for the most part, rather nicer than human beings.... Then, suddenly, we found that chimpanzees could be brutal – that they, like us, had a dark side to their nature" (Goodall 1999: 117). Such ignoble behaviours as infanticide, cannibalism, and killing between and within communities posed a threat to the noble chimpanzees idyll, but apparently, the damage remained limited. Not much later, the bonobo, with its abundant reconciliation through sex, came into the picture both as a cultural role model and technically as a model for early hominids. As an alternative, more positive, exemplar of humanness, it tended to be contrasted favourably with the common chimpanzee, which was prone to aggression and power-plays.

In the 1980s and 1990s, behavioural ecology emerged out of earlier socioecological and sociobiological approaches as a strong paradigm in field primatology. It used optimal-foraging theory and life-history theory to explain the complex and refined interactions of individuals and communities with their living and non-living environment. While most researchers tried to strike a balance, some did, in fact, place more stress on cooperation, while others emphasized conflict, often in bestsellers written for a broader audience, but influential in professional circles as well.

Harvard primatologist Richard Wrangham, who did extensive fieldwork on chimpanzees in Central Africa, highlighted male violence and male strategic alliances as pivotal survival strategies. Males were selected by females for their exploitive and aggressive behaviours, leading to competitive success. His 1996 book *Demonic Males: Apes and the Origin of Human Violence*, written with Dale Peterson, offers a dark view of ape and human nature, reminiscent of Hobbes, Huxley, and Freud. "We are cursed," they write, "with a demonic male temperament and a Machiavellian capacity to express it" – a "5-million year stain of our ape past" (Wrangham and Peterson 1996: 258). The idea of *simia figura diaboli* – the monkey as an image of the devil – is still remotely present here. The "Man-the-Hunter" model of the 1960s, which dropped out of favour during the 1970s, was recently revived by Craig Stanford and others who focussed on the crucial roles in the origins of human behaviour of the cognitive aspects of meat sharing, though to a much lesser degree meat acquisition, and females as central players in the mating game (Stanford and Bunn 2001).

The renewed stress on selfish aggression was counterbalanced by primatologist Frans de Waal. According to Hobbesian, Durkheimian, and

Freudian views, morality and reciprocal altruism were to be found in culture as a layer superimposed upon and constraining man's violent and selfish nature. De Waal, on the contrary, sees these behaviours as part and parcel of the biological make-up of humans and other primates. In a number of influential books, starting with his 1982 *Chimpanzee Politics*, he has revealed the complexity of social and political behaviour among non-human primates and its close similarity to that of humans. This includes aggression, altruism, and mechanisms for avoiding, reducing, and resolving conflicts in social life. *Peace-Making among Primates* (1989) concentrated on the latter mechanisms, and led to the empirical and philosophical claim that apes are basically *Good-Natured*, as the title of his 1996 book asserts, striving for harmonious relations, caring for the injured, and respecting social rules and contracts of give-and-take.

De Waal's approach diverges from the views of Thomas Huxley, Sigmund Freud, and, more recently, Richard Dawkins, who see no place for real unselfishness as a natural moral tendency, in any society, human or other. In their perspective, questions of right and wrong and human morality are outside of and at odds with the natural world. As to the moral implications of the theory that genetically determined altruistic behaviours serve the needs of genes and the individuals that carry those genes and are, thus, basically selfish, Dawkins (1976) applies a double standard: he makes an exception for human altruism, which is claimed to be of a different order.

De Waal's work (see Figure 7) has helped to combat the widespread inclination to see the bad habits of humans as exclusively animal and their good ones as exclusively human. Empathy and sympathy and reconciliation and forgiveness are in his view as natural as and ultimately more adaptive than Machiavellianism and aggression. Bonobos serve as a reminder "that people who keep shoving the murderous side of chimpanzees into our faces so as to make the point that humans are 'killer apes,' as Dart and Ardrey called us, have a biased agenda. They have seized upon the chimpanzee with an enthusiasm that doesn't do justice

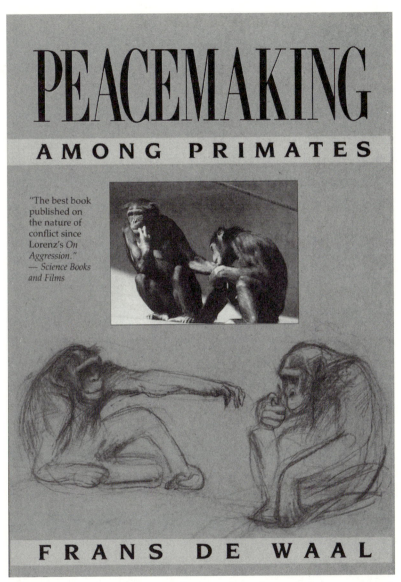

FIGURE 7. De Waal's stress on reconciliation and use of empathy in interpreting primate behaviour was not only scientifically and methodologically innovative, but also helped counterbalance traditional darker views of apes. Cover of the 1989 American edition of one of his books, courtesy of Harvard University Press.

to this species – which is cooperative and sociable most of the time – but that does expose the culturally colored glasses that have thus far kept the bonobo on the sidelines of the human evolution show" (2001: 130). Still, his approach is straightforwardly functionalist, and he is a firm believer in the acting individual's strategic rationality.

Like those of Jane Goodall, de Waal's interpretations of ape behaviour diverge from the mainstream in their use of human empathy. He has moved beyond the more objectivistic and mechanistic perspective of classic ethology, with its observable input–output relations, to cognitive ethology, a growing field that treats animals as knowing, believing, desiring and calculating actors. While remaining committed to observability and functionalist explanation, he talks about reasons in addition to causes, intentions in addition to observable actions. He does not shy away from concepts normally associated with humans exclusively, such as politics, friendship, and peacemaking, and was one of the first to speak of, for instance, "reconciliation" while most of his colleagues still preferred "post-conflict affiliative contact."

Like Goodall and many others who followed, de Waal names individuals and stresses their individual personalities, as well as idiosyncratic social and historical developments in specific groups. This gives an ethnographic quality to his writing and a hermeneutic or interpretive dimension to his scientific interpretations. Similarities between human and other primates are stressed over differences. A sophisticated, animal-centric anthropomorphism serves as a logical starting-point when it comes to animals as close to humans genetically and evolutionarily as apes; it is a heuristically useful tool which generates testable ideas. "I argue for breathing space in relation to cognitive interpretations," de Waal writes, "[I] don't mind drawing comparisons with human behaviour, and wonder how and why anthropomorphism got such a bad name" (de Waal 2001, 42; cf. 74 ff.).

Jane Goodall concurs: "If we ascribe human emotions to nonhuman animals we are accused of being anthropomorphic – a cardinal sin in ethology. But is it so terrible? If . . . we accept that there are dramatic similarities in chimpanzee and human brain and nervous system, is it not logical to assume that there will be similarities also in at least the more basic feelings, emotions, moods of the two species?" (Goodall 1990: 16). This has not gone uncriticized, but is certainly a parsimonious strategy. At least some of the reproach aimed at anthropomorphism and treating animals as humans would seem to be another expression of the anthropocentric concern with human unicity that has accompanied the study of non-human primates since Linnaeus. But the reproach may also reflect an austere methodology with strict standards of verifiability.

The previously mentioned shift from male-centred to female-centred accounts of non-human primates and early hominids – by female anthropologists – was analysed in considerable detail in a remarkable book by Donna Haraway (1989), a science historian and cultural theorist. The study itself constitutes a significant moment in the history of perceptions of primates it sets out to re- and deconstruct. Looking at twentieth-century primatology, Haraway sees race, species, gender, and science codes at work "to reinvent nature in the Third World for First World audiences within post-colonial, multinational capitalism" (1989: 135). She criticizes the discipline's predominant self-understanding in terms of a progress from immature free speculation to quantitative facts and falsifiable hypotheses as an ideology, and portrays primatology as a masculinist, speciesist, imperialist, and story-laden discourse which is inherently political – "simian Orientalism," as she terms it (*ibid.*: 10). The literary theorist Edward Said has used that latter term to denote the tendency in Western literature and sciences of the colonial period to construct a negative mirror-image of non-Western peoples serving the articulation of Western needs. Haraway sees a similar process at work in primatological narratives on male and female, culture and nature.

Primate Visions was widely read and discussed, favourably by most kindred spirits, but more critically by primatologists themselves, who felt the book seriously underestimated the role of hard empirical facts concerning primates in the development of their theories, whatever their context of discovery and social backgrounds. Primatology, Vernon Reynolds wrote, "is not just story-telling, it interfaces with the physical world as well. One goes out and observes . . . new things . . . hitherto disregarded facts." Haraway's deconstructionist perspective "has no handle on the possibility of an improved understanding of the non-human world . . . [it] does not touch on the real scientific enterprise" (Reynolds 1991: 168). Haraway's book is fascinating and has much to offer, but its intellectualist language, use of metaphors, and mixing of genres did not contribute to a favourable reception in primatological circles. It was also pointed out that Haraway's anti-racist and feminist analysis tended to set male primatology up as its own Orient, interpreted in terms of her own (too) radically postmodernist, deconstructionist intellectual preoccupations and political intentions; that to Haraway herself, likewise, non-human primates mattered primarily in terms of their meanings for humans and not so much for what they were themselves (Landau 1991b).

Once again, in a fashion that bore the mark of the 1980s, there was dissension concerning the interpretation of the ape–human boundary. Haraway's own agenda was dislocating and destabilizing that boundary, exploring its permeability, and thus remapping the borderlands between nature and culture and "facilitating revisionings of fundamental, persistent western narratives about difference, especially racial and sexual difference" (Haraway 1989: 377, cf. 15). Most primatologists, on the other hand, prefer to keep their research concerns and their often intense moral concerns separated (cf. Beck *et al.* 2001).

6.2 Tools, Mirrors, Symbols

Everything associated with mind and culture, thought to be essentially human attributes, was until quite recently as much of a taboo in biology as nature and biology were in the human sciences. This mindset was challenged by the discovery and in-depth study of a number of behaviours in apes which formerly were presumed to be unique to humans: cultural toolmaking, mirror self-recognition, the manipulation of symbols, food sharing, politics, cooperative hunting, and deliberate deception.

Homo faber, "man the toolmaker," was a widespread human self-definition, probably coined by Galen in the second century AD and connected with the idea of the unique human mind guiding manipulation. According to the thirteenth-century theologian and philosopher, Albert the Great, monkeys had hands, to be sure, but they used them only for locomotion and eating, while in humans the hand was the *organum organorum*, steered by the intellect. In the viewpoint of Friedrich Blumenbach, similarly, as was shown in Chapter 2, the grasping hand of humans with its versatile thumb, expressing their intelligent, free will and suiting their dignity, was one reason to situate them in a separate order, *contra* Linnaeus. In the same vein, Jacques Boucher de Perthes, the French pioneer of palaeolithic archaeology, interpreted the flint handaxes he had discovered in the sediments of the Somme river as "tools [which] are our first proof of reason, our first title to the rank of man, which no other terrestrial creature can show," situating humans, present-day as well as palaeolithic, at the summit of creation (Boucher de Perthes 1864, III: 459). Portuguese Roman Catholic missionaries had, however, already described tool use by chimpanzees in Sierra Leone during the sixteenth and seventeenth centuries. This did not become widely known, although Darwin was aware of it.

Archaeologists of the mid-twentieth century, with tens of thousands of palaeolithic handaxes already unearthed, mostly in Europe and Africa, generally saw tools as a unique adaptation, the hallmark of humanness, in line with neo-Darwinist biology. Man makes tools, tools make man. A classic expression of this conviction, which influenced the systematics of the *Homo* genus, was Kenneth Oakley's *Man the Toolmaker* (Oakley 1949), discussed in Chapter 4. When Louis Leakey received a telegram from Goodall in the Autumn of 1964 describing her discovery of chimpanzee termite fishing, he made his now famous response: "Now we must rede-fine tool, redefine Man, or accept chimpanzees as humans" – a reaction which reveals a strong commitment to the *homo faber* idea and a preoc-cupation with human unicity (Goodall 1998: 2184).

As has already become clear, the definitions of "man the toolmaker" and "technology" have been revised several times. Criteria such as us-ing tools made with tools or dependence on fabricated tools for sur-vival were added, thus disqualifying non-humans to which previous definitions were found to apply. One such revision warding off this new threat to human unicity was a controversial article with the tell-tale title "Culture: A *Human* Domain," by physical anthropologist Ralph Holloway (1969), a specialist in early hominid endocast studies. Giving voice to broadly felt concerns, Holloway pointed to the systematic impo-sition of arbitrary form upon the environment as specific and unique to human behaviour, and identifiable by the appearance of stone tools in the archaeological record. Holloway readjusted the human–animal bound-ary, "[giving] culture back [*sic*] to man, regardless of what the clever baboons, vultures, ants, macaques, or chimpanzees have done thus far" (*ibid.*: 47).

Much has been discovered on tool behaviours and other learned, cul-tural traditions in chimpanzees and other species in recent decades. The hammer-and-anvil technology of chimpanzees in Ivory Coast for crack-ing cola nuts was studied extensively (Joulian 1998). A systematic synthesis of seven studies in *Nature* entitled "Cultures in Chimpanzees" (Whiten *et al.* 1999; cf. McGrew 1992; Boesch *et al.* 1994) listed 39 forms of learned, cultural traditions habitual in some and absent in other, comparable communities of chimpanzees, with no ecological explanation. In addi-tion to cracking nuts with stone hammers on anvils, these included the use of leaf napkins and fly whisks, termite and ant fishing with sticks, hand clasping, rain dancing, grooming and courtship behaviours, and marrow picking. The patterns of variation, the article's nine authors, all primatologists, write, "are far more extensive than have previously been documented for any animal species except humans," and "the combined repertoire of these behaviour patterns in each chimpanzee community is itself highly distinctive, a phenomenon characteristic of human cultures but previously unrecognised in non-human species" (Whiten *et al.*: 682).

Despite Holloway's warning, the concepts of culture and cultural transmission are now widely applied to such behaviours, with a refreshing and heuristically useful disregard for the stress many cultural anthropologists place on linguistic mediation. Van Schaick and colleagues presented evidence supporting 24 culturally transmitted behaviors in orang-utans (Van Schaick *et al.* 2003). A captive nine-year-old male bonobo learned how to produce sharp stone flakes from cores by striking stones together, and to use these flakes as tools, for example, to cut a rope protecting food in a box (Toth *et al.* 1993; Schick *et al.* 1999). All in all, *Pan* the toolmaker, together with other apes, now stands firmly side-by-side with "man the toolmaker," and a cultural primatology, including a "cultural panthropology" (Whiten, Horner and Marshall-Pescini 2003), is positioning itself with respect to cultural anthropology.

Primatologists who study cultural traditions in non-human primates tend to play down the stress cultural anthropologists place on the role of syntactic language in "real," which to them is human, culture. Why should symbolic language be a more "essential" feature of culture than, for example, innovation, dissemination within and diffusion between groups, standardization, tradition, and nonsubsistence? De Waal sees culture as learned solutions to problems related to survival, "the nongenetic spreading of habits," while "the rest is nothing else than embellishment" (2001: 30–31). Cultural anthropologists who deny it in chimpanzees because they hold symbolic meaning to be essential wield an anthropocentric standard which keeps humans distinct. Human symbolic language is to primatologists just another, albeit powerful, means of survival. They try to bridge the gap and establish a continuum of small steps between humans and other primates (McGrew 1992: 144, 148, 199, 217).

163

The above-mentioned 1999 paper in *Nature* on chimpanzee cultures evoked "extensive coverage in the serious news media that extended to editorials in the major newspapers of both the USA and the UK, expressing concern that an assumed landmark of human disctinctiveness was under threat" (Whiten, Horner and Marshall-Pescini 2003: 92). Even two of the co-authors of the paper in *Nature*, themselves primatologists, express an ambiguous concern with human distinctiveness. Some people were quite disturbed by that paper, the two write, when they learned that the characteristic believed to separate humans starkly from animals was not an absolute difference after all. They felt that response to be misdirected, for "[the] differences between human customs and traditions, enriched and mediated by language as they are, are vast in contrast with what we see in the chimpanzee. The story of chimpanzee cultures sharpens our understanding of our unicity rather than threatening it in any way that need worry us" (Whiten and Boesch 2001).

The history of research into the subsistence behaviors of non-human primates illustrates a retreat from the notions of toolmaking and culture as tokens of human specialty, accompanied by efforts to save these human markers by redefining them. Presumed differences between human and other primates also came under fire through self-recognition experiments with mirrors, and research into the symbolic capacities of apes in experimental settings. "Man's structural peculiarities only suffice to place him in a monotypic zoological family, with a single living species," Theodosius Dobzhansky still wrote in 1974, but his mental abilities were "far more distinctive. If the zoological classification were based on psychological instead of mainly morphological traits, man would have to be considered a separate phylum or even kingdom" (Dobzhansky 1974: 333). This echoed evolutionary biologist Julian Huxley's (1941) claim that, despite their physical resemblance to apes, a kingdom should be reserved – next to the kingdom of the plants and the kingdom of the animals – for humans because of their psychological unicity. It also echoed a similar remark by Linnaeus, playing down the anatomical similarities that made him position humans and apes in the same genus: anatomically they were in the same genus, but mentally they were far apart.

While in the Middle Ages, the mirror-gazing monkey had been a symbol of foolish *vanitas*, the human folly of too mundane pursuits, in the 1970s the ape became a mirror for human self-consciousness. Psychologist Gordon Gallup offered some reflections on his ground-breaking experiments on chimpanzee mirror recognition in an article entitled "A Mirror for the Mind of Man, or Will the Chimpanzee Create an Identity Crisis for *Homo sapiens*?" (Gallup 1977). The answer to that question was a decisive yes, for here the self-conscious human mind, the most intimately human feature, the last refuge from the encroaching animal, was at stake. Gallup interpreted the fact that chimpanzees – as well as orang-utans and dolphins, as was subsequently discovered – were able to recognize their own image in mirrors as an indication of some form of self-awareness. More recent experiments have shown that they are even able to recognize themselves in distorting mirrors, correcting cognitively for the distortion of their features (Kitchen, Denton and Brent 1996). Tactical deception in non-human primates, likewise, seemed to presuppose some form or degree of reflexive self-awareness as well as, arguably, a certain awareness of beliefs, desires, and intentions, and thus of the mind, of conspecifics while monitoring and manipulating their behaviours. The precise implications of both self-recognition in mirrors and Machiavellian manipulations are, however, still controversial.

The other last bastion of the human soul or mind was, of course, language, traditionally seen as the outward appearance of mind, and cherished by cultural anthropologists and philosophers, among others. In recent decades, certain symbolic capacities have clearly been shown in apes by such researchers as David Premack with chimpanzee Sarah, Francine Patterson with gorilla Koko, Allen and Beatrice Gardner and Roger Fouts with chimpanzee Washoe, Lyn Miles with orang-utan Chantek, Duane Rumbaugh with chimpanzee Lana, and Sue Savage-Rumbaugh with bonobo Kanzi – "the ape who crossed the line" (Savage-Rumbaugh *et al.* 1998: 7). The ensuing controversies ran along many of the same lines as the ape language debate of the late eighteenth century, when Rousseau and Monboddo portrayed the "perfectible" Orang-Outang as being, in principle, capable of speech and thus human – a claim which was contested by Buffon and Camper (Wokler 1993).

Chimpanzees and bonobos have learned to comprehend spoken English to some degree. They have learned to communicate efficiently with the help of American Sign Language as used by hearing-impaired humans, or with the help of over two hundred arbitrary lexigrams – with such meanings as "tickle," "juice," "outdoors" – on a keyboard. They have gained some command of abstract concepts, such as the ability to categorize a screwdriver as a "tool" versus a banana as "fruit," or the capacity to work with numbers and amounts. They seem to understand simple syntactical differences such as between "doggie bites snake" and "snake bites doggie," referring to toys in the context of play. Intensive research with an African grey parrot, Alex, has also revealed considerable linguistic competence far beyond mere imitation, although even this latter behaviour is itself cognitively fairly complex (Pepperberg 1999).

While their exact interpretation has been and continues to be controversial, such performances have undermined the idea of *homo loquens*, humans as the only linguistic beings, closely linked with two other pervasive and exclusive human self-definitions, that of *homo symbolicus*, and that of *homo sapiens*. Chomskyan linguists see no real syntax in ape utterances comparable to that which humans possess. Those arguing in favour of ape language, mostly psychologists, on the other hand, feel that syntax as an abstract recursive algorithm or system of rules for generating permissible strings of lexical items is a far cry from natural as well as human-learned everyday ape communication – too anthropocentric a yardstick. Behaviourist psychologists think that the role of mechanical conditioning in ape "symbolic" behaviour is underestimated by the experimenters. It has also been suggested that human-reared apes are enculturated, and stimulated by their rich human environment to develop imitative capacities beyond their normal behavioural repertoire.

In the present context, we are not concerned with evaluating various claims, which would be all the more difficult given the lack of consensus on what constitutes "language," "symbolism," or "syntax." What is of primary interest here is their connection with sensitive issues concerning human identity and the ape–human boundary. The proponents of the idea of ape linguistic capacity have accused their opponents of anthropocentrist boundary-keeping time and again. Barbara King, whose work on social information transfer in primates, including humans and early hominids, was already referred to in Chapter 4, has criticized the fallacy of "assuming that the human form of a particular characteristic is the defining feature of that characteristic" (King 1994a: 134; cf. King 1994b; Gibson 1993). Two researchers on bonobo syntactical capacities have uttered a similar complaint: "Comparative developmental linguistics has been plagued by a double standard. . . . When children make up novel words on a one-shot basis, it is called lexical invention. When chimpanzees do the same thing, it is termed ambiguous" (Greenfield and Savage-Rumbaugh 1990: 571). "The way imitation is being defined and evaluated," primatologist Frans de Waal concurs, "disadvantages apes who fail to pay attention to the species that does the testing" (de Waal 2001: 224).

It is increasingly felt that the differences between humans and apes, however great, are in degree, not in kind, and that basically there is cognitive continuity. While in the eyes of some, discoveries pertaining to the linguistic, cognitive, and technological abilities of animals, especially non-human primates, have further problematized the animal–human boundary as it was traditionally drawn, others have time and again tried to fortify that boundary by redefining it. When apes turned out to be capable of wielding arbitrary symbols, it was pointed out that they were not capable of ordering them syntactically. When data became available pointing in the direction of at least some syntactic capacity, it was argued that they never used such syntactic utterances reflexively, as humans do. They may use tools, but we should not just look for tools but for tools made with tools. They may have cultural traditions in the sense of intergenerationally transmitted, learned solutions to problems, but we should look for the transmission of symbolic meaning. Technology, language, and culture were what humans were capable of, and when animals turned out to have similar capacities the definition was changed in order to make humans again unique – a matter of moving the goal posts. Such strategies kept apes at a comfortable distance.

However, Povinelli warns that we may have overestimated chimpanzees' understanding of the physical world, especially in the context of tool behaviour. On the basis of a long series of important and controversial experiments, conducted over a five-year period, he concludes that there is a profound, qualititative difference between the everyday causal understanding of humans and chimpanzees. While they are capable of certain tool behaviour similar to that of humans, the chimpanzees' ability to comprehend how things work, their "folk physics," is limited to perceptually available information. Humans, on the other hand, are able to mentally represent unobservable factors such as force and gravity (Povinelli 2000).

A relativizing note is added by primatologist Vernon Reynolds. We must not let the more outstanding abilities of apes such as the ability to make tools, manipulate symbols, or hunt cooperatively obscure the fact that normally these shy denizens of the African woodlands and rainforests engage in more common activities, he warns. They are what they are, and "not ersatz humans, nor failed humans, nor potential humans" (Reynolds 1990: 2), nor, we may add, idealized humans.

6.3 Ape and Human Rights

"In a series of forms graduating insensibly from some apelike creature to man as he now exists," Darwin wrote in Chapter 7 of *Descent of Man*, "it would be impossible to fix on any definite point where the term "man" ought to be used. But this is a matter of very little importance" (Darwin 1871, II: 380). The matter may be of little theoretical significance from the standpoint of evolutionary biology, but practically and morally speaking, the consequences are considerable because beings acknowledged as human enjoy a privileged status. Gordon Gallup ended his article on the implications of mirror recognition for the nature of chimpanzee minds with the following words: "Perhaps someday, in order to be logically consistent, man may have to seriously consider the applicability of his political, ethical and moral philosophy to chimpanzees" (Gallup 1977: 311).

Taxonomists and other scientists who classified humans more closely with apes have also regularly wondered about the moral implications thereof. Cladist Matt Cartmill concurs with the primate taxonomists Colin Groves and Jeffrey Schwartz, who both point to the moral implications of the fact that consistent application of cladist principles positions at least some great apes in the hominid family. For Groves – and many others – this is a reason to refrain from experiments on apes; Schwartz suggests giving up cladistics lest certain hominids will have to serve as experimental animals. "When stripped to its essence," Cartmill writes, "the animal–human boundary is not a taxonomic but a moral concept. It divides the moral universe into subjects and objects, separating responsible agents with rights and duties from mere things that we can use for our own purposes . . . [cladist] classification blurs and eradicates that boundary in several ways" (Cartmill 2001: 105).

Gallup's remark was prophetic. The day human moral philosophy was applied to great apes has come sooner than he may have thought, although it was certainly humans who stood up for ape rights, not the apes themselves. For a proper understanding of the ape rights movements of the past decades, a look at the human rights debate of the late 1940s and 1950s is indispensable. In the course of the twentieth century, scientific approaches to "races" in terms of a hierarchy of fixed types – under the influence of the metaphysical notion of a Great Chain of Being – had come under attack by the evolutionary and population-genetic approach of the New Synthesis in biology. This added to a similar critique developed earlier by cultural anthropologists, in particular the Boasians (cf. pp. 125 ff.) with their sharp distinction between physical and cultural characteristics. The Second World War and the Holocaust considerably amplified the tendency towards scientific humanism and the idea of one, culturally variable but genetically uniform humankind.

The General Assembly of the United Nations adopted and proclaimed the *Universal Declaration on Human Rights* in 1948 (United Nations 1952), and the UNESCO a *Statement on Race* in 1950 (UNESCO 1950). Biologists such as Julian Huxley and Theodosius Dobzhansky were involved, as well as physical anthropologists such as Ashley Montagu, and such cultural anthropologists as Claude Lévi-Strauss. Biologically, i.e., genetically, all humans were equal while culturally there could be considerable variability, it was claimed. The Preamble of the *Universal Declaration on Human Rights* states that "recognition of the inherent dignity and of the equal and inalienable rights of all members of the human family is the foundation of freedom, justice and peace in the world," referring explicitly to the "disregard and contempt for human rights [resulting] in barbarous acts which have outraged the conscience of mankind." Article 1 stipulates that "[all] human beings are born free and equal in dignity and rights. They are endowed with reason and conscience and should act towards one another in a spirit of brotherhood." Everyone has the right to life, liberty, and security of person, and to not be held in slavery or servitude (*ibid.*).

According to the UNESCO 1964 *Proposals on the Biological Aspects of Race*, "[all] men living today belong to a single species, *Homo sapiens*, and are derived from a common stock. . . . Neither in the field of hereditary potentialities concerning the over-all intelligence and the capacity for cultural development, nor in that of the physical traits, is there any justification for the concept of 'inferior' and 'superior' races" (in Dunn *et al.* 1975: 355, 358). In earlier views, presumed biological differences had been taken to imply moral and political inequality. Again, morals and biology were connected, but this time, the biological homogeneity of the species *Homo*, as defended by proponents of the New Synthesis in biology, served as an argument for moral and political equality and the right to full citizenship of all humans, whatever their cultural background or physical constitution (cf. Haraway 1989: 197 ff.). A preoccupation with differences gave way to one with similarities.

The widely circulated photography exhibition, *The Family of Man*, expressed the new idea and ideal vigorously. It was compiled by Edward Steichen in 1955 for the Museum of Modern Art, New York, and brought together some 500 photographs taken by 273 photographers from 68 countries, grouped thematically around subjects pertinent to all cultures, such as love, children, and death (Steichen 1955). After its initial showing in New York, the exhibition toured the world for eight years, making stops in thirty-seven countries on six continents. It formed a vast symbolic portrait of humankind, stressing the commonalities that bound people and cultures around the world.

In fact, the idea of a unity of humankind had never been entirely absent, despite theories and ideologies of racial hierarchy. Hierarchy was one aspect of the Great Chain of Being as a key concept of European cosmology, and essentialism, including the idea of a universal human essence, another. Rationalist and idealist philosophy assumed unity in humankind because of the rational human mind, even though rationality was assumed not to be expressed or developed to the same degree in all nations, races, or classes. For Christians, humankind was one because of its descendance from the same ancestral pair and the rational soul as an essence shared by all humans, corresponding to the Creator's archetypal idea. As Pope John Paul II phrased it in an address to the Pontifical Academy of Sciences on October 22, 1996, "[it] is by virtue of his spiritual soul that the whole person possesses such a dignity even in his body . . . if the human body takes its origin from pre-existent living matter the spiritual soul is immediately created by God. . . . Consequently, theories of evolution which, in accordance with the philosophies inspiring them, consider the mind as emerging from the forces of living matter, or as a mere epiphenomenon of this matter, are incompatible with the truth about man. Nor are they able to ground the dignity of the person. With man, then, we find ourselves in the presence of an ontological difference, an ontological leap" (John Paul II 1996). Christian views are still germane to the laws and moral views of Western societies.

Ironically, the inclusion of non-European "races" in the "family of man" was made possible by the persistent exclusion of non-human species. Humans were not to be treated like beasts. The racist, Eurocentric double standard for races – one for whites, another for non-whites – was torn down with the help of a persisting speciesist, *Homo*-centric standard for all other species as the foundation of society's moral order. The Caucasian yardstick for races was combated with a human yardstick for species. Being unique, the features all humans shared justified their dominion over beasts; being uniform, they forbade dominion of some humans over others.

This post-war biological humanism was the historical backdrop against which equality beyond, and not just within, humankind was claimed by the Great Ape Project's Declaration on Great Apes (Cavalieri and Singer 1993: 4–7), an initiative of philosophers, primatologists, anthropologists, and other academics. Styled after the American Declaration of Independence, it demands the extension of the community of moral equals to include all great apes, to wit humans, chimpanzees, gorillas, and orang-utans, and the enforcement of the right to life, individual liberty, and avoidance of suffering. Members of this moral community are not to be killed except in self-defence, not to be imprisoned without fair legal process, and not to suffer, wantonly or for the benefit of others (*ibid.*; cf. Beck 2001; Corbey 1993a). The moral stance taken by this charter contrasts starkly with the mainstream of most of the twentieth century as formulated repeatedly by, for example, the pioneer primate psychologist, Robert Yerkes, in the first decades of that century: chimpanzees are "infrahuman organisms" which contribute to human welfare and should be employed "as a means of approaching the solution of various human problems for which we may not freely and effectively use ourselves as materials of observation and experimentation" (quoted in Loy and Peters 1991: 5).

The Great Ape Project's relocation of the dividing line between "human" and "beast" out of grave concern for the life, well-being and dignity of apes suggests a wider humankind with increasingly blurred boundaries, including early hominids. The status and personhood of other animals – the question of when killing becomes murder and eating cannibalism – is left open to future reflection and initiatives. Cavalieri and Singer's edited volume also contains thirty-four essays supporting the Declaration on Great Apes in various ways, and concludes that there is no significant criterion of personhood apes cannot fulfil, and no natural category that includes apes but excludes humans. In the epilogue, the editors draw a parallel with the abolition of slavery, referring to Aristotle's view that slaves were animated property (Cavalieri and Singer 1993: 305).

The Declaration on Great Apes was instrumental in the New Zealand Animal Welfare Act, passed on October 8, 1999, which prohibits the use of all great apes – chimpanzees, bonobos, gorillas, orang-utans, and humans – in research and testing unless such use is in the best interests of the individual or species it concerns. It also had bearing on a government ban on the use of great apes for medical experiments in the United Kingdom, issued in 1998, and emphasizing that, however useful they might be as biological models for human diseases, their use for human purposes could not morally be allowed. An initiative with an agenda similar to that of the Great Ape Project was the foundation of the International Primate Protection League in 1973, which since that time has been working continuously for the well-being of primates. With Field Representatives in more than thirty countries and an Advisory Board composed of experts from the fields of zoology, anthropology, medicine, biology, veterinary medicine, and psychology, it monitors and tries to intervene on behalf of non-human primates worldwide.

Critics of the idea of great-ape rights were quick to point out that, while the exclusivity and anthropocentrism of the predominant view was being attacked, it was at the same time being incorporated – similarity to humans was still a standard non-human species were judged against. What about animal species other than humans and apes? The animal–human boundary was only displaced, it was argued, from the line sundering humans from apes to that sundering humans and apes from all other animals. The inclusion of apes was thus made possible by excluding species other than apes, analogous to the inclusion of non-European "races" at the expense of non-human species in the *Universal Declaration on Human Rights*. The reply was a pragmatic stance: one had to start somewhere. Great apes may serve as a convenient bridgehead to the animal world, and the mandate could conceivably be extended to other sentient beings.

Obviously, there are huge philosophical problems here. Where does one draw the line which, if not theoretically, has to be drawn practically, given the decisions concerning animals which have to be taken by humans every day? Should shrimp or mosquitoes be respected as much as cattle or cats, and the latter two categories as much as dolphins or macaques? A case has already been made by researchers of animal behaviour for elephants and certain dolphin species, for instance, as candidates for membership in the "community of equals" because they satisfy most of the traditional criteria for personhood. Dolphins recognize themselves in mirrors and, more generally, behave in a self-controlled fashion in the sense of being able "to act independently of instinct, biological drives or conditioning;" they are capable of actions that are "generated from within the person and are not the direct result of irresistible internal or external forces" (Herzing and White 1998: 69).

A related point of criticism addressed the focus on similarity: why respect beings that are similar in particular, while much of ethics is about respect for what is different, such as foreign cultural habits? In an evolutionary perspective, the relative biological uniformity of humans is a coincidence. Much of the time, there have been several contemporaneous and even sympatric species of hominids, for example, Neanderthals and humans of the modern type in Europe and the Near East, or *Homo habilis* and *Australopithecus robustus* in parts of Africa. Currently, there are humans and chimpanzees, among other primates. Still other points of reproach were that two fundamentally different discourses, biology and ethics, were being mixed up and the well-known so-called naturalistic fallacy was being committed – deriving an *ought* (moral respect) from what *is* (biological similarity), a *non sequitur* according to many moral philosophers. It has also been pointed out that it is imprudent to premise the case for parity of apes on approximately 99% overall similarity of their DNA, because this still leaves many genes that differ, the functional meaning of which and how they express development remaining unclear (Tuttle 2001: 186).

In a letter to *The New York Times*, two anthropologists, while expressing concern for apes, objected to blurring the animal–human boundary by comparing them to disabled persons: "There is an ominous undercurrent to the Great Ape Project that bears noting. In their zeal to humanize the apes, activists have begun to draw analogies between humans with disabilities and nonhuman primates. . . . 'They can reason and communicate at least as well as some of the children and disabled humans to whom we accord rights.' Is this relevant? Is this even true? All too frequently individuals with disabilities have been misjudged and their abilities underestimated. It is a perverse sense of morality indeed that seeks to blur the boundary between apes and people by dehumanising those for whom human rights are often the most precious" (Marks and Groves 1997).

The Declaration of the Rights of Great Apes in and by the Great Ape Project resembles so-called rites of passage as studied by ethnologists, those solemn changes of status such as a marriage or an initiation into an exclusive group. The great apes are declared part of a larger community of moral equals. Likewise significant is the lending of individual names, by which Koko, Gua, Viki, Lucy, Washoe, Nim, Kanzi, Matata, Sarah, Abang, Beethoven, Peanuts, and other great apes have been acknowledged as individuals, personalities, and subjects – not objects. Jane Goodall has described how naming the chimpanzees she studied in the wild was resisted and ridiculed at first. Editors and referees of scientific journals to which she submitted papers demanded "it" and "which" instead of "he/she" and "who", and numbers instead of individual names (Goodall 1998: 2184). In her writings, she also refers to killings among wild chimpanzees as "murders." The individuality of chimpanzees has since been underlined by detailed studies of characters, feelings, friendships, and lives, supported by passport-style and other photographs of chimpanzees identified by name in publications.

As was pointed out in Chapter 2 in relation to Linnaeus as a "second Adam" naming species, among humans, the naming of individuals generally situates the latter in the social hierarchy by identifying them as relatives, friends, or strangers; they are deigned higher, equal, or lower. Names express and create attitudes. As Durkheimian anthropologists, in particular, have pointed out, naming is a ritual of acknowledgment and incorporation. Bestowing a name or a title on someone is constitutive of the personal identity of the giver as well the receiver. It further articulates and specifies the relationship between them, expressing and creating specific attitudes, rights, and duties on both sides, and establishing a hierarchy. Animals people live or work with are often called by name. Linnaeus named the order humans as part of "Primates" – chief, first, or highest in rank. The previously mentioned proposal that humans and chimpanzees should carry the same generic name, therefore, carries much more than an exclusively taxonomic weight.

Calling a human an ape is still an offence. Calling apes human, as the Great Ape Project does, is another step in the human coming to terms with the moral implications of Darwinism, whatever those implications may ultimately turn out to be. Monboddo may have been correct: they are of our kind, but in the sense of present-day genetics and naturalist philosophy, stressing individual variation, contingency, historicity, and change in living nature, not in the Aristotelian sense of "kind," associated with eternal metaphysical essences.

SEVEN

Beyond Dualism

The study of the basic ideologies of scientists is very difficult because they are rarely articulated. They consist of silent assumptions taken so completely for granted that they are never mentioned. But anyone who attempts to question these 'eternal truths' encounters formidable resistance.

Ernst Mayr (1982: 835)

The preceding chapters have traced the struggle regarding the dignity and the animality of humans and apes, from the seventeenth-century physician–anatomists Nicholas Tulp and Edward Tyson (Chapter 2) to recent controversies on what apes are capable of and, ethically speaking, entitled to (Chapter 6). Along the way, the idea of an ascent up from the ape (Chapter 3), views of human nature in palaeoanthropology and archaeology (Chapter 4), and the disciplinary identity of ethnology (Chapter 5) have been explored. The struggle over the status of a number of primate species – the great apes, extant humans, and apelike early hominids – took place against the backdrop of the rise of new scientific conceptions of natural order. This generated considerable tensions between the *humanitas* of traditional metaphysics, on the one hand, and a growing awareness of the *hominitas* and *animalitas* of humans in natural history and biology, on the other. But alongside, or hidden within, the slowly emerging new view of natural order in terms of contingent evolution, elements of the traditional *scala naturae* view persisted, most importantly, teleology and hierarchy – in evolution in general, and in the prehistory and history of humankind, in particular. Even the United Nations *Universal Declaration on Human Rights*, meant to combat racism, places humans as a unified category above animals, as was made clear in Section 6.3.

Numerous anatomical and behavioural features have been used as markers of humanness, casting humans as uniquely superior. Such markers have regularly been adjusted whenever human hegemony was endangered by new data. Among the qualitative *Homo*-centric yardsticks were erect gait, tool making, self-recognition, and language. Quantitative criteria were Tyson's tally of differences between human and chimpanzee, Camper's facial angle, cranial capacity, and the extent of rational control over emotional impulse. Language, too, was quantified to some degree, by tallying the number of features the communication of animal species had in common with humans. One presumably uniquely human characteristic after another was redefined or abandoned when animals were likewise found to qualify.

In addition to the stubborn persistence of rebuffs of animality, there are some other remarkable continuities or parallels in the period under study. That apes are much closer to humans than generally assumed was a position defended by Rousseau and Monboddo, recently again by primatologists such as Jane Goodall and Frans de Waal, and by defenders of ape rights. Here, apes are, in a sense, humanized. Rousseau's and Monboddo's more specific claim that apes have linguistic capacities is at issue again in recent ape language research. Thomas Hobbes, Sigmund Freud, and Marcel Mauss, among many others, defended the idea of a wild primordial state of humankind which was constrained or overcome by civilized behaviour and society. The alternative idea of a paradisiacal natural state can be found in the writings of Rousseau, and also, less explicitly, as a trend in scientific as well as popular views of chimpanzees and early hominids since the 1960s. In line with these observations, Wiktor

Stoczkowski, a historian of anthropology, has pointed out many structural similarities and, therefore, considerable continuity between, on the one hand, scientific theories of human origins from the early nineteenth century to the present day and, on the other hand, Western folk theories, as well as the speculations of philosophers, from antiquity onwards (Stoczkowski 1995, 2002; but cf. Bowler 1991, 2001).

There seem to be two long-term trends in the history of anthropological dealings with humans and non-human primates, despite shifts in specific historical contexts. One is the rise of naturalistic views of humans which stress their continuity with nature; the other, the persistence of the tendency to set humans apart from all other living beings. The continuity view has roots in the materialism of ancient philosophers such as Democritus and Lucretius, and modern exponents such as La Mettrie and other thinkers of the Enlightenment, as well as various materialist or naturalistic traditions in nineteenth- and twentieth-century philosophy. The idea of one Chain of Being – with only tiny steps between adjacent species – and traditional European folk perceptions of nature (Thomas 1983) also implied continuity. In biological anthropology and primatology, discontinuity views have now nearly completely been overcome. One of their present-day strongholds is cultural anthropology as a human and humane science. Roughly speaking and with some minor exceptions, the order in which continuity views have grown stronger was that anatomical affinities between humans and apes were admitted first, followed by the admission of similarities in behaviour and motivation, genetic make-up, cognitive capacities, and, ultimately, moral rights.

The discrepancy between continuity and discontinuity approaches in scientific practice reflects a fundamental discord in philosophy. Much if not most of recent continental European philosophy – in the wake of scholastic metaphysics, Cartesian rationalism, Kantian epistemology and ethics, and even hermeneutics, despite the latter's anti-Cartesian tendency – advocates discontinuity views of the human place in nature, positioning apes on the other side of the animal–human boundary.

Continuity views would seem to be somewhat better represented in the North American philosophy of mind and philosophy of science where often the "naturalistic turn" (Callenbaut 1993) has been taken and no, or only a permeable, boundary between human and beast is assumed.

Reactions to discoveries with regard to the animal origins and animal nature of humans have varied from enthusiastic acceptance and philosophical reflection along new lines to denial with traditional or fresh arguments, indignation, shame, derision, and irony. Such negative reactions were analysed in Chapters 1 and 3 in terms of anthropological approaches to cultural dealings with ambiguity and pollution, narrative dealings with experienced paradoxes, symbolic inversion, and various other cultural mechanisms which help us to understand the why of the persistent repudiation of apes and apishness.

In this final chapter the readers' patience with vocabularies from various disciplinary fields is requested one last time, this time in the context of a number of technical concepts from recent philosophy. The baffling convolutions around the ape–human boundary in the previous chapters will now be recapitulated on a more abstract level, from an epistemological perspective, not analysing, that is, anthropological data as such but our various, often conflicting, methods of treating this data in terms of the cherished basic assumptions inevitably made. We will see once again how age-old presuppositions and controversies regarding the ape–human distinction persist or resurface in one form or another in present-day approaches. A moderately pluralist and constructivist perspective of knowledge which sheds more light on the role of dualist presuppositions in the history of anthropological research is sketched in Section 7.1.

The aim of this book was to make sense of the confusingly multi-paradigmatic scientific dealings with extant and extinct primates since the seventeenth century, including the human primate. A question which arises immediately, in particular for practicing researchers, and which, in fact, formed an implicit, somewhat "presentist" agenda throughout our historical explorations (cf. p. 12), is the determination of where we stand and where we should position ourselves in our present-day scientific practices: how should we deal with animal–human dichotomies? The perspective of knowledge presented in Section 7.1, in fact, suggests a strategy for dealing with multiparadigmatic situations and the tendency towards animal–human dualism that characterize much research of the present day. This strategy will be explored in Section 7.2.

7.1 An Epistemological Reminder

The epistemological and metaphysical stance taken in the foregoing analysis – of the "metaphysics of apes," primarily in the sense of fundamental assumptions connected to the researcher's world-view (cf. Section 1.1) – should not be left implicit. Theoretical dualities such as "Ancients–Moderns" and "nature–culture" are usually embedded in narrative scenarios which function as theoretical paradigms or conceptual schemes in anthropological disciplines. How such theoretical assumptions determine the manners in which empirical data are treated is studied by epistemology as well as by philosophy of science. Epistemology in general is the philosophical analysis of knowledge processes. Here the focus is specifically on the epistemology of the anthropological disciplines: the analysis is not primarily of the data itself but of the manner in which it is treated. Anthropology, in the wider sense, exhibits a baffling variety of paradigms between disciplines – e.g., human behavioural ecology versus interpretive cultural anthropology, as seen in Chapter 5 – as well as within disciplines, for example, in early hominid taxonomy, prehistoric archaeology, or the study of primate social cognition.

When trying to make explicit the most basic presuppositions of various anthropological approaches collaboration with philosophers can be fruitful. More so than practicing anthropologists, philosophers specialize in the study of the structure and history of empirical science and various world-views. They are well versed in conceptual analysis, in crossing disciplinary boundaries, taking a metaperspective, and searching for synopsis – as generalists "who can help specialists and local disputants to view their work from different perspectives, to make connections to new precedents and exemplars" (Nickles 1995: 149; cf. Corbey and Roebroeks 2001b). They can evaluate the founding presuppositions of empirical scientists, whose own disciplinary tools are geared to dealing with hominid fossils, primate social behaviour, or Bronze Age settlements, and thus less suitable for analysing the taken-for-granted assumptions on which those tools are founded.

My approach to knowledge in general and the empirical, that is, data-driven, anthropological disciplines in particular, is pluralist and moderately constructivist – these terms are explained below. It draws upon work by the American philosopher, Hilary Putnam, inspired by the late writings of Ludwig Wittgenstein, among others. There is much more of potential use in recent, post-positivist epistemology and philosophy of science, for example, in the discussions on the legacies of Willard V. O. Quine, Thomas Kuhn, Imre Lakatos, and Peter Winch, on Bruno Latour's controversial "anthropology of science," or in exchanges between (scientific) realists and anti-realists, but here I will confine myself to Putnam. I will explain why I find his work particularly useful in analysing the role of basic assumptions in anthropological research, in addition to the help provided by ethnological pollution theory (Section 1.3) and structuralist narratology (Section 3.3).

In his work of the 1980s and early 1990s, Putnam (1981, 1987, 1990, 1992) is no longer the strong philosophical realist and naturalist he used to be, a philosopher–logician who believed in a reality or nature consisting of hard facts which in principle could be established by hard, empirical science. He no longer believes in the privileged character of the vocabulary of the natural sciences as the best window on reality, the ultimate touchstone, justification, and world-guided calibration of other vocabularies. Nevertheless, he is not completely relativist, constructivist, or post-modern, like those who believe that forms of knowledge are social or cultural constructs, closely related and sensitive to the particular context in which they happen to have been produced.

According to the general theory of knowledge Putnam developed during these years, all, even the most elementary, concepts (such as "protoculture," "syntax," "intention," "species"), categorizations ("animal–human"), and periodizations ("Ancients–Moderns," "human adaptive grade") are always part of a specific theoretical discourse. They are inextricably connected to the other notions, rules, assumptions, values, narrative scenarios, and metaphors which occur in that specific discourse or language game. Their very meaning is defined in terms of these interconnections, which explains the frequent disagreement and misunderstandings when proponents of different paradigms meet. The specific paradigm not only defines the meaning of terms, but also what is considered to be a solid argument, a good reason to revise a view, reliable empirical evidence, or even what the subject matter of the particular discipline should be in the first place.

In this sense, Putnam is a holist: what is tested against reality is always a whole assemblage, not, as an atomistic view would maintain, a single proposition. Furthermore, the reality the assemblage is somehow tested against is always, to some extent, already perceived in terms of that theoretical assemblage or paradigm. There is no instant yes or no from the data under consideration to atomistic propositions, but a long-term process of various mutually incompatible paradigms being used to accomodate known and predict new data.

This stance makes eminent sense in the context of the foregoing reconstructions of presuppositions in anthropological research and fits the image arising from the foregoing chapters. Think, for example, of Blumenbach's interpretation of the human hand, Owen on the hippocampus minor, various conceptions of natural order, grade versus clade taxonomy, processual and postprocessual archaeologists, and behavioural–ecological versus culturalist approaches of tribal warfare. "Meaning comes from humans and not from Nature – not from the bones, stones, and DNA which are the objects of scrutiny in human ori-gins research," palaeoanthropologist Geoffrey Clark concurs after more than three decades experience in the discipline, criticizing the "received view" of a relentless advance to better knowledge based on increasingly precise data as a caricature. "One thing is certain. Human origins con-troversies will never be resolved merely by the acquisition of more data. The reason is that data are paradigm-dependent and have no meaning apart from the various conceptual frameworks that define them." (Clark 2001: 145–146). In his bleaker moments, he admits, "I tend to think that the metaphysical paradigms that govern [human] origins research pro-tocols are almost impervious to data. Enormously influential, but always implicit, the highest order conceptual frameworks seem to 'override' any patterns found inductively and operate independently of them" (Clark 2000: 853).

In a discussion of the concept of culture at a major conference on *Changing Images of Primate Societies* in Brazil in 1996, sponsored by the Wenner-Gren Foundation for Anthropological Research, one primatol-ogist explained how, in his view, each wild chimpanzee community has its own specific culture. He had barely gotten the word "culture" out of his mouth, he writes, looking back, "when I was made to feel the full weight of my blissful ignorance. The cultural anthropologists practically leaped across the seminar table to berate me for using the words 'culture' and 'chimpanzee' in the same sentence. . . . How dare you, they said, use a human term like 'cultural diversity'? Say 'behavioural variation,' they demanded . . . 'not only can humans alone claim culture, culture alone can explain humanity' " (Stanford 2001: 110–111).

But there were not just, predictably, major discrepancies between the approaches of cultural anthropologists and primatologists, but also among the latter themselves. This is how its organizers looked back upon the conference: "We had understood our guiding questions to be multifactorial, but . . . we came to realize that the issues were even more complex than we had previously thought. Each of the major factors that we had identified – method, theory, and gender – turned out on closer inspection to be heterogeneous, interdependent, and controversial. There was a disputation among the participants over how to define these factors, how to measure their influence, and even what words to use to talk about them" (Fedigan and Strum 1997: 678).

Part of this divergence was due to primatology having developed from at least three different academic disciplines – anthropology, zoology, and psychology – in several cultural settings and within various national traditions. In a session on "theory" in primatology, thirteen different uses of that term were counted. Even such, at first sight, rather unambiguous concepts as sociobiology, ethology, group selection, and behavioural ecology turned out to have different meanings and connotations for primatologists from different national, cultural, and theoretical backgrounds. In addition, the discrepancies at the conference between scientists and those who study them – science historians, philosophers of science, sociologists of science, scholars specializing in cultural studies – on the matter of what science itself is were conspicuously great. Moreover, there were several incompatible views of what science is and how to study it among those specialized in studying science and scientists.

There were similar problems at a large conference on *The Evolution of Language* at the École Nationale Supérieure des Télécommunications in Paris in the Spring of 2000. The lack of a coherent terminology facilitating communication between different disciplines, subdisciplines, and theoretical approaches was so considerable that it was decided to spend the entire first day of the next conference developing working definitions of "semantics," "syntax," "communication," "symbol," as well as other concepts. In accord with this feeling, Tim Ingold, in his contributions on the evolution of culture, language, and technology, has repeatedly uttered his frustration concerning the "basic disagreements about the meanings of the terms we are trying to connect. 'Language,' it seems, can mean almost what you will" (Ingold 1994b: 310).

A similar observation, to give yet another example of what Putnam means, was made by the editors of a volume on conceptual issues in modern human origins research regarding a series of palaeoanthropology conferences which they attended over a period of six or seven years: "What most impressed us about these meetings were the enormous differences in the preconceptions, assumptions, and biases that different workers brought to bear on the resolution of problems that, on the surface at least, were thought to be held in common. At times, these differences were so great as to preclude any common basis for discussion.... It quickly became evident that people were 'talking past one another,' guided by different assumptions and preconceptions of what the human past was like" (Clark and Willermet 1997: 1). The editors also pointed to a general unawareness of the role of multiple conceptual assumptions in research and an unwillingness to scrutinize these.

While the anthropological disciplines are data-driven, the conceptual schemes that influence interpretations of the data itself are so basic that they are hardly tested at all. They themselves constitute the framework that guides empirical research and even defines what counts as empirical corroboration or falsification. The attribution of a number of early Pleistocene hominid fossils to various species may be unambiguous from and within a cladist approach to early hominid taxonomy, as long as the cladist paradigm as such and how it compares to evolutionary taxonomy in terms of "grades" instead of "clades" is not under scrutiny (cf. pp. 103–105).

Returning to Putnam's view of knowledge, rationality, that is, thinking and acting reasonably, on the basis of good reasons, is seen as a local affair. There is no absolute, independent, timeless, universal criterion or touchstone which transcends all extant discursive or scientific activity, for example that of typically human scientists versus that of typical natural scientists. "The" reality, or natural order, is always that of a specific discourse. Therefore, it is better to speak of the plausibility or acceptability of a view (in terms of a specific, local set of rules and assumptions) than of "truth" or "certainty." Putnam calls this position "internal realism," for "it is a characteristic of this view to hold that 'what objects does the world consist of?' is a question that it only makes sense to ask *within* a theory or description" (Putnam, 1981: 49). As a consequence, there is more than one "true" theory or description of the world, in the following sense. "Truth, in this 'internalist' view, is idealized rational acceptability. It is an ideal coherence of our beliefs with each other and with our experiences as those experiences are themselves represented in our belief system – not corresponding with completely mind-independent or discourse-independent 'states of affairs.' . . . There is no God's Eye point of view that we can know or usefully imagine; there are only the various points of view of actual persons reflecting various interests and purposes that their descriptions and theories subserve" (*ibid.*: 50; cf. Putnam 1987; cf. Wittgenstein 1969). It is now clear in what sense Putnam is a pluralist.

Yet, as was previously remarked, no extreme relativism or "anything goes" is implied. Local definitions of concepts and standards of corroboration may vary, but are usually very strict. "Syntax" or "ritual" can be defined in various ways, but given a specific definition, embedded in the corresponding conceptual scheme, it will usually be quite clear whether a bonobo utterance or an archaeologically reconstructed behaviour pattern of Neanderthals qualify. In each case, the empirical data with its own robust structure dictates an answer which, within that particular conceptual scheme, is unambiguous. Each scheme, moreover, has to be internally consistent and can be judged as to its practicability for certain purposes. In both respects, researchers can be criticized by adherents of other paradigms who can understand, and communicate on, theoretical insights other than their own, helped by the fact that they share the same physical existence and world with their colleagues. Where there is a parting of ways is at higher levels of abstraction.

In addition, as Tim Murray has argued, specifically with respect to archaeology, empirical data can be so anomalous and unexpected "that they have the potential to destabilize conventional disciplinary relationships and throw up the possibility that the conventions of contemporary social theory may not be the natural interpretative and explanatory structures which many archaeologists think them to be," thus escaping from being "normalized" and defused by assimilation into prevailing conventions (Murray 1992: 730 ff.; cf. Murray 2001, and de Regt 2001).

I am not concerned here with the theoretical question whether, in the end, Putnam's internal realism is the definitive view of knowledge. There are certainly problems here, such as the question of the precise status of this epistemology itself. Does it ultimately undermine itself as just another locally favoured discourse, or is it, on the contrary, as such – as a local view – a fine illustration of its own vision, precisely because it is a workable but not definitive orientation of a field? I tend to the latter view, and in the present context the concern is a practical, pragmatic one, too. This is in line with the spirit of this epistemology, which draws upon the American pragmatist tradition. What is sought, given a baffling diversity of anthropological viewpoints in the discipline, is an approach which is workable and offers an orientation. It would seem this is the case with this epistemology.

It helps us to make sense of the divergent views of Linnaeus and Blumenbach, Monboddo and Camper, Huxley and Owen, gradists and cladists, and the various schools in the reconstruction of the origins of language. It helps us to understand the difference between culturalist ethnologists (or postprocessualist archaeologists) who tend to conceive of culture in terms of meanings and values in the heads of actors, on the one hand and, on the other, ecological anthropologists (or processual archaeologists) who study culture as an ecological system or process tied not so much to what is in the heads as what is in the stomachs of actors. It facilitates understanding the controversies and the miscommunication between such parties. "(A) sign that is actually employed in a particular way by a particular community of users," Putnam writes, "can correspond to particular objects *within the conceptual scheme of those users.* 'Objects' do not exist independently of conceptual schemes. *We* cut up the world into objects when we introduce one or another scheme of description. Since the objects *and* the signs are alike internal to the scheme of description, it is possible to say what matches what." (Putnam 1981: 52).

It has become clear in the foregoing chapters that the most basic convictions guiding anthropological research often took the form of narrative scenarios or plots. The epistemological exploration here ties in well with the analysis of such narratives in Section 3.3, as well as with Misia Landau's *Narratives of Human Evolution* (Landau 1991a; cf. p. 89, 90) and Donna Haraway's *Primate Visions* (Haraway 1989; cf. p. 159, 160). Two germane master narratives were that of a transcendent Creator and humans as a privileged category of creatures, informing the views of eighteenth-century natural historians, among others, and its secular, or secularized, successor, that of an ascent from bestiality to civilization and reason. The ape–human distinction as an authoritative categorial boundary was established and continuously renegotiated within the framework of these narrative constructions of natural and moral order. More particularly, both conceptual schemes in the sense of Putnam and narratives can be analysed as efforts to overcome ambiguity and inconsistency (cf. p. 25 ff.).

The fact that the pluralist and holistic epistemology presented here corresponds so well to the situation in the anthropological disciplines can be explained in its favour. A welcome implication is a tolerance for perspectives other than our own. Another attractive aspect is that it deals with knowledge not on an abstract level but as it occurs among people practically engaged with the world around them: palaeolithic archaeologists who have been excavating for twenty years, Chomskyan linguists with computer programs modelling language production, anatomist–palaeoanthropologists comparing skeletal material in the laboratory, primatologists doing fieldwork in the rain forest, or ethnographers talking to native informants in a local language.

The epistemological-cum-metaphysical stance taken here implies scepticism regarding the possibility of ultimate answers on such matters as whether humans with their symbolic minds transcend life as exemplified by ancestral and contemporaneous apes, or even their own living bodies. Therefore, it does not necessarily deny the possibility that the anthropocentrism and dualism which are implied by traditional European philosophy may be correct. That may be so, but we cannot be sure about it. It may even be the case that a strict animal–human boundary exists in some sense and that apes, in some respects or at some moments, for example, when they cheat intentionally, are or briefly reside on the human side of that boundary. An answer to the question of how things really are presupposes a metaphysical God's eye point of view, a panoptic narrator's position humans do not possess.

7.2 Rethinking Dichotomies

The outlined pragmatist and, indeed, to some extent sceptical view of knowledge helps to make sense of the history of anthropology. It helps us better understand the role of "metaphysical" assumptions in our own and others' research on humans, earlier hominids, great apes, other primates, and other animals. It also points in the direction of that other burning question, anathema to the professional science historian, but posing itself unavoidably to the practicing anthropologist: if the dualist paradigm still currently feeds into our research, how do we deal with it? How, after all, does one deal with dualist tendencies in present-day research in various anthropological disciplines as are present in such distinctions as nature–culture, world–mind, animal–human, and (cognitively and behaviourally) ancient–modern?

It is suggested that the dichotomies installed by the various conceptual schemes investigated in the preceding chapters be reconsidered in the light of new – as well as old – evidence which would seem to be at odds with too sharply dualist conceptualizations. This is not only in line with the anti-dualist tendency of Putnam's epistemology, but also with the evidence with respect to the biological aspects of culture and language which has been accumulating in recent decades. As palaeoanthropological, primatological, ethological, and genetic research has made abundantly clear, human nature has partially been shaped by the selective pressures of cultural behaviours and culturally fabricated elements of the environment. The functional morphology of the human hand, for instance, was shaped by the wielding of Oldowan chopping tools, Acheulean handaxes, and other tools during tens of thousands of generations. This added to and modified the characteristics of a primate organ preadapted by living in trees.

Analogously, parts of our brain and respiratory tract were selected through the use of epigenetically acquired, culturally traded lexicons and grammars. Indeed, many researchers, and not just proponents of the gene–culture coevolution theory, now refer to language and culture as biological adaptations. The acquisition and intergenerational, partially symbolic transmission of cultural and social abilities in humans is crucially dependent upon a whole gamut of cognitive and motivational capabilities that are part of our specific biological equipment. A complex, subtle, and well-timed interaction of these capacities with social–environmental influences in the course of the development of hominid children is of vital importance and can also be described on the level of epigenetic neuronal development.

Thus, human nature was, and is, social and cultural from its very beginning. That there is a brutish, impulsive animal nature at our phylogenetic roots as well as, ontologically, deep within humans, which requires restraint and coercion to make civilization and social order possible (cf. Chapter 3), is a grand narrative that can no longer be defended in the light of recent insights, at least not in this form. This dualistic perception of humans and reality at least partly issues from Platonic and Christian concepts of the spirit and the flesh, redemption and sin (cf. Sahlins 1996). Much of what is social does not come about through a Maussian symbolic contract or Freudian internalized cultural values restraining the biological, but is in and of itself biological, that is, natural. The degree to which Durkheimian, Freudian, structuralist, and other perspectives underestimate the role of that purportedly "raw" organic nature, again both phylogenetically and ontologically, has been illustrated forcefully by recent work on sociality, individuality, politics, motivation, and communication in non-human primates, for example, chimpanzees (Rodseth *et al.* 1991; Quiatt and Reynolds 1993; Ducros *et al.* 1998).

Marcel Mauss himself provided a starting point for overcoming the unproductive *homo duplex* view, with his previously-mentioned programmatic heuristic of "total social fact" and "total human" – a being not divided into faculties, but imbued totally and at the same time, with all aspects of body, soul, and society intertwined. Given what was known in his day about inclusive and reciprocal altruism, gene–culture coevolution, the neurological basis of cultural behaviour, and epigenetic development, it cannot be held against him that he did not entirely live up to this valuable methodological adage as far as the biology of behaviour was concerned. Durkheimian-oriented anthropologists now find themselves confronted with the exciting and important challenge of improving our understanding of the interaction between biology, sociality, and cultural meaning (cf. Carrithers 1996; Corbey 1998, 2000).

This line of argument suggests that Marcel Mauss' stimulating view of exchange, flawed by a too-radically dualistic view of humans, is in need not so much of being overthrown but of being rethought and updated. It can be put to good use in confrontation and concurrence with recent insights, going beyond what Mauss intended where necessary, but remaining faithful to his heuristic principle of a "totalising" approach which takes the natural into account, against the grain of dualist *homo duplex* approaches. It is worthwhile to try and bring *homo symbolicus*, constitutive of much of cultural anthropology as a discipline, back down to earth, to living nature, by bringing the wealth of recent evolutionary biology to bear upon the idea of "(hu)man the symbolic and cultural animal," rethinking and updating it. While Durkheim and Mauss defined altruism as the cultural suppression of selfish instincts, in evolutionary biology precisely the opposite is held: altruism is an expression of in the end selfish instincts.

Taking the evolutionary and natural basis of presumably unique human features more seriously is suggested by empirical data that, although it underdetermines interpretation, is robust in the sense of putting constraints on conceptualizations – Durkheimian, Boasian, or otherwise. Continuing to assert that the symbolic behaviour, altruism, and reciprocity that make human societies and identities possible are differences that set humans apart from nature is one possibility. The alternative is asking how they may be rooted *in* nature, which may be a timely move strategically and heuristically speaking (cf. Quiatt and Reynolds 1993: 265). Attempts could be made to go against the grain of double standards, blurring distinctions we think, research, and live by, to see what results, what changes, and where it leads. What is envisioned is not necessarily a definitive ontological but at least a methodological, pragmatic naturalism, which is aimed at undermining *homo duplex* approaches, and conceiving of natural entities in a non-reductionist manner, including not only natural laws and molecules but also meanings and intentions.

Going beyond dualism, as the editors of a volume on and against the typically modern Cartesianism of much anthropological thought write, "opens up an entirely different intellectual landscape, one in which states and substances are replaced by processes and relations" (Descola and Pálsson 1996: 12). This volume is one of the signs that, in the past two decades, the traditional nature/nurture, biology/culture, and nature/society dichotomies, so stubbornly resistant against change and replayed over and over again, are being pulled apart in favour of more sophisticated, unified approaches, at least in some circles.

One favourable development is the advent of piece-by-piece comparative studies which break down human culture into various components and compare them individually with non-human–primate behaviours (e.g, Whiten, Horner and Marshall-Pescini 2003). Such studies show that in some respects similarities are greater than in others, and offer a more fine-grained and differentiated picture than traditional all-or-nothing views, also regarding the likely mosaic character of the evolution of culture in hominids.

Another interesting development worth mention is recent anti-dualist, anti-Cartesian research under the key-words "embodied mind" or "(context-)embedded cognition." This research stresses the close connectedness of organism and environment, mind and body, subject and object, perception and action, and cognition and motivation. It is in line with convergent work by Martin Heidegger and Maurice Merleau-Ponty in continental philosophy, Ludwig Wittgenstein and Gilbert Ryle in British philosophy, the ecological approach to perception of James Gibson, and Pierre Bourdieu's sociology of "habitus" and *sens pratique.* Instead of being treated as detached from the physical and social environment, cognition is here seen as culturally and evolutionarily embedded in it (cf. Noble and Davidson 1996; Corbey and Roebroeks 1997; Donald 1991).

The idea of an essentially human nature and an essential difference between what is on one and what is on the other side of the animal–human boundary still determines part of our thought, scientific research, laws, and practices. It is connected with the traditional metaphysical view that species have eternal, immutable, and discrete essences which form a hierarchy. It is also connected with our common-sense habit of perceiving the world in terms of a natural and, at the same time, moral order of clear-cut natural kinds, the integrity of which is not to be tinkered with through, for example, gene transfer, organ transplantation between animal and human, the cloning of organisms, or indeed a too-proximate classification of non-human and human primates. The perception of patterning in life and evolution in Darwinist science to some extent is still informed and policed by Aristotelian essentialist or Cartesian dualist views of humans and human nature predating Darwin. In particular, there is a continuing reliance on pre-Darwinian philosophical principles in the study of culture, language, and apes.

What is it that anthropologists do? Are they cutting nature, human evolution, primate cognition at its joints, and is the animal–human boundary that at least some of them hold so precious such a joint? In the preceding chapters, the question of what continuity and discontinuity there really is between humans and (other) animals was addressed only indirectly, by the analysis of positions that had previously been taken. In particular when looking at present-day divergences and controversies, this strategy amounts to a gambit, perhaps of a queen more than a pawn. It is a move which clears a space for the analytical and historical clarification of the basic assumptions in terms of which we and others collect and interpret data, without the immediate detriment and heavy load of the question which view is the correct one. According to the position taken here, no singular definite answers to questions concerning natural order and the place of humans in it are presently identifiable. Accumulating empirical data constrains our views, but only to some extent as, at the same time, the data is interpreted in terms of those very views. Various answers are possible and have indeed been given, depending on the various conceptual schemes which suggest different identifications, or, better, constructions, of nature's joints, and, therefore, different categorizations of natural order.

The European metaphysical tradition with its strong dualist tendency has loomed large in anthropological research. It was supported by the articulation of human cultural identity in terms of animal alterity, and certain idiosyncrasies of making sense of the world narratively. Borders were erected and ambiguous borderline cases resulted. The currently burgeoning naturalistic approaches have been another influential conceptual scheme in anthropological research. The persisting tension between dualist and naturalistic stances is reflected by the fickle status and disciplinary identity of human sciences such as cultural anthropology and archaeology vis-à-vis the natural sciences, in particular biology. As there are various metaphysics of apes, the word "metaphysics" in the title of the present book, *The Metaphysics of Apes*, is emphatically plural, bearing more weight than the usual singular reading, as in, for example, "the metaphysics of Saint Thomas Aquinas."

Practicing anthropologists tend to cherish the view, implicitly or explicitly, that the history of their disciplines bears witness to progress towards more data and better theories. This may be correct to a considerable extent, but the anthology of that history offered by the preceding chapters also shows the persistence of traditional metaphysical views in the core of scientific theories. It may well be that, in the end, in trying to conceptualize natural order, we will be forced to keep certain dualities intact, though not so much as part of an essentialist metaphysical stance as due to empirical constraints placed upon our theorizing, and without knowledge of the true metaphysical meaning of this fact. For example, the earliest hominids may indeed not have been able to transcend the here and now and think abstractly, merely because of a lack of arbitrary symbols that make that possible, not because of a different metaphysical essence.

There is no easy method for disqualifying scientific approaches that keep apes at a distance as being somehow less scientific than those which stress continuities. Much of the scientific resistance to the idea of linguistic competence in apes, while of Cartesian inspiration, is methodologically very sophisticated. Defenders of the idea of ape language, on the other hand, adhere to assumptions which are as respectable philosophically, but are of a hermeneutical or interpretive nature.

The palaeoanthropologist and cladist Ian Tattersall moved too quickly when he wrote that although the New Synthesis "had the salutary effect of sweeping away a huge entrenched accumulation of mythology and misapprehension," it was "doomed to harden, much like a religion, into . . . a dogma whose heavy hand continues to oppress the science of human origins a half-century later," by casting human evolution as "a long, dogged, single-minded trudge from primitiveness to perfection" (Tattersall 2000: 2, 8; cf. Rosen, Nelson and Patterson 1979, as cited above on p. 104). Such observations cast the history of anthropology as a progress towards a perfection exemplified by their authors. Their lack of respect for other paradigms may be explained as a lack of epistemological sophistication. On the other hand, paradoxically, the history of science would seem to teach that moving doggedly and single-mindedly ahead is quite effective in terms of doing good research.

Naturalistic or Darwinist philosophy refuses to set humans apart from non-human primates and the rest of life as *the* unique species, and, instead, thinks of them as "just" another unique species. Other philosophical positions maintain that features such as mind, rationality, humanness, and morality do set humans apart, but that these are not perceived by empirical science because it does not probe deep enough. An instrumentalist or empiricist view of science – as a useful instrument, not as revealing truth – has served the latter kind of thinkers well. Here the two main metaphysical positions articulated in Western civilization – one postulating the primacy of mind, the other that of physical reality – clash.

Although from an epistemologically agnostic point of view it must be argued that the traditional, spiritualist metaphysics that forms the source and foundation of anthropological dualities is too anthropocentric, the matter cannot be resolved definitively. Opting for a naturalistic metaphysics, likewise, implies an overplaying of our hand. We have studied a paradigm shift, to wit, the reluctant naturalization of humans, to some degree accompanied by the humanization of apes. Has the human-centred views of apes, the natural world, and natural history been progressively undermined and have humans been dethroned? Empirically, yes, but philosophically or metaphysically speaking, the matter is far from clear. Can we subscribe to the naturalist view that any species, including the human one, is a purely historical entity, because if there is no essence to species, but only genetic variation, there is no essence to humans? Here again, one must be hesitant.

The present author opts for a naturalistic course, but only tentatively and pragmatically, not as a definitive ontology. One of the challenges for twenty-first–century anthropology lies in combining the efforts of biological and ethnological approaches, in an attempt to come to terms with the pervasive dualism of European metaphysics. This may not be an easy endeavour, since to many culture is still what transcends human biology, and the repudiation of biology is still constitutive of much of ethnology's disciplinary identity. Thinking against the grain of traditional European metaphysics is solicited by empirical evidence and it is an exciting experiment, a timely move that may make a difference, philosophically as well as ethically. To *in dubio pro reo* – an old principle of Western law: when in doubt a case is to be decided in favour of the defendant – one might add: *in dubio pro bestia*. A philosophically speaking naturalistic approach may be self-evident to most biologists, but it is certainly not self-evident to many cultural anthropologists, philosophers, nor indeed to Western and global legal and political systems at large.

There are no easy answers, but perhaps it is now possible to see things in sharper focus, in a clearer perspective. And this is as good as it gets, for let us be well aware, in line with the foregoing epistemological digression, that in the end we remain deeply caught up in the very strains of thought, the very metaphysics, we have set out to analyse. For humans, there can be no panoptic God's eye point of view. The present author does not side with those who think that the issues dealt with in this book are susceptible to an empirical or otherwise final or wholly intelligible solution, and encourages a less partisan and more exploratory attitude.

New problems have arisen: in dealing with primatophobia, we have moved away from anthropocentrism, but in the process we have focussed more on apes than on other non-human primates, and more on primates than on other animals. Beck (1982) warns against a certain "chimpocentric" tendency in research on primate cognition to stress chimpanzees, or all the great apes, as special, close to humans, and in some fundamental way different from other non-human primates and non-human species. A similar point has been made, ethically speaking, in connection with ape rights movements. Jan van Hooff ended a critical survey of two decades of research on chimpanzee understanding in 1994 with the remark that "[while] accepting the outstanding position of *Pan*, we should be careful not to create a new dichotomy in the animal kingdom" (van Hooff 1994: 279).

The exclusion of animals has been, and still is, constitutive of much of the Euro–American anthropological discourse on humanness, natural order, and culture. Condescending and distancing attitudes, connected to an obsession with human grandeur, have shifted towards more informed and egalitarian ones, and there is a growing awareness in the population at large that humans are not that different from apes. However, great apes and early hominids are still profoundly ambiguous, categorially, cognitively, and morally. The small group of apes that have become language-savvy through human training in particular, "are in a bizarre category. They are chimeras, not human but endowed with a human quality that their kind would not possess without years of human training. They are, in a sense, more sentient than their species is supposed to be.... [Some of them] have ended up in the dungeons of biomedical research laboratories ... [like] some sort of ape–human hybrid ... trapped in the netherworld between two species" (Stanford 2001: 161).

Betwixt and between as great apes are, they may serve as missing links in a new, more positive key: no longer as links in the Great Chain of Being, as was still the case in Linnaeus' natural history, nor primarily as evolutionary links in an "ascent" to civilization, but as go-betweens and mediators between humans and other animals, philosophically, scientifically, and morally. Like the trickster figures from the myths and rituals of so many peoples worldwide – Maui among the Polynesians, Semar among the Javanese, the Raven among American Indian and Arctic peoples (cf. above, p. 32) – they can break taboos, transgress borders, and bring together opposites as benefactors. In this respect, too, the trickster figure is a suitable counter-image to traditional depreciating perceptions of apes and apish beings that it is always, despite its ambiguous status, more than human, closer to the gods – a heroic benefactor, bringing good things.

Bibliography

American Anthropological Association 2001, "Preface," *El Dorado Task Force Papers*, http://www.aaanet.org/edtf/final/preface.htm.

Apted, Michael [director] 1988, *Gorillas in the Mist: The Story of Dian Fossey*, Universal Pictures/Warner Bros.

Arbuthnot, John 1732, "An Essay of the Learned Martinus Scriblerus, Concerning the Origin of Sciences," in Jonathan Swift and Alexander Pope (eds.), *Miscellanies in Prose and Verse*, vol. 3, London: B. Motte: 1727.

Ardrey, Robert 1961, *African Genesis*, London: Collins.

Ardrey, Robert 1966, *The Territorial Imperative: A Personal Inquiry into the Animal Origins of Property and Nations*, New York: Atheneum.

Ardrey, Robert 1976, *The Hunting Hypothesis*, New York: Atheneum.

Argyll, George Douglas Campbell, Duke of 1863, "Professor Huxley on Man's Place in Nature," *Edinburgh Review*, 117: 567–568.

Argyll, George Douglas Campbell, Duke of 1868, *The Reign of Law*, London: Strahan.

Argyll, George Douglas Campbell, Duke of 1869, *Primeval Man: An Examination of some Recent Speculations*, London: Strahan.

Asquith, Pamela J. 1981, *Some Aspects of Anthropomorphism in the Terminology and Philosophy underlying Western and Japanese Studies of the Social Behaviour of Non-Human Primates*, Ph.D. thesis, Oxford: University of Oxford.

Asquith, Pamela J. 1986, "Anthropomorphism and the Japanese and Western Traditions in Primatology," in J. G. Else and P. C. Lee (eds.), *Primate Ontogeny, Cognition and Social Behaviour*, Cambridge: Cambridge University Press: 61–71.

Asquith, Pamela J. 1995, "Of Monkeys and Men: Cultural Views in Japan and the West," in Raymond Corbey and Bert Theunissen (eds.), *Ape, Man, Apeman: Changing Views since 1600*, Leiden: Department of Prehistory of Leiden University: 309–326.

Babcock, Barbara A. 1978, *The Reversible World: Symbolic Inversion in Art and Society*, Ithaca and London: Cornell University Press.

Bibliography

Barnard, Alan 1994, "Rules and Prohibitions: The Form and Content of Human Kinship," in Tim Ingold (ed.), *Companion Encyclopedia of Anthropology*, London: Routledge: 783–812.

Barnard, Alan 1995, "Monboddo's Orang Outang and the Definition of Man," in Raymond Corbey and Bert Theunissen (eds.), *Ape, Man, Apeman: Changing Views since 1600*, Leiden: Department of Prehistory of Leiden University: 71–86.

Barraud, Cécile *et al.* 1994, *Of Relations and the Dead: Four Societies Viewed from the Angle of their Exchanges*, Oxford: Berg.

Barrett, Richard A. 1989, "The Paradoxical Anthropology of Leslie White," *American Anthropologist* 91: 986–999.

Barsanti, Giulio 1995, "Les singes de Lamarck," in Raymond Corbey and Bert Theunissen (eds.), *Ape, Man, Apeman: Changing Views since 1600*, Leiden: Department of Prehistory of Leiden University: 101–116.

Bartholomew, Michael 1973, "Lyell and Evolution: An Account of Lyell's Response to the Prospect of an Evolutionary Ancestry for Man," *The British Journal for the Philosophy of Science* 6 (23): 261–303.

Beck, B. B. 1982, "Chimpocentrism: Bias in Cognitive Ethology," *Journal of Human Evolution* 11: 3–17.

Beck, B. *et al.* (eds.), *Great Apes and Humans: The Ethics of Coexistence*, Washington, DC: Smithsonian Institution Press, 2001.

Benedict, Ruth 1943, *Race and Racism*, London: Scientific Book Club.

Bickerton, Derek 1990, *Language and Species*, Chicago and London: University of Chicago Press.

Bickerton, Derek 1995, *Language and Human Behaviour*, London: UCL Press.

Binford, Lewis R. 1981, *Bones: Ancient Men and Modern Myths*, New York: Academic Press.

Binford, Lewis R. 1989, "Isolating the Transition to Cultural Adaptations: An Organizational Approach," in Erik Trinkaus (ed.), *The Emergence of Modern Humans: Biocultural Adaptations in the Later Pleistocene*, Cambridge: Cambridge University Press: 18–41.

Bird-David, Nurit 1999, "'Animism' Revisited: Personhood, Environment, and Relational Epistemology," *Current Anthropology* 40, Supplement: Special Issue *Culture: A Second Chance?*: S67–S91.

Blanckaert, Claude 1987, "Les vicissitudes de l'angle facial et les débuts de la craniométrie (1765–1875)," *Revue de Synthèse*, IVe Série: 417–453.

Blanckaert, Claude 1991, "'Premier des singes, dernier des hommes'?," *Alliage* 7/8, Spring/Summer: 113–129.

Blanckaert, Claude 1998, "La naturalisation de l'homme de Linné à Darwin: Archéologie du débat nature/culture," in Albert Ducros, Jacqueline Ducros and

Frédéric Joulian (eds.), *La nature est-elle naturelle? Histoire, épistémologie et applications récentes du concept de culture*, Paris, Éditions Errance: 15–24.

Blanckaert, Claude, Albert Ducros and Jean-Jacques Hublin (eds.) 1989, *Histoire de l'Anthropologie: Hommes, Idées, Moments*, special issue of *Bulletins et Mémoires de la Société d'Anthropologie de Paris, Nouvelle Série* 1, 3/4.

Blok, Anton 2001, *Honour and Violence*, Cambridge: Polity.

Blumenbach, J. F. 1775, *De generis humani varietate nativa liber*, Gottingae: A. Vandenhoeck.

Blumenbach, J. F. 1779, *Handbuch der Naturgeschichte*, Göttingen: Dieterich.

Boesch, C. *et al.* 1994, "Is Nut Cracking in Wild Chimpanzees a Cultural Behaviour?" *Journal of Human Evolution* 26: 325–338.

Boucher de Perthes, Jacques 1847–1864, *Antiquités celtiques et antédiluviennes, mémoire sur l'industrie primitive et les arts à leur origine*, 3 vols., Paris: Treuttel et Würtz.

Bowler, Peter J. 1986, *Theories of Human Evolution: A Century of Debate, 1844–1944*, Baltimore: Johns Hopkins University Press.

Bowler, Peter J. 1991, "Science and the Narrative Structure of Theories," *Current Anthropology* 32: 364–366.

Bowler, Peter J. 2001, "Myths, Narratives and the Uses of History," in Raymond Corbey and Wil Roebroeks (eds.), *Studying Human Origins: Disciplinary History and Epistemology*, Amsterdam: Amsterdam University Press: 9–20.

Boule, Marcellin 1946, *Les hommes fossiles: Éléments de paléontologie humaine*, 3rd ed., Paris: Masson et Cie.

Bourdieu, Pierre 1984, *Distinction: A Social Critique of the Judgement of Taste*, transl. Richard Nice, London: Routledge & Kegan Paul.

Brace, C. Loring 1993, "The Creation of Specific Hominid Names: Gloria in Excelsis Deo? Or Ego? Or Praxis?" *Human Evolution* 8: 151–156.

Broberg, Gunnar 1980, "Linnaeus and *Genesis*: A Preliminary Survey," in *id.* (ed.), *Linnaeus: Progress and Prospects in Linnaean Research*, Stockholm: Almqvist and Wiksell International; Pittsburgh: Hunt Institute for Botanical Documentation.

Broberg, Gunnar 1983, "*Homo sapiens*: Linnaeus' Classification of Man," in Tore Frängsmyr (ed.), *Linnaeus: The Man and his Work*, Berkeley: University of California Press: 156–194.

Broom, Robert 1936, "A New Fossil Anthopoid Skull from South Africa," *Nature* 138: 486–488.

Broom, Robert 1938, "The Pleistocene Anthropoid Apes of South Africa," *Nature* 142: 377–379.

Callenbaut, Werner (ed.) 1993, *Taking the Naturalistic Turn or How Real Philosophy of Science is Done*, Chicago: University of Chicago Press.

Bibliography

Camper, Petrus 1782, *Natuurkundige Verhandelingen van Petrus Camper over den Orang Outang; en Eenige Andere Aap-Soorten*, Amsterdam: Erven P. Meijer en G. Warnars.

Camper, Petrus 1791, *Dissertation physique de mr. Pierre Camper, sur les différences réelles que présentent les traits du visage chez les hommes de différents pays et de différents âges*, transl. by D. B. Q. d'Isjonval, Utrecht: B. Wild & J. Altheer.

Caporael, Linda 1994, "Of Myth and Science: Origin Stories and Evolutionary Scenarios," *Social Science Information* 33, 1: 9–23.

Carrithers, Michael 1996, "Nature and Culture," in Alan Barnard and Jonathan Spencer (eds.), *Encyclopedia of Social and Cultural Anthropology*, London and New York: Routledge: 393–396.

Cartmill, Matt 1990, "Human Uniqueness and Theoretical Content in Palaeoanthropology," *International Journal of Primatology* 11: 173–191.

Cartmill, Matt 1993, *A View to a Death in the Morning: Hunting and Nature Through History*, Cambridge, Mass.: Harvard University Press.

Cartmill, Matt 2001, "Taxonomic Revolutions and the Animal–Human Boundary," in Raymond Corbey and Bert Theunissen (eds.), *Ape, Man, Apeman: Changing Views since 1600*, Leiden: Department of Prehistory of Leiden University: 97–106.

Cavalieri, Paola and Peter Singer (eds.) 1993, *The Great Ape Project: Equality beyond Humanity*, London: Fourth Estate.

Chagnon, Napoleon A. 1968, *Yanomamö: The Fierce People*, New York: Holt, Rinehart and Winston.

Chagnon, Napoleon A. 1992, *Yanomamö: The Last Days of Eden*, San Diego: Harcourt Brace Jovanovich.

Chagnon, Napoleon A. 1997, *Yanomamö*, 5th ed., Fort Worth: Harcourt Brace College.

Chambers, Robert 1844, *Vestiges of the Natural History of Creation*, London: J. Churchill.

Chilardi, S. *et al.* 1996, "Fontana Nuova di Ragusa (Sicily, Italy): Southernmost Aurignacian Site in Europe," *Antiquity* 70 (269): 553–563.

Clark, Geoffrey 2000, "On the Questionable Practice of Invoking the Metaphysic," *American Anthropologist* 102: 851–853.

Clark, Geoffrey 2001, "Observations on the Epistemology of Human Origins Research," in Raymond Corbey and Wil Roebroeks (eds.), *Studying Human Origins: Disciplinary History and Epistemology*, Amsterdam: Amsterdam University Press: 139–146.

Clark, Geoffrey and Catherine Willermet (eds.) 1997, *Conceptual Issues in Modern Human Origins Research*, New York: Aldine de Gruyter.

Conkey, M. W. 1985, "Ritual Communication, Social Elaboration and the Variable Trajectories of Paleolithic Material Culture," in T. D. Price and J. A. Brown (eds.),

Prehistoric Hunter-Gatherers: The Emergence of Cultural Complexity, Orlando: Academic Press: 299–323.

Coolidge. H. J. 1933, "*Pan paniscus*. Pygmy Chimpanzee from South of the Congo River." *American Journal of Physical Anthropology* 18: 1–59.

Corbey, Raymond 1988, *De mens een dier? Scheler, Plessner en de crisis van het traditionele mensbeeld*, Ph.D. Thesis, Nijmegen: Nijmegen University.

Corbey, Raymond 1991, "Freud's Phylogenetic Narrative", in Raymond Corbey and Joep Leerssen (eds.), *Alterity, Identity, Image: Selves and Others in Society and Scholarship*, Amsterdam Studies in Cultural Identity I, Amsterdam and Atlanta: Rodopi: 37–56.

Corbey, Raymond 1993a, "Ambiguous Apes," in Paola Cavalieri and Peter Singer (eds.), *The Great Ape Project: Equality beyond Humanity*, London: Fourth Estate: 126–136.

Corbey, Raymond 1993b, "Ethnographic Showcases, 1870–1930," *Cultural Anthropology: Journal of the Society for Cultural Anthropology* 8: 338–369.

Corbey, Raymond 1994, "Gift en Transgressie: Kanttekeningen bij Bataille," *Tijdschrift voor Filosofie* 56: 272–312.

Corbey, Raymond 1998, "De l'histoire naturelle à l'histoire humaine: Comment conceptualiser les origines de la culture?" in Albert Ducros, Jacqueline Ducros and Frédéric Joulian (eds.), *La nature est-elle naturelle? Histoire, épistémologie et applications récentes du concept de culture*, Paris: Éditions Errance: 223–238.

Corbey, Raymond 2000, "On Becoming Human: Mauss, the Gift, and Social Origins," in A. Vandevelde (ed.), *Gifts and Interests*, Leuven: Peeters: 157–174.

Corbey, Raymond and Bert Theunissen (eds.) 1995, *Ape, Man, Apeman: Changing Views since 1600*, Leiden: Department of Prehistory of Leiden University.

Corbey, Raymond and Wil Roebroeks 1997, "Ancient minds," *Current Anthropology* 38: 917–921.

Corbey, Raymond and Wil Roebroeks (eds.) 2001a, *Studying Human Origins: Disciplinary History and Epistemology*, Amsterdam: Amsterdam University Press.

Corbey, Raymond and Wil Roebroeks 2001b, "Does Disciplinary History Matter? An Introduction," in *id.* (eds.), *Studying Human Origins: Disciplinary History and Epistemology*, Amsterdam: Amsterdam University Press: 1–7.

Dart, Raymond 1953, "The Predatory Transition from Ape to Man," *International Anthropological and Linguistic Review* 1: 201–219.

Darwin, Charles 1859, *On the Origin of Species by means of Natural Selection, or the Preservation of favoured races in the struggle for life*, London: John Murray.

Darwin, Charles 1871, *The Descent of Man, and Selection in Relation to Sex*, 2 vols., London: Murray.

Bibliography

Darwin, Charles 1903, *More Letters of Charles Darwin*, 2 vols., Francis Darwin and A. C. Seward (eds.), London: John Murray.

Darwin, Charles 1985–1991, *The Correspondence of Charles Darwin*, 7 vols., Frederick Burkhardt *et al.* (eds.), Cambridge: Cambridge University Press.

Darwin, Charles 1987, *Charles Darwin's Notebooks, 1836–1844*, P. H. Barrett *et al.* (eds.), Cambridge: Cambridge University Press, with British Museum of Natural History.

Darwin, Francis (ed.) 1887, *The Life and Letters of Charles Darwin*, 3 vols., 2nd ed., London: John Murray.

Davidson, Iain and William Noble 1993, "Tools and Language in Human Evolution," in Kathleen R. Gibson and Tim Ingold (eds.), *Tools, Language and Cognition in Human Evolution*, Cambridge: Cambridge University Press: 363–388.

Dawkins, Richard 1976, *The Selfish Gene*, New York and Oxford: Oxford University Press.

Deacon, Terrence W. 1990, "Fallacies of Progression in Theories of Brain-Size Evolution," *International Journal of Primatology* 11: 193–236.

de Buffon, Georges Louis Leclerc and Louis Jean Marie Daubenton 1749 etc., *Histoire naturelle, générale et particulière, avec la description du Cabinet du roi*, 31 vols., Paris: Imprimierie Royale.

de Buffon, Georges Louis Leclerc and Louis Jean Marie Daubenton 1766–1799, *Histoire naturelle, générale et particulière*, nouv. ed., 21 vols., Amsterdam : J. H. Schneider.

de Buffon, Georges Louis Leclerc 1954, *Oeuvres philosophiques*, J. Piveteau (ed.), Paris: PUF.

de Lamarck, Jean-Baptiste 1809, *Philosophie Zoologique*, Paris: Dentu.

Delamétherie, J.-C. 1778, *Essai sur les Principes de la Philosophie Naturelle*, The Hague: Marc-Michel Reye.

de La Mettrie, Julien Jean Offray 1745, *Histoire naturelle de l'Âme*, La Haye: Jean Neaulme.

de La Mettrie, Julien Jean Offray 1748, *L'Homme machine*, Leyde: Elie Luzac.

Delisle, Richard 2001, "Adaptation versus Cladism in Human Evolution Studies," in Raymond Corbey and Wil Roebroeks (eds.), *Studying Human Origins: Disciplinary History and Epistemology*, Amsterdam: Amsterdam University Press: 107–121.

de Mortillet, Gabriel 1883, *Le Préhistorique: Antiquité de l'Homme*, Paris: Reinwald.

Démeunier, Jean-Nicolas 1785–1786, *L'esprit des usages et des coutumes des différens peuples*, 3 vols., London and Paris: Laporte.

Dennett, Daniel 1995, *Darwin's Dangerous Idea: Evolution and the Meanings of Life*, London: Penguin Group.

de Regt, Herman 2001, "Epistemic Attitudes and Palaeoanthropology," in Raymond Corbey and Bert Theunissen (eds.), *Ape, Man, Apeman: Changing Views since 1600*, Leiden: Department of Prehistory of Leiden University: 123–138.

de Rooy, Piet 1995, "In Search of Perfection: The Creation of a Missing Link," in Raymond Corbey and Bert Theunissen (eds.), *Ape, Man, Apeman: Changing Views since 1600*, Leiden: Department of Prehistory of Leiden University: 195–208.

Descartes, René 1664, *L'Homme*, Paris: Ch. Angot.

Descola, Philippe and Gísli Pálsson (eds.) 1996, *Nature and Society: Anthropological Perspectives*, London: Routledge.

Desmond, Adrian 1979, *The Ape's Reflection*, London: Blond and Briggs.

Desmond, Adrian 1989, *The Politics of Evolution: Morphology, Medicine and Reform in Radical London*. Chicago and London: The University of Chicago Press.

Desmond, Adrian and James Moore 1991, *Darwin*, London: M. Joseph.

de Vos, John *et al.* 1998, "The Evolution of Hominid Bipedalism," *Anthropologie* XXXVI (1–2): 5–16.

de Waal, Frans 1982, *Chimpanzee Politics: Power and Sex among Apes*, London: Cape.

de Waal, Frans 1989, *Peacemaking among Primates*, Cambridge, Mass.: Harvard University Press.

de Waal, Frans 1996, *Good Natured: The Origins of Right and Wrong in Humans and Other Animals*, Cambridge, Mass.: Harvard University Press.

de Waal, Frans, 2001, *The Ape and the Sushi Master: Cultural Reflections by a Primatologist*, New York: Basic Books.

Diamond, Jared 1993, "The Third Chimpanzee," in Paola Cavalieri and Peter Singer (eds.), *The Great Ape Project: Equality beyond Humanity*, London: Fourth Estate: 88–101.

Diderot, Denis 1975 etc., *Oeuvres Complètes*, Herbert Dieckmann *et al.* (eds.), Paris: Hermann.

Dobzhansky, Theodosius 1962, *Mankind Evolving: The Evolution of the Human Species*, New Haven: Yale University Press.

Dobzhansky, Theodosius 1974, "Chance and Creativity in Evolution," in F. J. Ayala and T. Dobzhansky (eds.), *Studies in the Philosophy of Biology*, Los Angeles and Berkeley: University of California Press: 307–337.

Donald, Merlin 1991, *Origins of the Modern Mind: Three Stages in the Evolution of Culture and Cognition*, Cambridge, Mass.: Harvard University Press.

Dougherty, Frank (ed.) 1984, *Commercium Epistolicum J.F. Blumenbachii*, Göttingen: Niedersächsische Staats- und Universitätsbibliothek.

Dougherty, Frank 1996, *Gesammelte Aufsätze zu Themen der klassischen Periode der Naturgeschichte/Collected Essays on Themes from the Classical Period of Natural History*, Göttingen: Norbert Klatt Verlag.

Bibliography

Douglas, Mary 1966, *Purity and Danger*, London and Henley: Routledge and Kegan Paul.

Douglas, Mary 1970, *Natural Symbols: Explorations in Cosmology*, London: Barrie Cresset.

Douglas, Mary 1975, *Implicit Meanings: Essays in Anthropology*, London and Boston: Routledge and Kegan Paul.

Dubois, Eugène 1894, *Pithecanthropus erectus, eine menschenähnliche Übergangsform aus Java*, Batavia: Landesdruckerei.

Ducros, Albert and Jacqueline Ducros 2000, "Du gorille à l'homme fossile," in *id.* (eds.), *L'homme préhistorique: Images et imaginaire*, Paris: l'Harmattan.

Ducros, Albert, Jacqueline Ducros and Frédéric Joulian (eds.) 1998, *La nature est-elle naturelle? Histoire, Épistémologie et applications récentes du concept de culture*, Paris: Éditions Errance.

Dumont, Louis 1970, *Homo Hierarchicus: An Essay on the Caste System*, Chicago: University of Chicago Press.

Dunbar, Robin 1994, "Sociality among Humans and Non-Human Animals," in Tim Ingold (ed.), *Companion Encyclopedia of Anthropology*, London: Routledge: 756–782.

Dunn, Leslie Clarence *et al.* 1975, *Race, Science and Society*, Paris: Unesco Press.

Durkheim, Émile 1960, "The Dualism of Human Nature and its Social Conditions,'" in Kurt H. Wolff (ed.), *Emile Durkheim, 1858–1917*, Columbus: Ohio State University Press: 325–340.

Fedigan, Linda and Shirley Strum 1997, "Changing Images of Primate Societies," *Current Anthropology* 38: 677–681.

Ferrie, Helke 1997, "An Interview with C. Loring Brace," *Current Anthropology* 38: 851–869.

Fossey, Dian 1970, "Making Friends with Mountain Gorillas," *National Geographical Magazine* 137: 48–67.

Fouts, Roger with Stephen Mills 1997, *Next of Kin: What My Conversations with Chimpanzees Have Taught Me about Intelligence, Compassion and Being Human*, London: Joseph.

Fox, Robin 1989, *The Search for Society: Quest for a Biosocial Science and Morality*, New Brunswick and London: Rutgers University Press.

Fox, Robin 1994, *The Challenge of Anthropology: Old Encounters and New Excursions*, New Brunswick and London: Transaction Publishers.

Frayssinous, D. 1853, *Défense du Christianisme et conférence sur la Religion*, 2 vols., Paris: Delahays.

Freeman, Derek 1983, *Margaret Mead and Samoa: The Making and Unmaking of an Anthropological Myth*, Cambridge, Mass.: Harvard University Press.

Freeman, Derek 1997, "Paradigms in Collision: Margaret Mead's Mistake and What It Has Done to Anthropology," *Skeptic* 5 (3): 66–73.

Freud, Sigmund 1953–1966, *Standard Edition of the Complete Psychological Works of Sigmund Freud*, James Strachey *et al.* (eds.), London: Hogarth Press.

Freud, Sigmund 1987, *A Phylogenetic Phantasy: Overview of the Transference Neuroses*, I. Grubrich-Simitis (ed.), transl. by A. Hoffer and P. T. Hoffer, Cambridge Mass.: Belknap Press of Harvard University Press.

Frykman, Jonas and Orvar Löfgren 1987, *Culture Builders: A Historical Anthropology of Middle-Class Life*, New Brunswick and London: Rutgers University Press.

Galdikas, Birute 1995, *Reflections of Eden: My Life with the Orangutans of Borneo*, London: Victor Gollancz.

Gallup, Gordon G. 1977, "A Mirror for the Mind of Man, or Will the Chimpanzee Create an Identity Crisis for *Homo sapiens?*" *Journal of Human Evolution* 6: 301–313.

Gamble, Clive 1994, "Human Evolution: The Last One Million Years," in Tim Ingold (ed.), *Companion Encyclopedia of Anthropology*, London: Routledge: 79–107.

Gamble, Clive 1998, "Palaeolithic Society and the Release from Proximity: A Network Approach to Intimate Relations," *World Archaeology* 29: 426–449.

Gaudzinski, Sabine and Wil Roebroeks 2000, "Adults Only: Reindeer Hunting at the Middle Palaeolithic Site Salzgitter Lebenstedt, Northern Germany," *Journal of Human Evolution* 38: 497–521.

Geertz, Clifford 1973, *The Interpretation of Cultures: Selected Essays*, New York: Basic Books.

Geertz, Clifford 1995, *After the Fact: Two Countries, Four Decades, One Anthropologist*, Cambridge, Mass.: Harvard University Press.

Geoffroy St. Hilaire, Etienne 1798, "Observations on the Account of the Supposed Orang-Outang of the East-Indies," *Philosophical Magazine* 1: 337–342.

Geoffroy St. Hilaire, Etienne 1836, "Extrait d'un mémoir sur l'Orang-Outang, vivant actuellement à la Ménagerie," *Comptes rendues des séances de l'Académie des Sciences* II: 581–585.

Gibson, Kathleen R. 1993, "Animal Minds, Human Minds," in Kathleen R. Gibson and Tim Ingold (eds.), *Tools, Language and Cognition in Human Evolution*, Cambridge: Cambridge University Press: 3–19.

Gilmore, H. A. 1981, "From Radcliffe-Brown to Sociobiology: Some Aspects of the Rise of Primatology within Physical Anthropology," *American Journal of Physical Anthropology* 56: 387–392.

Goodall, Jane 1990, *Through a Window*, Boston: Houghton Mifflin Publishing.

Goodall, Jane 1998, "Learning from the Chimpanzees: A Message Humans Can Understand," *Science* 282, 18 December: 2184–2185.

Bibliography

Goodall, Jane and Dale Peterson 1993, *Visions of Caliban: On Chimpanzees and People*, Boston: Houghton Mifflin.

Goodall, Jane with Phillip Berman 1999, *Reason for Hope: A Spiritual Journey*, London: Thorsons.

Goodman, Morris 1962, "Immunochemistry of the Primates and Primate Evolution," *Annals of the New York Academy of Sciences* 102: 219–234.

Goodman, Morris *et al.* 1998, "Toward a Phylogenetic Classification of Primates Based on DNA Evidence Complemented by Fossil Evidence," *Molecular Phylogenetics and Evolution* 9: 585–598.

Gould, Stephen Jay 1981, *The Mismeasure of Man*, Harmondsworth: Penguin Books.

Gould, Stephen Jay 1997, *Life's Grandeur: The Spread of Excellence from Plato to Darwin*, London: Vintage.

Greenfield, Patricia Marks and Sue Savage-Rumbaugh 1990, "Grammatical Combinations in *Pan paniscus*: Processes of Learning and Invention in the Evolution and Development of Language," in Sue T. Parker and Kathleen Gibson (eds.), *"Language" and Intelligence in Monkeys and Apes: Comparative Developmental Perspectives*, Cambridge: Cambridge Univesity Press: 540–578.

Gregory of Nyssa 1944, *La création de l'homme*, ed. and transl. by Jean Laplace, annotated by Jean Daniélou, Paris: Cerf.

Greimas, Algirdas Julien 1990, *Narrative Semiotics and Cognitive Discourses*, transl. by Paul Perron and Frank H. Collins, London : Pinter.

Haeckel, Ernst 1866, *Generelle Morphologie der Organismen*, 2 vols., Berlin: Reimer.

Haeckel, Ernst 1874, *Anthropogenie, oder, Entwickelungsgeschichte des Menschen*, Leipzig: Engelmann.

Haraway, Donna 1989, *Primate Visions: Gender, Race and Nature in the World of Modern Science*, New York and London: Routledge.

Haydn, Brian 1993, "Cultural Capacities of Neandertals: A Review and a Reevaluation," *Journal of Human Evolution* 24: 113–146.

Heidegger, Martin 1983, *Die Grundbegriffe der Metaphysik: Welt, Endlichkeit, Einsamkeit*, Gesamtausgabe vol. 29/30, Frankfurt am Main: Klostermann.

Herzing, Denise L. and Thomas I. White 1998, "Dolphins and the Question of Personhood," *Etica & Animali* 9: 64–84.

Hobbes, Thomas, 1972 [1651], *Leviathan*, Harmondsworth: Pelican.

Høeg, Peter 1996, *The Woman & the Ape*, transl. by Barbara Haveland, London: The Harvill Press.

Holloway, Ralph L. 1969, "Culture: A Human Domain," *Current Anthropology* 10: 395–412.

Hooton, Earnest 1931, *Up from the Ape*, New York: The Macmillan Company.

Husband, Timothy 1980, *The Wild Man: Medieval Myth and Symbolism*, New York: The Metropolitan Museum of Art.

Huxley, Julian 1941, *The Uniqueness of Man*, London: Chatto & Windus.

Huxley, Thomas 1861, "On the Zoological Relations of Man with the Lower Animals," *Natural History Review: A Quarterly Journal of Biological Science* 1: 67–84.

Huxley, Thomas 1863, *Evidence as to Man's Place in Nature*, London: Williams and Norgate.

Huxley, Thomas 1889, "Agnosticism," *The Nineteenth Century* 25 (144), February: 170–194.

Huxley, Thomas 1893, *Evolution and Ethics: The Romanes lecture 1893, delivered in the Sheldonian Theatre, May 18, 1893*, Oxford: Clarendon Press.

Ingold, Tim 1994a, "From Trust to Domination. An Alternative History of Human-Animal Relations," in A. Manning and J. Serpell (eds.), *Animals and Human Society. Changing Perspectives*, London and New York: Routledge: 1–22.

Ingold, Tim 1994b, "Tool-Using, Toolmaking, and the Evolution of Language," in Duane Quiatt and Junichiro Itani (eds.), *Hominid Culture in Primate Perspective*, Niwot: University Press of Colorado: 279–314.

Isaac, Glynn 1972, "Early Phases of Human Behavior: Models in Lower Paleolithic Archaeology," in David Clark (ed.), *Models in Archaeology*, London: Methuen: 167–200.

Isaac, Glynn and Barbara Isaac 1977, *Olorgesailie: Archaeological Studies of a Middle Pleistocene Lake Basin in Kenya*, Chicago: University of Chicago Press.

Janson, H. W. 1952, *Apes and Ape Lore in the Middle Ages and the Renaissance*, London: The Warburg Institute.

Jensen, Stine 2002, *Waarom vrouwen van apen houden: Een liefdesgeschiedenis in cultuur en wetenschap*, Amsterdam: Bert Bakker.

Johanson, D. C., T. D. White, and Y. Coppens 1978, "A New Species of the Genus *Australopithecus* (Primates: Hominidae) from the Pliocene of Eastern Africa," *Kirtlandia* 28: 1–14.

John Paul II, Pope 1996, "Truth Cannot Contradict Truth: Address to the Pontifical Academy of Sciences" (October 22), *L'Osservatore Romano* (English edition), October 30.

Joulian, Frédéric 1998, "Le casse-noix du chimpanzé: Lectures anthropologiques d'un objet simien," in Albert Ducros, Jacqueline Ducros and Frédéric Joulian (eds.), *La nature est-elle naturelle? Histoire, épistémologie et applications récentes du concept de culture*, Paris: Éditions Errance: 115–137.

Keeley, Lawrence 1997, *War before Civilization: The Myth of the Peaceful Savage*, New York: Oxford University Press.

Keith, Arthur 1948, *A New Theory of Human Evolution*, London: Watts.

Bibliography

Khare, R. S. 1996, "Purity and Pollution," in Alan Barnard and Jonathan Spencer (eds.), *Encyclopedia of Social and Cultural Anthropology*, London and New York: Routledge: 437–439.

King, Barbara J. 1994a, *The Information Continuum: Evolution of Social Information Transfer in Monkeys, Apes, and Hominids*, Santa Fe: SAR Press.

King, Barbara J. 1994b, "Evolutionism, Essentialism, and an Evolutionary Perspective on Language: Moving Beyond a Human Standard," *Language & Communication* 14: 1–13.

King, M. C. and A. C. Wilson 1975a, "Evolution at Two Levels in Humans and Chimpanzees," *Science* 188: 107–116.

King, M. C. and A. C. Wilson 1975b, "Our Close Cousin the Chimpanzee," *New Scientist* 67: 16–18.

Kingsley, Charles 1863, *The Water-Babies: A Fairy Tale for a Land-Baby*, London: Macmillan.

Kitchen, Ann, Derek Denton and Linda Brent 1996, "Self-recognition and abstraction abilities in the common chimpanzee studied with distorting mirrors," *Proceedings National Academy of Sciences* 93: 7405–7408.

Knauft, Bruce 1987, "Reconsidering Violence in Simple Human Societies: Homicide among the Gebusi of New Guinea," *Current Anthropology* 28: 457–500.

Köhler, Wolfgang 1921, *Intelligenzprüfungen an Anthropoiden*, Berlin: Springer.

Köhler, Wolfgang 1925, *The Mentality of Apes*, transl. E. Winter, London: Kegan Paul, Trench, Trubner.

Kuspit, Donald, "A Mighty Metaphor: The Analogy of Archaeology and Psychoanalysis," in L. Gamwell and R. Wells (eds.), *Sigmund Freud and Art. His Personal Collection of Antiquities*, New York and London: 133–151.

Lamarck, Jean-Baptiste de 1809, *Philosophie zoologique*, Paris: Dentu.

Landau, Misia 1991a, *Narratives of Human Evolution*, New Haven and London: Yale University Press.

Landau, Misia 1991b, review of Haraway 1989, *Journal of Human Evolution* 20: 433–437.

Latour, B. and S. Strum 1986, "Human Social Origins: Oh, Please, Tell Us Another Story," *Journal of Social and Biological Structures* 9: 169–187.

Leach, Edmund 1982, *Social Anthropology*, London: Fontana Paperbacks.

Leakey, L. S. B. 1959, "A New Fossil Skull from Olduvai," *Nature* 184: 491–493.

Leakey, L. S. B., P. V. Tobias and J. R. Napier 1964, "A New Species of Genus *Homo* from Olduvai Gorge," *Nature* 202: 7–9.

Lee, Richard B. and Irving DeVore (eds.) 1968, *Man the Hunter*, Chicago, Il.: Aldine.

Lee, Richard 1979, *The !Kung San: Men, Women and Work in a Foraging Society*, Cambridge: Cambridge University Press.

Le Gros Clark, Wilfred 1934, *Early Fore-Runners of Man: A Morphological Study of the Evolutionary Origin of the Primates*, London: Ballière, Tindall & Cox.

Leroi-Gourhan, André 1964, *Le geste et la parole, I: Technique et language*, Paris: Albin Michel.

Lévi-Strauss, Claude 1956, "The Family," in H. Shapiro (ed.), *Man, Culture and Society*, New York: Oxford University Press: 261–285.

Lévi-Strauss, Claude 1969 [1949], *The Elementary Structures of Kinship*, Boston: Beacon Press.

Lévi-Strauss, Claude 1963, *Totemism*, transl. by Rodney Needham, Boston: Beacon Press.

Lieberman, Philip 1991, *Uniquely Human: The Evolution of Speech, Thought and Speechless Behavior*, London and Cambridge, Mass.: Harvard University Press.

Liliequist, Jonas 1990, "Peasants against Nature: Crossing the Boundaries between Man and Animal in Seventeenth- and Eighteenth-Century Sweden," *Focaal: Tijdschrift voor Antropologie* 13: 28–54.

Linnaeus, Carolus 1746, *Fauna Svecica*, Stockholm: Salvius, Laurentius.

Linnaeus, Carolus 1758: *Systema Naturae*, 10th ed., Stockholm: Salvius, Laurentius.

Linnaeus, Carolus 1766, *Systema Naturæ*, 12th ed., Stockholm: Salvius, Laurentius.

Linnaeus, Carolus 1972 [1749], *L'Équilibre de la Nature*, transl. by Bernard Jasmin, introd. and annot. by Camille Limoges, Paris: Vrin.

Linnaeus, Carolus 1976, *Letters on Natural History to Carolus Linnaeus*, Vol. V, London: Linnaean Society.

Littré, Émile 1872, *Dictionnaire étymologique, historique et grammaticale de la langue française*, Paris: Bibliothèque de l'Institut.

Lombroso, Cesare 1876, *L'Uomo Delinquente, Studiato in Rapporto alla Antropologia, alla Medicina Legale ed alle Discipline Carcerarie*, Milano: U. Hoepli.

Loy, James D. and Calvin B. Peters, "Mortifying Reflections: Primatology and the Human Disciplines," in *id.* (eds.) 1991, *Understanding Behaviour. What Primate Studies Tell Us about Human Behaviour*, New York and Oxford: Oxford University Press: 3–16.

Lucas, J. R. 1979, "Wilberforce and Huxley: A Legendary Encounter," *The Historical Journal* 22: 313–330.

Lyell, Charles 1830–1833, *Principles of Geology, Being an Attempt to Explain the Former Changes of the Earth's Surface, by Reference to Causes now in Operation*, 4 vols., London: John Murray.

Lyell, Charles 1867–1868, *Principles of Geology, or The Modern Changes of the Earth and its Inhabitants Considered as Illustrative of Geology*, 10th and entirely rev. ed., London: John Murray.

Bibliography

Lyell, Charles 1970, *Sir Charles Lyell's Scientific Journals on the Species Question*, Leonard G. Wilson (ed.), New Haven, London: Yale University Press.

Malinowski, B. 1921, "The Primitive Economics of the Trobriand Islanders," *Economic Journal* 31: 1–16.

Marks, Jonathan and Nora Ellen Groce 1997, Letter to the *New York Times* (on Cavalieri and Singer 1993), February 18.

Mauss, Marcel 1990, *The Gift: The Form and Reason for Exchange in Archaic Societies*, transl. by W. D. Halls, London: Routledge.

Mauss, Marcel 1995, *Sociologie et Anthropologie*, Paris: PUF.

Mayr, Ernst 1950, "Taxonomic Categories in Fossil Hominids," *Cold Spring Harbor Symposium on Quantitative Biology* 15: 109–117.

Mayr, Ernst 1982, *The Growth of Biological Thought*, Cambridge, Mass.: Belknap Press.

Mead, Margaret 1928, *Coming of Age in Samoa: A Psychological Study of Primitive Youth for Western Civilization*, New York: Morrow.

McGrew, William C. 1992, *Chimpanzee Material Culture: Implications for Human Evolution*, Cambridge: Cambridge University Press.

McLennan, John F. 1865, *Primitive Marriage*, Edinburgh: Black.

Meijer, Miriam 1999, *Race and Aesthetics in the Anthropology of Petrus Camper (1722–1789)*, Amsterdam and Atlanta: Rodopi.

Monboddo, James Burnett Lord 1773–1792, *Of the Origin and Progress of Language*, vols. I–VI, Edinburgh: J. Balfour.

Monboddo, James Burnett Lord 1779–1799, *Antient Metaphysics*, vols. I–VI, Edinburgh: J. Balfour.

Morris, Ramona and Desmond Morris 1968, *Men and Apes*, London: Sphere Books.

Moser, Stephanie 1998, *Ancestral Images: The Iconography of Human Origins*, Stroud: Sutton, and Ithaca (NY): Cornell University Press.

Mowat, Farley 1987, *Woman in the Mists: The Story of Dian Fossey and the Mountain Gorillas of Africa*, New York: Warner Books.

Murray, Tim 1992, "The Tasmanians and the Constitution of the 'Dawn of Humanity'," *Antiquity* 66: 730–743.

Murray, Tim 2001, "On 'Normalizing' the Paleolithic: An Orthodoxy Questioned," in Raymond Corbey and Bert Theunissen (eds.), *Ape, Man, Apeman: Changing Views since 1600*, Leiden: Department of Prehistory of Leiden University: 29–43.

Nash, Richard 1995, "Tyson's Pygmie: The Orang-Outang and Augustan 'Satyr'," in Raymond Corbey and Bert Theunissen (eds.), *Ape, Man, Apeman: Changing Views since 1600*, Leiden: Department of Prehistory of Leiden University: 51–62.

Nickles, T. 1995, "Philosophy of Science and History of Science," *OSIRIS* 10: 139–163.

Nietzsche, Friedrich 1999, *Sämtliche Werke: Kritische Studienausgabe*, Giorgio Colli and Mazzino Montinari (eds.), Berlin: De Gruyter; München: Deutscher Taschenbuch Verlag.

Noble, William and Iain Davidson 1993, "Tracing the Emergence of Modern Human Behavior. Methodological Pitfalls and a Theoretical Path," *Journal of Anthropological Archaeology* 12: 121–149.

Noble, William and Iain Davidson 1996, *Human Evolution, Language and Mind: A Psychological and Archaeological Enquiry*, Cambridge: Cambridge University Press.

Oakley, Kenneth 1949, *Man the Tool-Maker*, London: British Museum.

Oakley, Kenneth 1968, *Man the Tool-Maker: An Up-to-date and Authoritative Account of the Early History of Man's Distinguishing Trait, His Ability to Make Tools*, Chicago: Phoenix Books.

Oakley, Kenneth 1972, *Man the Tool-Maker*, 6th ed., London: Trustees of the British Museum.

Ohnuki-Tierney, Emiko 1987, *The Monkey as a Mirror. Symbolic Transformations in Japanese History and Ritual*, Princeton: Princeton University Press.

Ohnuki-Tierney, Emiko 1995, "Representations of the Monkey (*saru*) in Japanese Culture," in Raymond Corbey and Bert Theunissen (eds.), *Ape, Man, Apeman: Changing Views since 1600*, Leiden: Department of Prehistory of Leiden University: 297–308.

Otterbein, Keith F. 2000, "A History of Research on Warfare in Anthropology," *American Anthropologist* 101: 794–805.

Owen, Richard 1857, "On the Characters, Principles of Division, and the Primary Groups of the Class Mammalia," *Proceedings of the Linnaean Society* 2: 1–37.

Pearsall, Judy and Patrick Hanks (eds.) 1998, *The New Oxford Dictionary of English*, Oxford: Clarendon Press.

Pennant, Thomas 1768–1770, *British Zoology*, 4 vols., London: White.

Pepperberg, Irene 1999, *The Alex Studies: Cognitive and Communicative Abilities of Grey Parrots*, Cambridge, Mass.: Harvard University Press.

Platenkamp, Jos D. M. 1988, *Tobelo: Ideas and Values of a North-Moluccan Society*, Ph.D. thesis, Leiden: Leiden University.

Plato 1982, *Hippias major*, transl. and ed. by Paul Woodruff, Oxford: Blackwell.

Plessner, Helmuth 1928, *Die Stufen des Organischen und der Mensch: Einleitung in die philosophische Anthropologie*, Berlin: De Gruyter.

Plessner, Helmuth 1983, *Conditio humana, Gesammelte Schriften* vol. 8, Günter Dux *et al.* (eds.), Frankfurt am Main: Suhrkamp.

Plieninger, G. H. T. (ed.) 1861, *Joannis Georgii Gmelini reliquias quae supersunt commercii epistolici*, Stuttgart: Typis C. F. Heringianis.

Bibliography

Poe, Edgar A. 1841, "The Murders in the Rue Morgue," *Graham's Magazine* XVIII, 4 (April): 166–179.

Povinelli, Daniel 2000, *Folk Physics for Apes: The Chimpanzee's Theory of How the World Works*, Oxford: Oxford University Press.

Putnam, Hilary 1981, *Reason, Truth and History*, Cambridge: Cambridge University Press.

Putnam, Hilary 1987, *The Many Faces of Realism: The Paul Carus Lectures*, La Salle: Open Court.

Putnam, Hilary 1990, *Realism with a Human Face*, ed. by James Conant, Cambridge, Mass.: Harvard University Press.

Putnam, Hilary 1992, *Renewing Philosophy*, London and Cambridge, Mass.: Harvard University Press.

Quiatt, Duane and Vernon Reynolds 1993, *Primate Behaviour: Information, Social Knowledge, and the Evolution of Culture*, Cambridge: Cambridge University Press.

Reader, John 1988, *Missing Links: The Hunt for Earliest Man*, 2nd ed., Harmondsworth: Penguin Books.

Reynolds, Vernon 1967, *The Apes: The Gorilla, Chimpanzee, Orangutan, and Gibbon: Their History and Their World*, New York: Dutton.

Reynolds, Vernon 1990, "Images of Chimpanzees," *Anthropology Today* 6 (6): 1–3.

Reynolds, Vernon 1991, review of Haraway 1989, *Man* 26: 167–168.

Richard, Nathalie 1993, "De l'art ludique à l'art magique: Interprétations de l'art pariétal au XIXe siècle," *Bulletin de la Société Préhistorique française* 90 (1–2): 60–68.

Rodseth, Lars *et al.* 1991, "The Human Community as a Primate Society," *Current Anthropology* 32: 221–254.

Rooijakkers, Gerard 1995, "European Ape Lore in Popular Prints, 17th–19th Centuries," in Raymond Corbey and Bert Theunissen (eds.), *Ape, Man, Apeman: Changing Views since 1600*, Leiden: Department of Prehistory of Leiden University: 327–336.

Rosen, Donne E., Gareth Nelson and Colin Patterson 1979, "Foreword," in Willi Hennig, *Phylogenetic systematics*, transl. by D. Dwight Davis and Rainer Zanger, Urbana: University of Illinois Press.

Rousseau, Jean-Jacques 1755, *Discours sur l'Origine et les Fondements de l'Inégalité parmi les Hommes*, Amsterdam: Marc Michel Rey.

Sahlins, Marshall 1972, "The Spirit of the Gift," in *id., Stone Age Economics*, London: Routledge: 149–183.

Sahlins, Marshall 1976a, *The Use and Abuse of Biology: An Anthropological Critique of Sociobiology*, Ann Arbor: University of Michigan Press.

Sahlins, Marshall 1976b, *Culture and Practical Reason*, Chicago: University of Chicago Press.

Sahlins, Marshall 1996, "The Sadness of Sweetness: The Native Anthropology of Western Cosmology," *Current Anthropology* 37: 395–428.

Savage, Thomas S. 1847, "Notice of the External Characters and Habits of Troglodytes Gorilla, a New Species of Orang from the Gaboon River," *Proceedings of the Boston Society of Natural History* II: 245–247.

Savage-Rumbaugh, Sue, Stuart G. Shanker and Talbot J. Taylor 1998, *Apes, Language, and the Human Mind*, New York and Oxford: Oxford University Press.

Schefold, Reimar 1988, *Lia: Das grosse Ritual auf den Mentawai-Inseln (Indonesien)*, Berlin: Dietrich Reimer.

Schefold, Reimar 2002, "Visions of the Wilderness on Siberut in a Comparative Southeast Asian Perspective," in Geoffrey Benjamin and Cynthia Chou (eds.), *Tribal Communities in the Malay World: Historical, Cultural and Social Perspectives*, Leiden, Singapore and Richmond, Surrey: IIAS, ISEAS and Curzon Press, 2002: 422–438.

Scheler, Max 1961, *Mans' Place in Nature*, transl. and introd. by Hans Meyerhoff, New York: Noonday.

Schick, Kathy D. *et al.* 1999, "Continuing Investigations into the Stone Tool-making and Tool-using Capabilities of a Bonobo (*Pan paniscus*)," *Journal of Archaeological Science*: 821–832.

Schneider, David M. 1984, *A Critique of the Study of Kinship*, Ann Arbor: University of Michigan Press.

Serpell, James 1986, *In the Company of Animals: A Study of Human-Animal Relationships*, Oxford: Basil Blackwell.

Shakespeare, William 2001, *The Arden Shakespeare Complete Works*, rev. edition, Richard Proudfoot *et al.* (eds.), London: Arden Shakespeare.

Spence, Donald 1987, *The Freudian Metaphor: Towards Paradigm Change in Psychoanalysis*, New York: Norton.

Spencer, Frank 1986, *Ecce Homo: An Annotated Bibliographic History of Physical Anthropology from its Beginnings*, New York and London: Greenwood Press.

Spencer, Frank (ed.) 1995, *History of Physical Anthropology: An Encyclopaedia*, New York: Garland.

Sperling, Susan 1991, "Baboons with Briefcases: Feminism, Functionalism, and Sociobiology in the Evolution of Primate Gender," *Signs*, Autumn: 1–27.

Sponsel, Leslie 1996, "Peace and Nonviolence," in David Levinson and Melvin Ember (eds.), *Encyclopedia of Cultural Anthropology*, New York: Holt: 908–912.

Sponsel, Leslie and Thomas Gregor 1994, *The Anthropology of Peace and Nonviolence*, Boulder: Lynne Rienner Publishers.

Bibliography

Stallybrass, Peter and Allon White 1986, *The Politics and Poetics of Transgression*, London: Methuen.

Stanford, Craig 2001, *Significant Others: The Ape-Human Continuum and the Quest for Human Nature*, New York: Basic Books.

Stanford, Craig T. and Henry T. Bunn (eds.) 2001, *Meat-Eating and Human Evolution*, New York: Oxford University Press.

Steichen, Edward 1955, *The Family of Man: The Greatest Photographic Exhibition of All Time, 503 Pictures from 68 Countries*, New York: Museum of Modern Art.

Stoczkowski, Wiktor 1995a, "Le bipède et sa science: Histoire d'une structure de la pensée naturaliste," *Gradhiva* 17: 17–43.

Stoczkowski, Wiktor 1995b, "Portrait de l'Ancêtre en Singe. L'Hominisation sans Évolutionnisme dans la Pensée Naturaliste du XVIIIe Siècle," in Raymond Corbey and Bert Theunissen (eds.), *Ape, Man, Apeman: Changing Views since 1600*, Leiden: Department of Prehistory of Leiden University: 141–156.

Stoczkowski, Wiktor 2002, *Explaining Human Origins: Myth, Imagination and Conjecture*, transl. by Mary Turton, Cambridge: Cambridge University Press.

Stuart, Martinus 1802–1807, *De mensch zoo als hij voorkomt op den bekenden aardbol*, 6 vols., Amsterdam: Johannes Allart.

Stringer, Chris and Clive Gamble 1993, *In Search of the Neanderthals*, London: Thames and Hudson.

Strum, Shirley C. 1987, *Almost Human: A Journey into the World of Baboons*, New York: Random House.

Tanner, Nancy M. and Adrienne Zihlman 1976, "Women in Evolution, Part I: Innovation and Selection in Human Origins," *Signs* 1: 585–608.

Tattersall, Ian 2000, "Paleoanthropology: The Last Half-Century," *Evolutionary Anthropology* 9: 2–16.

Theunissen, Bert 1989, *Eugène Dubois and the Ape-Man from Java*, Dordrecht: Kluwer Academic Press.

Theweleit, Klaus 1987, *Männerphantasien*, 2 vols., Reinbek bei Hamburg: Rowohlt.

Thijssen, Hans 1995, "Reforging the Great Chain of Being. The Medieval Discussion of the Human Status of 'Pygmies' and its Influence on Edward Tyson," in Raymond Corbey and Bert Theunissen (eds.), *Ape, Man, Apeman: Changing Views since 1600*, Leiden: Department of Prehistory of Leiden University: 43–50.

Thomas, Elizabeth Marshall 1959, *The Harmless People*, New York: Random House.

Thomas, Keith 1983, *Man and the Natural World. A History of the Modern Sensibility*, New York: Pantheon Books.

Thulié, Henri 1907, "L'École d'Anthropologie depuis sa fondation," in *1876–1906. L'Ecole d'anthropologie de Paris*, no editor, Paris: Félix Alcan: 1–27.

Tierney, Patrick 2000, *Darkness in El Dorado: How Scientists and Journalists Devastated the Amazon*, New York: Norton.

Tiger, Lionel and Robin Fox 1971, *The Imperial Animal*, New York: Holt, Rinehart and Winston.

Tobias, Phillip V. 1965a, "Australopithecus, Homo habilis, Tool-Using and Tool-Making," *South-African Archaeological Bulletin* 20: 167–192.

Tobias, Phillip V. 1965b, "Early Man in East Africa," *Science* 149: 22–3.

Tobias, Phillip V. 1979, *The Evolution of the Human Brain, Intellect and Spirit*, 1st Abbie Memorial lecture, Adelaide, Australia: University of Adelaide.

Tobias, Phillip V. 1983, "Recent Advances in the Evolution of the Hominids, with Special Reference to Brain and Speech," *Pontifical Academy of Sciences Scripta Varia* 50: 85–140.

Tobias, Philip V. 1991, *Olduvai Gorge, Vol. 4: The Skulls, Endocasts and Teeth of* Homo habilis, Cambridge: Cambridge University Press.

Tobias, Phillip V. 1994, "The Evolution of Early Hominids," in Tim Ingold (ed.), *Companion Encyclopedia of Anthropology*, London: Routledge: 33–78.

Tobias, Philip V. 1995, *The Communication of the Dead: Earliest Vestiges of the Origin of Articulate Language*, Amsterdam: Stichting Nederlands Museum voor Anthropologie en Praehistorie.

Tobias, Philip V. and John R. Napier 1964, letter to *The Times*, 29 May.

Toth, N. *et. al.* 1993, "Pan the Tool-Maker: Investigations into the Stone Tool-Making and Tool-Using Capabilities of a Bonobo (*Pan Paniscus*)," *Journal of Archaeological Science* 20: 81–91.

Trinkaus, Erik and Pat Shipman 1993, *The Neanderthals: Changing the Image of Mankind*, London: Jonathan Cape.

Tulp, Nicolaes 1641, *Observationes medicae*, Amstelodami: Elzevirium.

Turner, Terence and Leslie Sponsel Nov. 13, 2000, "The Turner-Sponsel Memo," http://www.umich.edu/~idpah/SEP/sep_ts.html.

Turner, Victor 1969, *The Ritual Process*, Chicago: Aldine.

Tuttle, Russell H. 2001, "Phylogenies, Fossils, and Feelings," in Benjamin B. Beck *et al.* (eds.), *Great Apes & Humans: The Ethics of Coexistence*, Washington, D.C.: Smithsonian Institution Press: 178–190.

Tyson, Edward 1699, *Orang-Outang, sive Homo Sylvestris: Or, The Anatomy of a Pygmie Compared with that of a Monkey, an Ape, and a Man. To which is Added, a Philological Essay Concerning the Pygmies, the Cynocephali, the Satyrs, and Sphinges of the Ancients*, London: T. Bennett and D. Brown.

UNESCO 1950, *Statement on Race*, Paris: United Nations Educational, Scientific and Cultural Organisation.

Bibliography

United Nations 1952, *Universal Declaration of Human Rights: Final Authorized Text*, New York: United Nations.

van der Dennen, Matheus Gerardus 1995, *The Origin of War: The Evolution of a Male-Coalitional Reproductive Strategy*, 2 vols., Groningen: Origin Press.

van Gulick, Robert 1967, *The Gibbon in China. An Essay in Chinese Animal Lore*, Leiden: E. J. Brill.

van Hooff, Jan A. R. A. M. 1994, "Understanding Chimpanzee Understanding," in Richard W. Wrangham *et al.* (eds.), *Chimpanzee Cultures*, Cambridge, Mass.: Harvard University Press: 267–284.

van Hooff, Jan 2000, "Primate Ecology and Socioecology in the Netherlands," in Shirley C. Strum and Linda M. Fedigan (eds.), *Primate Encounters: Models of Science, Gender, and Society*, Chicago: University of Chicago Press: 116–137.

van Lawick-Goodall, Jane 1971, *In the Shadow of Man*, London: Collins.

Van Reybrouck, David 2000, *From Primitives to Primates: A History of Ethnographic and Primatological Analogies in the Study of Prehistory*, Ph. D. thesis, Leiden: Department of Archaeology.

Van Schaick, C. P. *et al.* 2003, "Orangutan cultures and the evolution of material culture," *Science* 299: 102–105.

Verwey, Gerlof 1995, "The Quest for Natural Man: Reflections on Atavism, Degeneration, and Fin de Siècle," in Raymond Corbey and Bert Theunissen (eds.), *Ape, Man, Apeman: Changing Views since 1600*, Leiden: Department of Prehistory of Leiden University: 181–184.

Virey, Julien-Joseph 1819, "Art nègre," *Dictionnaire des sciences médicales*, Paris: Crapart, vol. 35: 378–432.

Virey, Julien-Joseph 1834, *Histoire naturelle du genre humain*, Brussels: Louis Hauman.

von Haller, Albrecht 1787, *Tagebuch seiner Beobachtungen über Schriftsteller und über sich selbst*, 2 vols., Bern: Haller.

Vosmaer, Arnout 1778, *Beschryving van de zo Zeldzaame als Zonderlinge Aap-Soort, Genaamd Orang-Outang, van het Eiland Borneo*, Amsterdam: Meijer.

Wallace, Alfred Russell 1905, *My Life: A Record of Events and Opinions*, 2 vols., London: Chapman & Hall.

Wallace, Irving 1983, *Freud and Anthropology: A History and Reappraisal*, New York: International Universities Press.

Walker, Alan and Pat Shipman 1996, *The Wisdom of Bones: In Search of Human Origins*, London: Weidenfeld and Nicolson; New York: A. Knopf.

Walter, A. 1993, "An interview with Robin Fox," *Current Anthropology* 34: 441–452.

Washburn, Sherwood L. 1951, "The New Physical Anthropology," *Yearbook of Physical Anthropology* 7: 298–304.

Washburn, Sherwood L. 1960, "Tools and Human Evolution," *Scientific American* 203: 63–75.

Washburn, Sherwood L. 1982, "Fifty Years of Studies on Human Evolution," *The Bulletin of Atomic Scientists*, May: 37–43.

Washburn, Sherwood L. and Irving DeVore 1961, "The Social Life of Baboons," reprinted in Shirley C. Strum, Donald G. Lindburg and David Hamburg (eds.), *The New Physical Anthropology: Science, Humanism, and Critical Reflection*, Upper Saddle River, N.J.: Prentice Hall: 254–260.

Washburn, Sherwood L. and C. S. Lancaster 1999 [1968], "The Evolution of hunting," reprinted in Shirley C. Strum, Donald G. Lindburg and David Hamburg (eds.), *The New Physical Anthropology: Science, Humanism, and Critical Reflection*, Upper Saddle River, N.J.: Prentice Hall: 244–253.

Watson, E. E., S. Eastael and D. Penny 2001, "*Homo* genus: A Review of the Classification of Humans and the Great Apes," in Phillip V. Tobias *et al.* (eds.), *Humanity from African Naissance to Coming Millennia: Colloquia in Human Biology and Palaeoanthropology*, Firenze: Firenze University Press; Johannesburg: Witwatersrand University Press: 317–318.

Weiner, Annette 1992, *Inalienable Possessions: The Paradox of Keeping-While-Giving*, Berkeley and Oxford: University of California Press.

White, Leslie 1949, *The Science of Culture: A Study of Man and Civilization*, New York: Farrar, Straus & Co.

White, Leslie 1959, *The Evolution of Culture*, New York: McGraw-Hill.

Whiten, A. *et al.* 1999, "Cultures in Chimpanzees," *Nature* 399: 682–685.

Whiten, A. and Chr. Boesch 2001, "The Cultures of Chimpanzees," *Scientific American*, January: 49–55.

Whiten, A. *et al.* 2003, "Cultures in Chimpanzees," *Nature* 399: 682–685.

Wildman, Derek E. *et al.* 2003, "Implications of Natural Selection in Shaping 99.4% Nonsynonymous DNA Identity between Humans and Chimpanzees: Enlarging Genus *Homo*," *Proceedings National Academy of Sciences* 100: 7181–7188.

Wilson, Edward O. 1975, *Sociobiology: The New Synthesis*, Cambridge, Mass.: Belknap Press of Harvard University Press.

Wilson, Edward O. 1978, *On Human Nature*, Cambridge, Mass.: Harvard University Press.

Wittgenstein, Ludwig 1969, *On Certainty*, G. E. M. Anscombe and G. H. von Wright (eds.), transl. by Denis Paul and G. E. M. Anscombe, Oxford: Blackwell.

Wokler, Robert 1993, "Enlightening Apes: 18th-Century Speculation and Current Experiments on Linguistic Competence," in Raymond Corbey and Bert Theunissen (eds.), *Ape, Man, Apeman: Changing Views since 1600*, Leiden: Department of Prehistory of Leiden University: 87–100.

Bibliography

Wood, Bernard and Marc Collard 1999, "The Human Genus," *Science* 284: 65–71.

Wrangham, Richard and Dale Peterson 1996, *Demonic Males: Apes and the Origin of Human Violence*, Boston: Houghton Mifflin.

Wynn, Thomas 1994, "Tools and Tool Behavior," in Tim Ingold (ed.), *Companion Encyclopedia of Anthropology*, London: Routledge: 133–161.

Zacharias, Kristen L. 1980, *The Construction of a Primate Order: Taxonomy and Comparative Anatomy in Establishing the Human Place in Nature, 1735–1916*, Ph.D. thesis, Baltimore: Johns Hopkins University.

Zilhão, João 2001, *Anatomically Archaic, Behaviorally Modern: The Last Neanderthals and Their Destiny*, Amsterdam: Stichting Nederlands Museum voor Anthropologie en Praehistorie.

Index

Index